MATHEMATICS REVISION FOR LEAVING CERTIFICATE

ORDINARY LEVEL

EURO EDITION

GEORGE HUMPHREY

Gill & Macmillan

CONTENTS

Preface

Guidelines on Doing the Exam

PAPER 1

PAPER 2

Gill & Macmillan Ltd
Hume Avenue
Park West, Dublin 12
with associated companies throughout the world
© George Humphrey 1996, 2000, 2001
0 7171 3176 9
Print origination in Ireland by
DTP Workshop

PREFACE

This book was written to help you revise for the Leaving Certificate Ordinary Level Mathematics Examination. Chapters 1 to 5 deal with Paper 1 and Chapters 6 to 13 deal with Paper 2. This book has been developed to help you to achieve the best result you can in the examination. Unlike a textbook, this book has been organised to make your revision easier.

Throughout your course you can use the book to:

• remind you of what you have been taught

• help you with your homework

• do some extra practice at the kind of questions you will meet in the examination

• sort out things you did not quite follow in class

• focus on the essential points in each topic

• organise your revision and preparation for the actual examination.

To make the best use of this book, attempt to solve the problems yourself before looking at the solutions given. Re-do any questions you answer incorrectly. Get into the habit of making your own notes as you work throughout the book and use these notes in later revision sessions.

I would like to thank Michael Dunne, Maryfield College, who read the entire manuscript and made many valuable suggestions which I have included in the final text. I would also like to thank Jane Finucane, 6th year pupil at the Holy Faith Girls Secondary School, Clontarf, Dublin, who also read the entire manuscript and greatly reduced my errors!

I also wish to express my thanks to the staff at Gill & Macmillan for their advice, guidance and untiring assistance in the preparation and presentation of the text.

George Humphrey
St Andrew's College
Booterstown Avenue
Blackrock
Co. Dublin

September 1995

Dedicated to the memory of my brother Larry

GUIDELINES ON DOING THE EXAM

Each question carries a total of 50 marks. Therefore, you should not spend more than 25 minutes answering any one question. Attempt each part of each question as there is an 'attempt mark' given for each part which is normally worth one third of the marks. Marks may be lost if all your work is not shown. If you use a calculator show the result of each stage of the calculation. Do what the question asks and always write any formula that you use. Give clear reasons for your answers if asked. Make sure you understand the words *solve, verify, evaluate, show, prove, plot, investigate, hence, calculate*. Be familiar with the relevant pages of the mathematical tables in particular, pages 6, 7, 9 and 42. Drawing diagrams in coordinate geometry, or complex numbers, can help you in obtaining a solution but do not answer questions from the diagram where the use of a formula would be expected. It is good practice to make the units on both axes the same and is essential when drawing circles.

Marking Scheme

There is an attempt to divide each question into 3 parts:

(a)   Straight forward, testing only one or two basic concepts and carrying a total of 10 marks.
(b)   More difficult but still straight forward and carrying a total of 20 marks.
(c)   Much more challenging and may have several parts, all related to the one situation and carrying a total of 20 marks.

Structure of the examination

Paper 1
Time: $2\frac{1}{2}$ hours   Marks: 300
Attempt any 6 questions from a choice of 8

Q1.	Arithmetic
Q2,3,4.	Algebra (including Complex Numbers)
Q5.	Sequences and Series
Q6,7,8.	Functions and Calculus

Paper 2
Time: $2\frac{1}{2}$ hours   Marks: 300
Section A: Attempt any 5 questions from a choice of 7

Q1.	Area and Volume
Q2,3,4.	Geometry (Line, Circle, Theorems and Enlargements)
Q5.	Trigonometry
Q6,7.	Permutations, Combinations, Probability and Statistics

Section B: Attempt any 1 question from a choice of 4

Q8.	Further Geometry
Q9.	Vectors
Q10.	Further Sequences and Series
Q11.	Linear Programming

1. ARITHMETIC

Ratios

Example

(i) Express as a ratio of whole numbers $\frac{1}{2} : \frac{2}{3} : \frac{3}{4}$

(ii) Hence, or otherwise, divide €920 in the ratio $\frac{1}{2} : \frac{2}{3} : \frac{3}{4}$

Solution:

(i) $\frac{1}{2} : \frac{2}{3} : \frac{3}{4}$

The common denominator of 2, 3 and 4 is 12.

$$\frac{1}{2} : \frac{2}{3} : \frac{3}{4}$$

$$= \frac{6 : 8 : 9}{12}$$

$$\therefore \frac{1}{2} : \frac{2}{3} : \frac{3}{4} = 6 : 8 : 9$$

Alternatively, multiply each fraction by 12.

(ii) $\frac{1}{2} : \frac{2}{3} : \frac{3}{4} = 6 : 8 : 9$

$6 + 8 + 9 = 23$

$\therefore$ there are 23 parts altogether

$$1 \text{ part } = \frac{€920}{23} = €40$$

6 parts $= €40 \times 6 = €240$

8 parts $= €40 \times 8 = €320$

9 parts $= €40 \times 9 = €360$

$\therefore$ €920 in the ratio $\frac{1}{2} : \frac{2}{3} : \frac{3}{4}$

$= €240, €320, €360$

Sometimes we are given an equation in disguise.

Example

A glass rod falls and breaks into 3 pieces whose lengths are in the ratio $8 : 9 : 5$. If the sum of the lengths of the two larger pieces is 119 cm, find the length of the third piece.

Solution:

$8 + 9 + 5 = 22$

$\therefore$ there are 22 parts altogether

Given: sum of two larger lengths is 119 cm

$\Rightarrow \quad (8 + 9) \text{ parts} = 119 \text{ cm}$

$\Rightarrow \qquad 17 \text{ parts} = 119 \text{ cm}$

$\Rightarrow \qquad\quad 1 \text{ part} = 7 \text{ cm}$

third piece

$=$ smallest piece

$= 5$ parts

$= 5 \times 7$ cm

$= 35$ cm

Example

A, B, C and D shared €493. B and C each received twice as much as A while D received 350% of what A received. Calculate how much each received.

Solution:

A received the smallest amount.

Let A receive one part.

$\therefore$ B and C receive two parts each (as B and C received twice as much as A) and D receives $3\frac{1}{2}$ parts (as D received $3\frac{1}{2}$ times as much as A).

(Note: $350\% = 3\frac{1}{2}$ as a fraction)

$\therefore$ $\qquad A : B : C : D = 1 : 2 : 2 : 3\frac{1}{2}$

$\qquad\qquad\qquad = 2 : 4 : 4 : 7$ (multiply each part by 2)

In other words, we are asked to divide €493 in the ratio $2 : 4 : 4 : 7$.

$2 + 4 + 4 + 7 = 17$	A's share = 2 parts = €29 $\times$ 2 = €58
$\therefore$ there are 17 parts altogether	B's share = 4 parts = €29 $\times$ 4 = €116
one part $= \dfrac{€493}{17}$	C's share = 4 parts = €29 $\times$ 4 = €116
$= €29$	D's share = 7 parts = €29 $\times$ 7 = €203

Example

If $a : b = \frac{2}{3} : \frac{1}{2}$ and $b : c = \frac{3}{5} : \frac{7}{10}$, find $a : c$.

Solution:

First remove all fractions:

$\dfrac{2}{3} : \dfrac{1}{2}$ $\qquad\qquad\qquad\qquad\qquad$ $\dfrac{3}{5} : \dfrac{7}{10}$

$= 4 : 3$ (multiply both by 6) $\qquad$ $= 6 : 7$ (multiply both by 10)

$\therefore$ $\quad a : b = 4 : 3$ $\qquad$ and $\qquad$ $b : c = 6 : 7$

$\Rightarrow \dfrac{a}{b} = \dfrac{4}{3}$ and $\dfrac{b}{c} = \dfrac{6}{7}$ $\qquad$ (write both as fractions)

$\Rightarrow \dfrac{a}{b} \times \dfrac{b}{c} = \dfrac{4}{3} \times \dfrac{6}{7}$ $\qquad$ (multiply both to eliminate b)

$\Rightarrow \quad \dfrac{a}{c} = \dfrac{24}{21} = \dfrac{8}{7}$

$\Rightarrow \quad a : c = 8 : 7$

Example

If $a : b = \dfrac{2}{3} : \dfrac{5}{6}$ and $b : c = \dfrac{1}{2} : \dfrac{7}{12}$, find the ratio $a : b : c$.

Solution:

First remove all fractions.

$$\dfrac{2}{3} : \dfrac{5}{6} \qquad\qquad\qquad \dfrac{1}{2} : \dfrac{7}{12}$$

$= 4 : 5 \qquad$ (multiply both by 6) $\qquad = 6 : 7 \qquad$ (multiply both by 12)

$\therefore \quad a : b = 4 : 5 \qquad$ and $\qquad b : c = 6 : 7$

What we do next is make the b's the same in each ratio.

Multiply both sides of the first ratio by 6 and both sides of the second ratio by 5.

$\therefore \quad a : b = 24 : 30$ (multiply both by 6) and $b : c = 30 : 35$ (multiply both by 5)

$$\therefore \quad a : b : c = 24 : 30 : 35$$

Percentages

In many questions dealing with percentages we will be given an equation in disguise. The best way to tackle this type of problem is to write down the equation given in disguise. From this we can find 1%, and, hence, any percentage we like. Consider the next examples.

Example

A solicitor's fee for the sale of a house is $1\dfrac{1}{2}\%$ of the selling price.

If the fee is €870, calculate the selling price.

Solution:

Given: Solicitor's fee is €870

$\Rightarrow \quad 1\dfrac{1}{2}\% = €870 \qquad$ (equation given in disguise)

$\Rightarrow \qquad 3\% = €1\,740 \qquad$ (multiply both sides by 2)

$\Rightarrow \qquad 1\% = €580 \qquad$ (divide both sides by 3)

$\Rightarrow \quad 100\% = €58\,000 \qquad$ (multiply both sides by 100)

$\therefore$ the selling price of the house was €58 000.

Example

The selling price of a car was €13 125 which includes 25% VAT. Before being sold the VAT rate was reduced from 25% to 15%. Find:

(i) the new selling price of the car

(ii) the cost to the customer if the salesman allowed a 7% discount on this new selling price.

Solution:

(i) Given : Cost of car, including VAT of 25%, is €13 125

∴   125% = €13 125   (equation given in disguise)

⇒   1% = €105   (divide both sides by 125)

⇒   115% = €12 075   (multiply both sides by 115)

∴ the new selling price, including VAT at 15%, is €12 075

(ii) Discount of 7%

      100% = €12 075   (equation given in disguise)

⇒   1% = €120·75   (divide both sides by 100)

⇒   93% = €11 229·75   (multiply both sides by 93, i.e. 100 − 7 = 93)

∴ Cost to the customer, including a 7% discount, is €11 229·75

Example

Express $\frac{7}{8}$ of 0·21 as a percentage of 0·588.

Solution:

     $\frac{1}{8}$ of 0·21 = 0·02625   (divide by 8)

⇒ $\frac{7}{8}$ of 0·21 = 0·18375   (multiply by 7)

Now the question is, express 0·18375 as a percentage of 0·588.

$$= \frac{0 \cdot 18375}{0 \cdot 588} \times \frac{100}{1}$$

$$= 31 \cdot 25\%$$

Foreign Exchange

In Ireland the euro, €, is the basic unit of currency.

Example

If €1 = 109 Japanese yen, how much in € would a person receive for 17 113 Japanese yen, if the commission is $1\frac{1}{2}\%$?

Solution:

It is good practice to put the units of currency we require on the RHS.

$$109 \text{ yen} = €1 \qquad \text{(put what you want on the RHS)}$$

$$1 \text{ yen} = €\frac{1}{109} \qquad \text{(divide both sides by 109)}$$

$$17\,113 \text{ yen} = €\frac{17\,113}{109} \qquad \text{(multiply both sides by 17 113)}$$

$$= €157$$

Now, $1\frac{1}{2}\%$ commission must be paid on this.

$$\text{Commission} = 1\frac{1}{2}\% \text{ of } €157 = €2\cdot36$$

Thus the person will receive = €157 − €2·36 = €154·64

Example

A person changes €1 200 into SF (Swiss francs). A charge is made for this service. The exchange rate is €1 = 2·2 SF. If the person receives 2 593·8 SF, calculate the percentage charge.

Solution:

First express €1 200 in SF

$$€1\,200 = 1\,200 \times 2\cdot2 \text{ SF} = 2\,640 \text{ SF}$$

$$\text{Amount received} = 2\,593\cdot8$$

$$\therefore \qquad \text{charge} = 2\,640 - 2\,593\cdot8 = 46\cdot2 \text{ SF}$$

$$\text{Percentage charge} = \frac{\text{charge}}{\text{original amount}} \times \frac{100}{1}$$

$$= \frac{46\cdot2}{2\,640} \times \frac{100}{1}$$

$$= 1\cdot75\%$$

Example

If €1 = 9 Norwegian krone and €1 = 2·25 SF, how many Swiss francs would you get for 1 388 krone?

Solution:

Our answer os to be in SF, ∴ put SF on the RHS.

Given €1 = 9 krone and €1 = 2·25 SF

$$\therefore \qquad 9 \text{ krone} = 2\cdot25 \text{ SF} \qquad \text{(as both equal €1)}$$

$$1 \text{ krone} = \frac{2\cdot25}{9} \text{ SF} \qquad \text{(divide both sides by 9)}$$

$$1\,388 \text{ krone} = \frac{1\,388 \times 2\cdot25}{9} \text{ SF (multiply both sides by 1 388)}$$

$$= 347 \text{ SF}$$

Thus, you would get 347 Swiss francs for 1388 krone

Income Tax

The following is called the '**income tax equation**':

$$\boxed{\text{Gross tax} - \text{Tax credits} = \text{Tax payable}}$$

Gross tax is calculated as follows:

Standard rate on all income up to the standard rate cut-off point	+	A higher rate on all income above the standard rate cut-off point

Example

A man has a gross yearly income of €24 750. He has a standard rate cut-off point of €26 000 and a tax credit of €1 370. The standard rate of tax is 16% of income up to the standard rate cut-off point. Calculate:

(i) the amount of gross tax for the year

(ii) the amount of tax paid for the year

(iii) net income for the year.

Solution:

(i) Gross tax = 16% of €24 750 = €24 750 × 0.16 = €3 960

(ii) Income tax equation: Gross tax – Tax credits = Tax payable
                          €3 960   –   €1 370   =   €2 590
Therefore, the amount of tax paid = €2 590

(iii) Net income = Gross income – Tax paid
                 =   €24 750   –   €2 590   =   €22 160

When a person earns more than their standard rate cut-off point we have to split their gross income into two parts, which are taxed at different rates. The first part, up to the standard rate cut-off point, is taxed at the standard rate and the amount of income above the standard rate cut-off point is taxed at a higher rate.

Example

A man has a gross yearly income of €47 000. He has a standard rate cut-off point of €26 000 and a tax credit of €2 010. The standard rate of tax is 15% of income up to the standard rate cut-off point and 38% on all income above the standard rate cut-off point. Calculate:

(i) the amount of gross tax for the year

(ii) the amount of tax paid for the year.

Express the amount of tax paid as a percentage of gross income.

Solution:

(i) Gross tax = 15% of €26 000 + 38% of €21 000

$\qquad$ = €26 000 × 0.15 + €21 000 × 0.38

$\qquad$ = €3 900 + €7 980

$\qquad$ = €11 880

> Income above the standard rate cut-off point
> = €47 000 − €26 000
> = €21 000

(ii) Income tax equation: Gross tax − tax credits = tax payable

$\qquad$ €11 880 − €2 010 = €9 870

Therefore, he paid €9 870 in tax.

Tax paid as a percentage of gross income $= \dfrac{\text{tax paid}}{\text{gross income}} \times 100\%$

$$= \frac{9\,870}{47\,000} \times 100 = 21\%$$

Example

A woman paid €6 820 in tax for the year. She had a tax credit of €1 974 and a standard rate cut-off point of €24 800. The standard rate of tax is 16% of income up the standard rate cut-off point and 38% on all income above the standard rate cut-off point. Calculate:
(i) the amount of income taxed at the rate of 38%
(ii) the woman's gross income for the year.

Solution:

(i) Income tax equation:

$$\text{Gross tax} - \text{tax credits} = \text{Tax payable}$$

$$16\% \text{ of } €24\ 800 + 38\% \text{ of (income above cut-off point)} - €1\ 974 = €6\ 820$$

$$€3\ 968 + 38\% \text{ of (income above cut-off point)} - €1\ 974 = €6\ 820$$

$$38\% \text{ of (income above cut-off point)} + €1\ 994 = €6\ 820$$

$$38\% \text{ of (income above cut-off point)} = €4\ 826$$

$$1\% \text{ of (income above cut-off point)} = €127$$

divide both sides by 38

$$100\% \text{ of (income above cut-off point)} = €12\ 700$$

multiply both sides by 100

Therefore, the amount of income taxed at the higher rate of 38% was €12 700

(ii) Gross income = standard rate cut-off point + income above the standard rate cut-off point

$$= €24\ 800 + €12\ 700 = €37\ 500$$

Interest and Depreciation

Example

€800 was invested at $r\%$ per annum. The interest earned was subject to tax at 48%. After one year tax of €32.64 was paid. Calculate r.

Solution:

Equation given in disguise:

$$48\% \text{ of interest} = €32.64$$

$$1\% \text{ of interest} = €0.68 \quad \text{(divide both sides by 48)}$$

$$\therefore \qquad \text{interest} = €68 \quad \text{(multiply both sides by 100)}$$

$$\text{interest rate} = \frac{\text{interest}}{\text{principal}} \times \frac{100}{1}$$

$$= \frac{68}{800} \times \frac{100}{1}$$

$$= 8.5\%$$

$$r = 8.5$$

When dealing with compound interest the easiest way to calculate the amount at each stage is to multiply the principal at the beginning of each year by $(1 + \frac{r}{100})$. For depreciation we multiply by $(1 - \frac{r}{100})$.

Example

€2 900 was invested for 3 years at compound interest. The rate for the first year was 8%, the rate for the second year was 12% and the rate for the third year was 9%.

Calculate (i) the amount and (ii) the compound interest at the end of the third year, correct to the nearest cent.

Solution:

$$P_1 = €2\,900$$

$$A_1 = €2\,900 \times 1{\cdot}08 \qquad = €3\,132$$

$$P_2 = €3\,132$$

$$A_2 = €3\,132 \times 1{\cdot}12 \qquad = €3\,507{\cdot}84$$

$$P_3 = €3\,507{\cdot}84$$

$$A_3 = €3\,507{\cdot}84 \times 1{\cdot}09 \qquad = €3\,823{\cdot}5456$$

(i) Thus, the amount after 3 years = €3 823·55 (nearest cent)

(ii) The compound interest after 3 years $= A_3 - P_1$

$$= €3\,823{\cdot}55 - €2\,900$$

$$= €923{\cdot}55$$

Be careful when some money is repaid at the end of a year.

Example

A man borrowed €10 000. He agreed to repay €2 000 after one year, €3 000 after two years and the balance at the end of the third year. If interest was charged at 8% in the first year, 5% in the second year and 6% in the third year, how much was paid at the end of the third year to clear the debt?

Solution:

R_1 = repayment after one year and R_2 = repayment after two years.

$$P_1 = €10\,000$$

$$A_1 = €10\,000 \times 1{\cdot}08$$

$$= €10\,800$$

$$R_1 = \underline{€2\,000}$$

$$P_2 = €8\,800 \qquad \text{(subtract as } R_1 \text{ was repaid)}$$

$$A_2 \quad = \quad \text{€8 800} \times 1\cdot05$$

$$\quad = \quad \text{€9 240}$$

$$R_2 \quad = \quad \underline{\text{€3 000}}$$

$$P_3 \quad = \quad \text{€6 240} \qquad \text{(subtract as } R_2 \text{ was repaid)}$$

$$A_3 \quad = \quad \text{€6 240} \times 1\cdot06$$

$$\quad = \quad \text{€6 614·40}$$

Thus, €6 614·40 was paid at the end of the third year to clear the debt.

Example

A man borrowed €x for three years at compound interest. The rate for the first year was $12\frac{1}{2}\%$ and at the end of that year he repaid €1 000. The rate for the second year was 15% and at the end of that year he repaid €2 000. The rate for the third year was 10% and at the end of that year he repaid €5 073·75, the full amount due. Calculate the value of x.

Solution:

End of the year 3: $\qquad$ 110% = €5 073·75

$\qquad\qquad\qquad\qquad$ 1% = €46·125 $\qquad$ (divide both sides by 110)

$\qquad\qquad\qquad\qquad$ 100% = €4 612·50 $\qquad$ (multiply both sides by 100)

He repaid €2 000,
∴ amount owed at the end of year 2 = €4 612·50 + €2 000 = €6 612·50

End of year 2: $\qquad$ 115% = €6 612·50

$\qquad\qquad\qquad\qquad$ 1% = €57·50 $\qquad$ (divide both sides by 115)

$\qquad\qquad\qquad\qquad$ 100% = €5 750 $\qquad$ (multiply both sides by 100)

He repaid €1 000,
∴ amount owed at the end of year 1 = €5 750 + €1 000 = €6 750

End of year 1: $\qquad$ $112\frac{1}{2}\%$ = €6 750

$\qquad\qquad\qquad\qquad$ 1% = €60 $\qquad$ (divide both sides by $112\frac{1}{2}$)

$\qquad\qquad\qquad\qquad$ 100% = €6 000 $\qquad$ (multiply both sides by 100)

∴ $x = 6 000$

Example

A person put €W at compound interest in a Savings Bank. The rate for the first year was 10%. At the end of the first year the person put another €$2W$ in the Savings Bank. The rate for the second year was 8% and the rate for the third year was 5%. If the total investment at the end of the three years amounted to €8 788·50, calculate W.

Solution:

We leave out the € symbol for clarity.

$$P_1 = W$$

$$A_1 = W \times 1 \cdot 1 = 1 \cdot 1W$$

$$P_2 = 1 \cdot 1W + 2W = 3 \cdot 1W \qquad \text{(add on } 2W\text{)}$$

$$A_2 = 3 \cdot 1W \times 1 \cdot 08 = 3 \cdot 348W$$

$$P_3 = 3 \cdot 348W$$

$$A_3 = 3 \cdot 348W \times 1 \cdot 05 = 3 \cdot 5154W$$

We are given $A_3 = 8\,788 \cdot 50$

Thus $3 \cdot 5154W = 8\,788 \cdot 50$

$$\Rightarrow \qquad W = \frac{8\,788 \cdot 50}{3 \cdot 5154}$$

$$\Rightarrow \qquad W = 2\,500$$

Compound Interest Formula

There is a formula to calculate what a principal will amount to under compound interest. It can only be used if the following two conditions hold throughout the time period the principal is invested:

1. The rate of interest is unchanged

2. No money is added or subtracted

The amount, A, to which a principal, P, will grow over n years at $r\%$ per annum compound interest is given by

$$A = P\left(1 + \frac{r}{100}\right)^n$$

Example

€2 500 is invested for 8 years at 6% per annum compound interest.
Find **(i)** the amount and **(ii)** the compound interest after 8 years, to the nearest cent.

Solution:

(i) Given : $\qquad P = 2\,500, \qquad r = 6 \qquad$ and $\qquad n = 8, \qquad$ find A.

$$A = P\left(1 + \frac{r}{100}\right)^n$$

$$= 2\,500\left(1 + \frac{6}{100}\right)^8$$

$$= 2\,500(1 + 0 \cdot 06)^8$$

$$= 2\,500(1 \cdot 06)^8$$

$$= 3\,984 \cdot 6\,202$$

Thus, the amount is €3 984·62

(ii) Compound interest $= A - P =$ €3 984·62 $-$ €2 500 $=$ €1 484·62

Example

A machine bought for €8 000 depreciates at a compound rate of 8% per annum.
Find its value after 6 years, correct to the nearest €.

Solution:

When dealing with depreciation, the formula becomes $A = P\left(1 - \dfrac{r}{100}\right)^n$

$\qquad$ Given : $\qquad P = 8\,000, \qquad r = 8 \qquad$ and $\qquad n = 6, \qquad$ find A.

$$A = P\left(1 - \frac{r}{100}\right)^n$$

$$= 8\,000\left(1 - \frac{8}{100}\right)^6$$

$$= 8\,000(1 - 0 \cdot 08)^6$$

$$= 8\,000(0 \cdot 92)^6$$

$$= 4\,850 \cdot 84$$

Thus, the machine is worth €4 851 after 6 years (to the nearest €)

Sometimes we are given the amount, A, and asked to find the principal, P. To do this we rearrange the formula to get P on its own.

Example

A certain sum of money, invested for 9 years at 5% per annum compound interest, amounted to €6 000. Find this sum of money, correct to the nearest cent.

Solution:

Given: $A = 6\,000$, $r = 5$ and $n = 9$,   find P.

$$A = P\left(1 + \frac{r}{100}\right)^n$$

$$\Rightarrow P\left(1 + \frac{r}{100}\right)^n = A \qquad \text{[swop sides]}$$

$$\Rightarrow \qquad P = \frac{A}{\left(1 + \frac{r}{100}\right)^n} \qquad \text{[divide both sides by } \left(1 + \frac{r}{100}\right)^n \text{]}$$

$$= \frac{6\,000}{\left(1 + \frac{5}{100}\right)^9} \qquad [A = 6\,000, r = 5, n = 9]$$

$$= \frac{6\,000}{(1 + 0{\cdot}05)^9}$$

$$= \frac{6\,000}{(1{\cdot}05)^9}$$

$$= 3\,867{\cdot}6\,535$$

Thus, the sum of money invested was €3 867·65

13

Sometimes we are given A, P and n and asked to find r. This is best achieved by putting in the values of A, P and n into the formula and rearranging to get r on its own.

Example

At what rate per annum compound interest would €750 amount to €983·10 in 4 years?

Solution:

Given: $\qquad A = 983{\cdot}10, \qquad P = 750, \qquad n = 4, \qquad$ find r.

$$P\left(1 + \frac{r}{100}\right)^n = A$$

$\Rightarrow \qquad 750\left(1 + \frac{r}{100}\right)^4 = 983{\cdot}10 \qquad (A = 983{\cdot}10, P = 750, n = 4)$

$\Rightarrow \qquad \left(1 + \frac{r}{100}\right)^4 = \dfrac{983{\cdot}10}{750} \qquad$ (divide both sides by 750)

$\Rightarrow \qquad \left(1 + \frac{r}{100}\right)^4 = 1{\cdot}3108 \qquad$ (simplify RHS, using a calculator)

$\Rightarrow \qquad 1 + \frac{r}{100} = (1{\cdot}3108)^{\frac{1}{4}} \qquad$ (take fourth root of both sides)

$\Rightarrow \qquad 1 + \frac{r}{100} = 1{\cdot}07 \qquad$ (simplify RHS, using a calculator)

$\Rightarrow \qquad \frac{r}{100} = 1{\cdot}07 - 1$

$\Rightarrow \qquad \frac{r}{100} = 0{\cdot}07$

$\Rightarrow \qquad r = 7 \qquad$ (multiply both sides by 100)

Estimation and Approximation

Error = (True value – Estimated value)
and is always considered positive

$$\text{Relative error} = \frac{\text{Error}}{\text{True value}}$$

or if the true value is not known

$$\text{Relative error} = \frac{\text{Error}}{\text{Estimated value}}$$

$$\text{Percentage error} = \text{Relative error} \times \frac{100}{1}$$

Note: For any value given to the nearest unit of measurement, the maximum, or minimum, possible error is '**half of that unit of measurement**'.

Example

It is estimated that the cost of building a table will be €350. The actual cost was €360. Calculate **(i)** the relative error (as a fraction) and **(ii)** the percentage error, correct to two decimal places.

Solution:

Error = Actual cost − Estimated cost = €360 − €350 = €10

(i) Relative error = $\dfrac{\text{Error}}{\text{True cost}} = \dfrac{10}{350} = \dfrac{1}{35}$

(ii) Percentage error = Relative error $\times \dfrac{100}{1} = \dfrac{1}{35} \times \dfrac{100}{1} = \dfrac{100}{35} = 2 \cdot 86\%$

Example

Calculate the percentage error in taking 50 + 60 as an approximation for 52·47 + 64·87, correct to three decimal places.

Solution:

True value = 52·47 + 64·87 = 117·34

Estimated value = 50 + 60 = 110

Error = True value − Estimated value = 117·34 − 110 = 7·34

Relative error = $\dfrac{\text{Error}}{\text{True value}} = \dfrac{7 \cdot 34}{117 \cdot 34}$

Percentage error = Relative error $\times \dfrac{100}{1} = \dfrac{7 \cdot 34}{117 \cdot 34} \times \dfrac{100}{1} = 6 \cdot 255\%$

Example

Lengths x and y are measured to the nearest centimetre and reported to be 2·23 m and 3·31 m, respectively. Calculate:

(i) the smallest possible value of the length $4x + 5y$ and

(ii) the largest possible value of $(2x + 4y)^2$, giving your answer correct to four significant figures.

Solution:

Minimum value of x = 2·225 and maximum value of x = 2·235

Minimum value of y = 3·305 and maximum value of y = 3·315

(i) smallest value of $4x + 5y = 4(2 \cdot 225) + 5(3 \cdot 305)$

$$= 8 \cdot 9 + 16 \cdot 525$$

$$= 25 \cdot 425$$

(ii)   largest value of $2x + 4y = 2(2\cdot235) + 4(3\cdot315)$

$$= 4\cdot47 + 13\cdot26$$

$$= 17\cdot73$$

$\therefore$ largest value of $(2x + 4y)^2 = (17\cdot73)^2$

$$= 314\cdot4 \text{ (correct to four significant figures)}$$

Example

The mass of three parcels correct to the nearest kg are 7 kg, 9 kg and 12 kg, respectively. If the total mass of the three parcels is taken as 28 kg, calculate the maximum percentage error to one place of decimals.

Solution:

The maximum values of 7 kg, 9 kg and 12 kg are 7·5 kg, 9·5 kg and 12·5 kg, respectively.

$\therefore$ maximum error $= 0\cdot5 + 0\cdot5 + 0\cdot5 = 1\cdot5$ kg

$$\text{maximum relative error} = \frac{\text{maximum error}}{\text{estimated value}} = \frac{1\cdot5}{28} = \frac{3}{56}$$

$\therefore$ maximum percentage error $= \dfrac{3}{56} \times \dfrac{100}{1} = 5\cdot4\%$

Note: We could also have used the minimum values, 6·5 kg, 8·5 kg and 11·5 kg to obtain the same result.

Scientific Notation

A number is said to be in 'scientific notation' or 'standard form' when it is written in the form $a \times 10^n$, where $1 \le a < 10$ and $n \in \mathbf{Z}$.

Standard Form:

$a \times 10^n$ where $1 \le a < 10$ and $n \in \mathbf{Z}$

or

(a number between 1 and 10) × (power of 10)

For example:

$$8\,000\,000 = 8 \times 10^6$$

$$0\cdot0000258 = 2\cdot58 \times 10^{-5}$$

Example

(i) Express $\dfrac{1\,512}{0.36}$ in the form $a \cdot 10^n$, where $1 \le a < 10$ and $n \in \mathbf{Z}$.

(ii) Find x if $\dfrac{560}{0.008} = 7 \times 10^x$.

Solution:

(i) $\dfrac{1\,512}{0.36} = 4\,200$

$\qquad = 4.2 \times 1\,000$

$\qquad = 4.2 \times 10^3$

(ii) $\dfrac{560}{0.008} = 7 \times 10^x$

$\qquad = 70\,000$

$\qquad = 7 \times 10\,000$

$\qquad = 7 \times 10^4$

$\qquad \therefore x = 4$

Addition and Subtraction

To add or subtract numbers in standard form do the following:

1. Write as ordinary numbers.
2. Add or subtract these numbers.
3. Write the number in standard form.

Example

Express (i) $1.2 \times 10^4 + 17.9 \times 10^3$ (ii) $3.91 \times 10^{-2} + 1.9 \times 10^{-3}$

in the form $a \times 10^n$, where $1 \le a < 10$ and $n \in \mathbf{Z}$.

Solution:

(i) $1.2 \times 10^4 + 17.9 \times 10^3$

  1. $1.2 \times 10^4 = 12\,000$

    $17.9 \times 10^3 = \underline{17\,900}$

  2. $\qquad\qquad 29\,900$

  3. $\qquad\qquad = 2.99 \times 10^4$

(ii) $3.91 \times 10^{-2} + 1.9 \times 10^{-3}$

  1. $3.91 \times 10^{-2} = 0.0391$

    $1.9 \times 10^{-3} = \underline{0.0019}$

  2. $\qquad\qquad 0.0410$

  3. $\qquad\qquad = 4.1 \times 10^{-2}$

Multiplication and Division

To multiply or divide numbers in standard form do the following:

> 1. Multiply or divide the 'a' parts.
> 2. Multiply or divide the powers of 10.
> 3. Write your answer in standard form.

Example

Express **(i)** $(2 \cdot 25 \times 10^4) \times (1 \cdot 6 \times 10^3)$ **(ii)** $(3 \cdot 91 \times 10^3) \div (1 \cdot 7 \times 10^7)$

in the form $a \times 10^n$, where $1 \leq a < 10$ and $n \in \mathbf{Z}$.

Solution:

(i) $(2 \cdot 25 \times 10^4) \times (1 \cdot 6 \times 10^3)$

$= 2 \cdot 25 \times 10^4 \times 1 \cdot 6 \times 10^3$

$= 2 \cdot 25 \times 1 \cdot 6 \times 10^4 \times 10^3$

$= 3 \cdot 6 \times 10^{4+3}$

$= 3 \cdot 6 \times 10^7$

ii) $(3 \cdot 91 \times 10^3) \div (1 \cdot 7 \times 10^7)$

$= \dfrac{3 \cdot 91 \times 10^3}{1 \cdot 7 \times 10^7}$

$= \dfrac{3 \cdot 91}{1 \cdot 7} \times \dfrac{10^3}{10^7}$

$= 2 \cdot 3 \times 10^{3-7}$

$= 2 \cdot 3 \times 10^{-4}$

Example

Express $\dfrac{(6 \times 10^5)^2}{6 \times 10^{-7}}$ in the form 6×10^n where $n \in \mathbf{Z}$.

Solution:

$\dfrac{(6 \times 10^5)^2}{6 \times 10^{-7}} = \dfrac{6 \times 10^5 \times 6 \times 10^5}{6 \times 10^{-7}}$

$= \dfrac{\not{6} \times 6 \times 10^5 \times 10^5}{\not{6} \times 10^{-7}}$

$= \dfrac{6 \times 10^{10}}{10^{-7}}$

$= 6 \times 10^{10} \times 10^7$

$= 6 \times 10^{10+7}$

$= 6 \times 10^{17}$

Example

Simplify $\dfrac{1 \cdot 4 \times 10^3 + 5 \cdot 6 \times 10^2}{7 \times 10^{-1}}$ and write your answer in the form $a \cdot 10^n$, $1 \le a < 10$ and $n \in \mathbf{Z}$.

Solution:

$$\underline{\text{Top}}$$
$$1 \cdot 4 \times 10^3 = 1\,400$$
$$5 \cdot 6 \times 10^2 = 560$$
$$\overline{}$$
$$1\,960$$

$$\underline{\text{Bottom}}$$
$$7 \times 10^{-1} = 0 \cdot 7$$

$\therefore \dfrac{\text{Top}}{\text{Bottom}}$

$= \dfrac{1\,960}{0 \cdot 7}$

$= 2\,800$

$= 2 \cdot 8 \times 1\,000$

$= 2 \cdot 8 \times 10^3$

2. ALGEBRA

Multiplication and Division of Algebraic Fractions

Operations with algebraic fractions follow the same rules as in arithmetic. Before attempting to simplify when multiplying or dividing algebraic fractions, factorise where possible and divide top and bottom by common factors. The contents of a bracket should be considered as a single term.

Example

Simplify   (i) $\dfrac{8x^2}{14y} \div \dfrac{4x}{7y^2}$ (ii) $\dfrac{x^2 - 2x}{x^2 - 4}$

Solution:

(i) $\dfrac{8x^2}{14y} \div \dfrac{4x}{7y^2}$

    $= \dfrac{8x^2}{14y} \times \dfrac{7y^2}{4x}$ [turn the fraction we divide by upside down and multiply]

    $= xy$ [divide top and bottom by common factors]

(ii) $\dfrac{x^2 - 2x}{x^2 - 4}$

    $= \dfrac{x(x - 2)}{(x - 2)(x + 2)}$ [factorise top and bottom]

    $= \dfrac{x}{x + 2}$ [divide top and bottom by the common factor $(x - 2)$]

Example

Simplify $\dfrac{x^2 + 8x + 15}{x^2 - 9} \div \dfrac{xy + 5y}{x^2 - 3x}$

Solution:

$\dfrac{x^2 + 8x + 15}{x^2 - 9} \div \dfrac{xy + 5y}{x^2 - 3x}$

$= \dfrac{x^2 + 8x + 15}{x^2 - 9} \times \dfrac{x^2 - 3x}{xy + 5y}$ [turn the fraction we divide by upside down and multiply]

$= \dfrac{(x + 5)(x + 3)}{(x - 3)(x + 3)} \times \dfrac{x(x - 3)}{y(x + 5)}$ [factorise top and bottom]

$= \dfrac{x}{y}$ [divide top and bottom by the common factors $(x + 5)$, $(x + 3)$ and $(x - 3)$]

Addition and Subtraction of Algebraic Fractions

To add or subtract algebraic fractions do the following:

> **1.** Factorise denominators (if necessary).
>
> **2.** Find the L.C.M. of the denominators.
>
> **3.** Express each fraction in terms of this L.C.M. and simplify.

Example

Simplify $\dfrac{3x}{x^2 - x - 6} + \dfrac{5}{x + 2} - \dfrac{2}{x - 3}$

Solution:

$$\dfrac{3x}{x^2 - x - 6} + \dfrac{5}{x + 2} - \dfrac{2}{x - 3}$$

$$= \dfrac{3x}{(x - 3)(x + 2)} + \dfrac{5}{(x + 2)} - \dfrac{2}{(x - 3)} \quad \text{[factorise denominators, their L.C.M. is } (x-3)(x+2)]$$

$$= \dfrac{3x + 5(x - 3) - 2(x + 2)}{(x - 3)(x + 2)} \quad \text{[each fraction expressed in terms of this L.C.M.]}$$

$$= \dfrac{3x + 5x - 15 - 2x - 4}{(x - 3)(x + 2)} \quad \text{[remove brackets on top]}$$

$$= \dfrac{6x - 19}{(x - 3)(x + 2)} \quad \text{[simplify the top]}$$

Note: It is common practice not to multiply out the expressions on the bottom.

Example

Express $\dfrac{5}{2x - 3} - \dfrac{3}{2x^2 - 3x} - \dfrac{1}{x}$ as a single fraction.

Solution:

$$\dfrac{5}{2x - 3} - \dfrac{3}{2x^2 - 3x} - \dfrac{1}{x}$$

$$= \dfrac{5}{(2x - 3)} - \dfrac{3}{x(2x - 3)} - \dfrac{1}{x} \quad \text{[factorise denominators, their L.C.M. is } x(2x - 3)]$$

$$= \dfrac{5x - 3 - 1(2x - 3)}{x(2x - 3)} \quad \text{[each fraction expressed in terms of this L.C.M.]}$$

$$= \dfrac{5x - 3 - 2x + 3}{x(2x - 3)} \quad \text{[remove brackets on top]}$$

$$= \frac{3x}{x(2x-3)} \qquad \text{[simplify the top]}$$

$$= \frac{3}{2x-3} \qquad \text{[divide top and bottom by } x \text{]}$$

Changing the Subject of a Formula

When we rearrange a formula so that one of the variables is given in terms of the others we are said to be 'changing the subject of the formula'. The rules in changing the subject of a formula are the same as when solving an equation, that is we can:

1. **Add** or **subtract** the same quantity to both sides.

   (In practice this involves moving a term from one side to another and changing its sign)

2. **Multiply** or **divide** both sides by the same quantity.

3. **Square** both sides.

4. Take the **square root** of both sides.

Whatever letter comes after the word 'express' is to be on its own.

Example

If $r = \dfrac{1}{p} + \dfrac{1}{q}$, express p in terms of q and r.

Solution:

Method 1:

$$r = \frac{1}{p} + \frac{1}{q}$$

$$pqr = pq\frac{1}{p} + pq\frac{1}{q} \qquad \text{[multiply each part by } pq \text{]}$$

$$pqr = q + p \qquad \text{[simplify right hand side]}$$

$$pqr - p = q \qquad \text{[terms with } p \text{ on the left hand side]}$$

$$p(qr - 1) = q \qquad \text{[take out common factor } p \text{ on left hand side]}$$

$$p = \frac{q}{qr-1} \qquad \text{[divide both sides by } (qr-1) \text{]}$$

Method 2: (using a common denominator)

$$r = \frac{1}{p} + \frac{1}{q}$$

$$\frac{r}{1} = \frac{1}{p} + \frac{1}{q} \quad \text{[make left hand side a fraction, the common denominator is } pq\text{]}$$

$$\frac{pqr = q + p}{pq} \quad \text{[each fraction expressed in terms of the common denominator } pq\text{]}$$

$$pqr = q + p \quad \text{[remove common denominator]}$$

$$pqr - p = q \quad \text{[terms with } p \text{ on the left hand side]}$$

$$p(qr - 1) = q \quad \text{[take out common factor } p \text{ on left hand side]}$$

$$p = \frac{q}{qr - 1} \quad \text{[divide both sides by } (qr - 1)\text{]}$$

Example

If $a = \frac{3bc}{b + c}$, express c in terms of a and b.

Solution:

$$a = \frac{3bc}{b + c}$$

$$a(b + c) = 3bc \qquad \text{[multiply both sides by } (b + c)\text{]}$$

$$ab + ac = 3bc \qquad \text{[remove brackets on the left hand side]}$$

$$-3bc + ac = -ab \qquad \text{[terms with } c \text{ on the left hand side]}$$

$$3bc - ac = ab \qquad \text{[change all signs]}$$

$$c(3b - a) = ab \qquad \text{[take out common factor } c \text{ on the left hand side]}$$

$$c = \frac{ab}{3b - a} \qquad \text{[divide both sides by } (3b - a)\text{]}$$

Example

If $\frac{x - y}{y} = \frac{r}{s}$, express y in terms of r, s and x.

Solution:

$$\frac{x - y}{y} = \frac{r}{s}$$

$$\frac{ys(x - y)}{y} = ys \frac{r}{s} \qquad \text{[multiply both sides by } ys\text{]}$$

$$s(x - y) = yr \qquad \text{[simplify both sides]}$$

$$sx - sy = yr \qquad \text{[remove brackets on the left hand side]}$$

$$-sy - yr = -sx \qquad \text{[terms with } y \text{ on the left hand side]}$$

$$sy + yr = sx \qquad \text{[change all signs]}$$

$$y(s + r) = sx \qquad \text{[take out common factor } y \text{ on left hand side]}$$

$$y = \frac{sx}{s + r} \qquad \text{[divide both sides by } (s + r)\text{]}$$

Example

If $v = \sqrt{\dfrac{u - s}{ut}}$, express t in terms of u, v and s.

Solution:

$$v = \sqrt{\frac{u - s}{ut}}$$

$$v^2 = \frac{u - s}{ut} \qquad \text{[square both sides, square root sign disappears]}$$

$$v^2 ut = u - s \qquad \text{[multiply both sides by } ut\text{]}$$

$$t = \frac{u - s}{v^2 u} \qquad \text{[divide both sides by } v^2 u\text{]}$$

Example

If $\dfrac{8 - q^2}{2a^2} = m$, express a in terms of m and q.

Find the **values** of a when $q = 2$ and $m = 4\cdot 5$.

Solution:

$$\frac{8 - q^2}{2a^2} = m$$

$$8 - q^2 = 2a^2 m \qquad \text{[multiply both sides by } 2a^2\text{]}$$

$$2a^2 m = 8 - q^2 \qquad \text{[swap sides to have '}a\text{' on the left hand side]}$$

$$a^2 = \frac{8 - q^2}{2m} \qquad \text{[divide both sides by } 2m\text{]}$$

$$a = \pm\sqrt{\frac{8 - q^2}{2m}} \qquad \text{[take the square root of both sides]}$$

$$q = 2, \quad m = 4\cdot 5$$

$$a = \pm\sqrt{\frac{8 - q^2}{2m}} = \pm\sqrt{\frac{8 - 2^2}{2(4\cdot 5)}} = \pm\sqrt{\frac{8 - 4}{9}} = \pm\sqrt{\frac{4}{9}} = \pm\frac{\sqrt{4}}{\sqrt{9}} = \pm\frac{2}{3}$$

Note: If $x^2 = k$, then $x = \pm\sqrt{k}$, always include both the positive and negative solutions.

Quadratic Equations

There are three types of quadratic equations we shall meet on our course:

1.	$ax^2 + bx + c = 0$	
2.	$ax^2 + bx = 0$	(no constant)
3.	$ax^2 + c = 0$	(no x term)

Steps in solving a quadratic equation.

Method 1:

1.	Bring every term to the left hand side
	(If necessary make the coefficient of x^2 positive)
2.	Factorise the left hand side
3.	Let each factor $= 0$
4.	Solve each simple equation

Method 2:

Use the formula: $x = \dfrac{-b \pm \sqrt{b^2 - 4ac}}{2a}$

The whole of the top of the right hand side, including $-b$, is divided by $2a$.

It is often called the ' $-b$' or 'quadratic' formula.

Before using the formula, make sure every term is on the left hand side, i.e. write the equation in the form $ax^2 + bx + c = 0$.

Type 1

Example

Solve $x(2x + 7) + 6 = 0$

Solution:

Method 1:

$x(2x + 7) + 6 = 0$

$2x^2 + 7x + 6 = 0$ (write in the form $ax^2 + bx + c = 0$)

$(2x + 3)(x + 2) = 0$ (factorise the left hand side)

$2x + 3 = 0$ or $x + 2 = 0$ (let each factor $= 0$)

$2x = -3$ or $x = -2$

$x = -\dfrac{3}{2}$ or $x = -2$

Method 2:

$$x(2x + 7) + 6 = 0$$

$$2x^2 + 7x + 6 = 0 \qquad \text{(write in the form } ax^2 + bx + c = 0)$$

$$a = 2, b = 7, c = 6$$

$$x = \frac{-b \pm \sqrt{b^2 - 4ac}}{2a}$$

$$x = \frac{-7 \pm \sqrt{(7)^2 - 4(2)(6)}}{2(2)}$$

$$x = \frac{-7 \pm \sqrt{49 - 48}}{4}$$

$$x = \frac{-7 \pm \sqrt{1}}{4}$$

$$x = \frac{-7 \pm 1}{4}$$

$$x = \frac{-7 + 1}{4} \qquad \text{or} \qquad x = \frac{-7 - 1}{4}$$

$$x = \frac{-6}{4} \qquad \text{or} \qquad x = \frac{-8}{4}$$

$$x = -\frac{3}{2} \qquad \text{or} \qquad x = -2$$

Example

Solve $3(x - 1)^2 - 4 = 11 - x$

Solution: (Using Method 1)

$$3(x - 1)^2 - 4 = 11 - x$$
$$\downarrow$$

$$3(x^2 - 2x + 1) - 4 = 11 - x \qquad \text{(multiply out } (x - 1)^2)$$

$$3x^2 - 6x + 3 - 4 = 11 - x \qquad \text{(remove brackets on the left hand side)}$$

$$3x^2 - 6x + 3 - 4 - 11 + x = 0 \qquad \text{(every term to the left)}$$

$$3x^2 - 5x - 12 = 0 \qquad \text{(write in the form } ax^2 + bx + c = 0)$$

$$(3x + 4)(x - 3) = 0 \qquad \text{(factorise the left hand side)}$$

$$3x + 4 = 0 \qquad \text{or} \quad x - 3 = 0 \qquad \text{(let each factor = 0)}$$

$$3x = -4 \qquad \text{or} \qquad x = 3$$

$$x = -\frac{4}{3} \qquad \text{or} \qquad x = 3$$

Type 2

Example

Solve for x,   **(i)** $x^2 + 3x = 0$ and   **(ii)** $2x^2 = 3x$

Solution:

(i) $x^2 + 3x = 0$

      $x(x + 3) = 0$ (factorise the left hand side)

      $x = 0$ or $x + 3 = 0$ (let each factor $= 0$)

      $x = 0$ or $x = -3$

(ii) $2x^2 = 3x$

      $2x^2 - 3x = 0$ (every term to the left)

      $x(2x - 3) = 0$ (factorise the left hand side)

       $x = 0$ or $2x - 3 = 0$ (let each factor $= 0$)

       $x = 0$ or $2x = 3$

       $x = 0$ or $x = \dfrac{3}{2}$

Note: It is important not to divide both sides by x, otherwise you lose the root $x = 0$.

Type 3

Example

Solve   **(i)** $x^2 - 1 = 0$ **(ii)** $x^2 - 9 = 0$ **(iii)** $4x^2 - 25 = 0$

Solution:

(i) $x^2 - 1 = 0$ **(ii)** $x^2 - 9 = 0$

       $x^2 = 1$ $x^2 = 9$

       $x = \pm \sqrt{1}$ $x = \pm \sqrt{9}$

(take square root of both sides)   (take square root of both sides)

               $x = \pm 1$ $x = \pm 3$

       $x = 1$ or $x = -1$ $x = 3$ or $x = -3$

(iii) $4x^2 - 25 = 0$

        $4x^2 = 25$

        $x^2 = \dfrac{25}{4}$ (divide both sides by 4)

        $x = \pm \sqrt{\dfrac{25}{4}}$ (take square root of both sides)

$$x = \pm\frac{5}{2}$$

$$x = \frac{5}{2} \qquad \text{or} \qquad x = -\frac{5}{2}$$

Quadratic Equations Where the Formula Must Be Used

Many quadratic equations cannot be resolved into factors. When this happens the formula **must** be used. To save time trying to look for factors, a clue that you must use the formula is often given in the question. When the question requires an approximate answer, e.g. 'correct to two decimal places', 'correct to three significant figures', 'correct to the nearest integer' or 'express your answers in surd form', then the formula must be used.

Example

Solve the equation, $3x^2 - 8x - 2 = 0$, giving your answers correct to two decimal places.

Solution:

$3x^2 - 8x - 2 = 0$ (two decimal places $\therefore$ use formula)

$a = 3, \quad b = -8, \quad c = -2$

$$x = \frac{-b \pm \sqrt{b^2 - 4ac}}{2a}$$

$$x = \frac{8 \pm \sqrt{(-8)^2 - 4(3)(-2)}}{2(3)}$$

$$x = \frac{8 \pm \sqrt{64 + 24}}{6}$$

$$x = \frac{8 \pm \sqrt{88}}{6}$$

$$x = \frac{8 \pm 9\cdot3808}{6} \qquad (\sqrt{88} = 9\cdot3808 \text{ correct to 4 decimal places})$$

$$x = \frac{8 + 9\cdot3808}{6} \qquad \text{or} \qquad x = \frac{8 - 9\cdot3808}{6}$$

$$x = \frac{17\cdot3808}{6} \qquad \text{or} \qquad x = \frac{-1\cdot3808}{6}$$

$$x = 2\cdot8968 \qquad \text{or} \qquad x = -0\cdot2301$$

$\therefore \; x = 2\cdot90 \quad \text{or} \quad x = -0\cdot23$, correct to two decimal places.

Quadratic Equations in Fractional Form

When fractions are involved do the following:

1. Factorise denominators (if necessary).
2. Find the L.C.M. of the denominators.
3. Express each part of the equation with its denominator equal to this L.C.M.
4. Remove the L.C.M.
5. Solve as before (using factors or formula).
6. Any answer that makes one of the original denominators = 0 must be rejected.

Example

Solve the equation $\dfrac{2x}{x+3} + \dfrac{4x+5}{x^2-x-12} = \dfrac{3}{x-4}$, $x \neq 4, -3$

Solution:

$$\frac{2x}{x+3} + \frac{4x+5}{x^2-x-12} = \frac{3}{x-4}$$

$$\frac{2x}{(x+3)} + \frac{4x+5}{(x+3)(x-4)} = \frac{3}{(x-4)} \qquad \left(\begin{array}{l} \text{factorise denominators.} \\ \text{Their L.C.M. is } (x+3)(x-4x) \end{array} \right)$$

$$\frac{2x(x-4) + 1(4x+5) = 3(x+3)}{(x+3)(x-4)} \qquad \text{(each part expressed in terms of the L.C.M.)}$$

$$2x(x-4) + 1(4x+5) = 3(x+3) \qquad \text{(remove L.C.M.)}$$

$$2x^2 - 8x + 4x + 5 = 3x + 9 \qquad \text{(remove brackets)}$$

$$2x^2 - 8x + 4x + 5 - 3x - 9 = 0 \qquad \text{(every term to the left)}$$

$$2x^2 - 7x - 4 = 0 \qquad \text{(clear up left hand side)}$$

$$(2x+1)(x-4) = 0 \qquad \text{(factorise left hand side)}$$

$$2x + 1 = 0 \quad \text{or} \quad x - 4 = 0 \qquad \text{(let each factor = 0)}$$

$$2x = -1 \quad \text{or} \qquad x = 4$$

$$x = -\frac{1}{2} \quad \text{or} \qquad x = 4$$

$x = -\dfrac{1}{2}$ will satisfy the original equation and is a solution.

$x = 4$ will make $\dfrac{3}{x-4} = \dfrac{3}{0}$ which is undefined.

Hence, $x = 4$ is rejected as a solution.

$\therefore$ the solution is $x = -\dfrac{1}{2}$.

So when solving an equation given in fractional form, reject any solution that would make any expression on the bottom equal to zero in the original equation.

Forming a Quadratic Equation When Given Its Roots

Example

Form a quadratic equation whose roots are (i) -3 and 7 (ii) $-\frac{4}{5}$ and $\frac{1}{3}$

Solution:

Method 1:

$$x^2 - (\text{add the roots})\, x + (\text{multiply the roots}) = 0$$

(i) -3 and 7

$$x^2 - (-3 + 7)x + (-3)(7) = 0$$
$$x^2 - (4)\,x + (-21) = 0$$
$$x^2 - 4x - 21 = 0$$

(ii) $-\frac{4}{5}$ and $\frac{1}{3}$

$$x^2 - \left(-\frac{4}{5} + \frac{1}{3}\right) x + \left(-\frac{4}{5}\right)\left(\frac{1}{3}\right) = 0$$
$$x^2 - \left(-\frac{7}{15}\right)x + \left(-\frac{4}{15}\right) = 0$$
$$x^2 + \frac{7}{15}\,x - \frac{4}{15} = 0$$
$$15x^2 + 7x - 4 = 0$$

Method 2:

(i) -3 and 7

Let $x = -3$ and $x = 7$

$\Rightarrow \quad x + 3 = 0$ and $x - 7 = 0$

$\Rightarrow \quad\quad\quad (x + 3)(x - 7) = 0$

$\Rightarrow \quad\quad x^2 - 7x + 3x - 21 = 0$

$\Rightarrow \quad\quad\quad x^2 - 4x - 21 = 0$

(ii) $-\frac{4}{5}$ and $\frac{1}{3}$

Let $x = -\frac{4}{5}$ and $x = \frac{1}{3}$

$\Rightarrow \quad 5x = -4$ and $3x = 1$

$\Rightarrow \quad 5x + 4 = 0$ and $3x - 1 = 0$

$\Rightarrow \quad\quad\quad (5x + 4)(3x - 1) = 0$

$\Rightarrow \quad\quad 15x^2 - 5x + 12x - 4 = 0$

$\Rightarrow \quad\quad\quad 15x^2 + 7x - 4 = 0$

Simultaneous Linear Equations

Simultaneous linear equations are solved with the following steps:

1. Write both equations in the form $ax + by = k$.
2. Make the coefficients of one of the variables the same in both equations.
3. Add or subtract (depending on signs) one equation from the other to form a new equation in one variable.
4. Solve the new equation obtained in Step 3.
5. Put the value obtained in Step 4 into one of the given equations to find the corresponding value of the other variable.

Example

Solve for x and y, $\quad 2x + y = 3(y - x) + 7$ and $\dfrac{x}{3} = 2 - \dfrac{y}{4}$.

Solution:

Step 1: First write both equations in the form $ax + by = k$

$$2x + y = 3(y - x) + 7$$

$2x + y = 3y - 3x + 7 \qquad$ (remove brackets)

$2x + y - 3y + 3x = 7 \qquad$ (letters to the left, number to the right)

$\boxed{5x - 2y = 7 \;\; \textbf{\textit{A}}} \qquad$ (in the form $ax + by = k$)

$$\dfrac{x}{3} = 2 - \dfrac{y}{4}$$

$(12)\dfrac{x}{3} = (12)2 - (12)\dfrac{y}{4} \qquad$ (multiply each part by 12)

$4x = 24 - 3y \qquad$ (simplify)

$\boxed{4x + 3y = 24 \;\; \textbf{\textit{B}}} \qquad$ (in the form $ax + by = k$)

$$5x - 2y = 7 \qquad \textbf{\textit{A}}$$
$$\underline{4x + 3y = 24} \qquad \textbf{\textit{B}}$$

Step 2: Make coefficient of x the same.

Multiply $\textbf{\textit{A}}$ by 4 and $\textbf{\textit{B}}$ by 5.

$$20x - 8y = 28 \qquad \textbf{\textit{A}} \times 4$$
$$\underline{20x + 15y = 120} \qquad \textbf{\textit{B}} \times 5$$

Step 3: Subtract the second equation from the first.

$$-23y = -92$$

Step 4: Solve this new equation.

$$\Rightarrow \quad 23y = 92$$
$$\Rightarrow \quad y = 4$$

Step 5: Put $y = 4$ into equation $\textbf{\textit{A}}$ or $\textbf{\textit{B}}$.

$$5x - 2y = 7 \qquad \textbf{\textit{A}}$$
$$\downarrow$$
$$5x - 2(4) = 7$$
$$\Rightarrow 5x - 8 = 7$$
$$\Rightarrow \quad 5x = 7 + 8$$
$$\Rightarrow \quad 5x = 15$$
$$\Rightarrow \quad x = 3$$

Thus, the solution is $x = 3$, $y = 4$

Solution Containing Fractions

If the solution contains fractions the substitution can be difficult.

In such cases the following method is useful:

Example

Solve for x and y, $\qquad 2x + y = 4 \qquad$ and $\qquad 3x - 4y = -2$

Solution:

Both equations are written in the form $ax + by = k$

Step 1: Eliminate y

$$2x + y = 4 \qquad \qquad \text{(A)}$$
$$\underline{3x - 4y = -2} \qquad \qquad \text{(B)}$$
$$8x + 4y = 16 \qquad \qquad \text{(A)} \times 4$$
$$\underline{3x - 4y = -2} \qquad \qquad \text{(B)} \times 1$$
$$11x = 14 \qquad \qquad \text{(add)}$$
$$x = \frac{14}{11}$$

Step 2: Eliminate x

$$2x + y = 4 \qquad \qquad \text{(A)}$$
$$\underline{3x - 4y = -2} \qquad \qquad \text{(B)}$$
$$6x + 3y = 12 \qquad \qquad \text{(A)} \times 3$$
$$\underline{6x - 8y = -4} \qquad \qquad \text{(B)} \times 2$$
$$11y = 16 \qquad \qquad \text{(subtract)}$$
$$y = \frac{16}{11}$$

Thus, the solution is $x = \frac{14}{11}$ and $y = \frac{16}{11}$.

Linear – Quadratic Systems

The **method of substitution** is used to solve between a linear equation and a quadratic equation.

The method involves three steps:

> **Step 1:** From the linear equation get one of the variables on its own.
>
> **Step 2:** Substitute this into the quadratic equation and solve.
>
> **Step 3:** Substitute separately the value(s) obtained in step 2 into the linear equation in step 1 to find the corresponding value(s) of the other variable.

Example

Solve for x and y, $\qquad x - y + 2 = 0 \qquad$ and $\qquad x^2 + y^2 = 10$.

Solution:

Step 1: $\qquad \qquad x - y + 2 = 0 \qquad \qquad$ [get x on its own from the linear equation]

$\Rightarrow \qquad \qquad \qquad x = (y - 2)$

Step 2: $\qquad x^2 + y^2 = 10$

$\Rightarrow \qquad (y - 2)^2 + y^2 = 10 \qquad$ [substitute $(y - 2)$ for x]

$\Rightarrow \qquad y^2 - 4y + 4 + y^2 = 10 \qquad$ [remove brackets]

$\Rightarrow \quad y^2 - 4y + 4 + y^2 - 10 = 0 \qquad$ [everything to the left]

$\Rightarrow \qquad 2y^2 - 4y - 6 = 0 \qquad$ [simplify]

$\Rightarrow \qquad y^2 - 2y - 3 = 0 \qquad$ [divide each part by 2]

$\Rightarrow \qquad (y - 3)(y + 1) = 0 \qquad$ [factorise the left hand side]

$\Rightarrow \quad y - 3 = 0 \quad$ or $\quad y + 1 = 0 \qquad$ [let each factor = 0]

$\Rightarrow \quad y = 3 \qquad$ or $\qquad y = -1$

Step 3: Substitute separately $y = 3$ and $y = -1$ into the linear equation:

	$y = 3$		$y = -1$
	$x = y - 2$		$x = y - 2$
$\Rightarrow$	$x = 3 - 2$	$\Rightarrow$	$x = -1 - 2$
$\Rightarrow$	$x = 1$	$\Rightarrow$	$x = -3$
	$x = 1,\ y = 3$		$x = -3,\ y = -1$

Thus, there are two solutions: $x = 1, y = 3 \quad$ or $\quad x = -3, y = -1$.

Example

Solve for x and y, $\qquad 2x - y + 1 = 0 \qquad$ and $\qquad y^2 = 2x^2 + x$.

Solution:

Step 1: $\qquad 2x - y + 1 = 0 \qquad$ [get y on its own from the linear equation]

$\Rightarrow \qquad -y = -2x - 1$

$\Rightarrow \qquad y = (2x + 1) \qquad$ [change all signs]

Step 2: $\qquad y^2 = 2x^2 + x$

$\Rightarrow \qquad (2x + 1)^2 = 2x^2 + x \qquad$ [substitute $(2x + 1)$ for y]

$\Rightarrow \qquad 4x^2 + 4x + 1 = 2x^2 + x \qquad$ [remove brackets]

$\Rightarrow \quad 4x^2 + 4x + 1 - 2x^2 - x = 0 \qquad$ [everything to the left]

$\Rightarrow \qquad 2x^2 + 3x + 1 = 0 \qquad$ [simplify]

$\Rightarrow \qquad (2x + 1)(x + 1) = 0 \qquad$ [factorise the left hand side]

$\Rightarrow \quad 2x + 1 = 0 \quad$ or $\ x + 1 = 0 \qquad$ [let each factor = 0]

$\Rightarrow \qquad 2x = -1 \quad$ or $\qquad x = -1$

$\Rightarrow \qquad x = -\dfrac{1}{2} \quad$ or $\qquad x = -1$

Step 3: Substitute separately $x = -\frac{1}{2}$ and $x = -1$ into the linear equation:

$$x = -\frac{1}{2}$$
$$y = 2x + 1$$
$$y = 2\left(-\frac{1}{2}\right) + 1$$
$$y = -1 + 1$$
$$y = 0$$
$$x = -\frac{1}{2}, y = 0$$

$$x = -1$$
$$y = 2x + 1$$
$$y = 2(-1) + 1$$
$$y = -2 + 1$$
$$y = -1$$
$$x = -1, \qquad y = -1$$

Thus, there are two solutions: $x = -\frac{1}{2}, y = 0$ or $x = -1, y = -1$

Cubic Expressions and Cubic Equations

Factor Theorem

> If $f(a) = 0$ for a polynomial $f(x)$, then:
>
> $x = a$ is a root (solution)
>
> and $(x - a)$ is a factor.

Example

If $x - 5$ is a factor of $x^3 - kx^2 - 13x - 10$, find the value of k.

Solution:

Let $f(x) = x^3 - kx^2 - 13x - 10$

If $x - 5$ is a factor, then $x = 5$ is a root and $f(5) = 0$

$$f(5) = 0$$

$\Rightarrow \quad (5)^3 - k(5)^2 - 13(5) - 10 = 0$ (replace x with 5)

$\Rightarrow \quad 125 - 25k - 65 - 10 = 0$

$\Rightarrow \quad -25k = 65 + 10 - 125$

$\Rightarrow \quad -25k = -50$

$\Rightarrow \quad 25k = 50$

$\Rightarrow \quad k = 2$

Example

If $(x + 1)$ and $(x - 2)$ are factors of $x^3 + 2x^2 + ax + b$, find the values of $a, b, \in \mathbf{R}$.

Solution:

Let $f(x) = x^3 + 2x^2 + ax + b$

If $(x + 1)$ is a factor, then $x = -1$ is a root and $f(-1) = 0$

If $(x - 2)$ is a factor, then $x = 2$ is a root and $f(2) = 0$

$f(-1) = 0$	$f(2) = 0$
$(-1)^3 + 2(-1)^2 + a(-1) + b = 0$	$(2)^3 + 2(2)^2 + a(2) + b = 0$
$-1 + 2 - a + b = 0$	$8 + 8 + 2a + b = 0$
$-a + b = 1 - 2$	$2a + b = -8 - 8$
$-a + b = -1$ (**A**)	$2a + b = -16$ (**B**)

We now solve the simultaneous equations (**A**) and (**B**):

$$-a + b = -1 \quad \textbf{A}$$
$$\underline{2a + b = -16 \quad \textbf{B}}$$
$$-3a = 15 \quad \text{(subtract)}$$
$$\Rightarrow \quad 3a = -15$$
$$\Rightarrow \quad a = -5$$

$$-a + b = -1 \quad \textbf{A}$$
$$\downarrow$$
$$-(-5) + b = -1$$
$$\Rightarrow \quad 5 + b = -1$$
$$\Rightarrow \quad b = -1 - 5$$
$$\Rightarrow \quad b = -6$$

Put in $a = -5$ into (**A**) or (**B**)

Thus, $a = -5$ and $b = -6$

A cubic equation is solved with the following steps:

1. Find the first root, a, by trial and error, i.e. try $f(1), f(-1), f(2), f(-2)$ etc.
   (Only try numbers that divide evenly into the constant in the equation.)
2. If $x = a$ is a root, then $(x - a)$ is a factor.
3. Divide $f(x)$ by $(x - a)$ which always gives a quadratic expression.
4. Let this quadratic $= 0$ and solve.

Example

Solve the equation $2x^3 - 9x^2 + 7x + 6 = 0$

Solution:

Let $f(x) = 2x^3 - 9x^2 + 7x + 6$

1. The first root will be a factor of 6 (i.e. $\pm 1, \pm 2, \pm 3, \pm 6$)

$$f(1) = 2(1)^3 - 9(1)^2 + 7(1) + 6 \qquad = 2 - 9 + 7 + 6 \qquad = 6 \neq 0$$

$$f(-1) = 2(-1)^3 - 9(-1)^2 + 7(-1) + 6 \quad = -2 - 9 - 7 + 6 \quad = -12 \neq 0$$

$$f(2) = 2(2)^3 - 9(2)^2 + 7(2) + 6 \qquad = 16 - 36 + 14 + 6 = 0$$

$$\therefore x = 2 \text{ is a root}$$

2. $$\therefore (x - 2) \text{ is a factor}$$

3. Divide $2x^3 - 9x^2 + 7x + 6$ by $(x - 2)$

$$
\begin{array}{r}
2x^2 - 5x - 3 \\
x - 2 \overline{)\, 2x^3 - 9x^2 + 7x + 6} \\
\underline{2x^3 - 4x^2} \\
-5x^2 + 7x \\
\underline{-5x^2 + 10x} \\
-3x + 6 \\
\underline{-3x + 6} \\
0
\end{array}
$$

4. Let $2x^2 - 5x - 3 = 0$

$\Rightarrow \quad (2x + 1)(x - 3) = 0 \qquad$ [factorise]

$\Rightarrow \quad 2x + 1 = 0 \quad$ or $\quad x - 3 = 0 \quad$ [let each factor = 0]

$\qquad 2x = -1 \quad$ or $\qquad x = 3$

$\qquad x = -\frac{1}{2} \quad$ or $\qquad x = 3$

Thus the roots of the equation are $-\frac{1}{2}$, 2 and 3.

Simple Inequalities

Algebraic expressions which are linked by one of the following four symbols are called inequalities.

$>$ greater than $<$ less than

$\geq$ greater than or equal to $\leq$ less than or equal to

Solving inequalities is exactly the same as solving equations with the following exception:

> If we multiply or divide both sides of an inequality by a negative number, we must reverse the direction of the inequality.
>
> '>' becomes '<'   or   '<' becomes '>'

The following rules apply to graphing inequalities on a number line.

> Number line for $x \in N$ or $x \in Z$, use dots.
>
> Number line for $x \in R$, use a 'full' heavy line.

Example

Find the range of values of $x \in R$ for which $3(x - 4) > 5(2x - 3) + 17$ and graph your solution on the number line.

Solution:

$$3(x - 4) > 5(2x - 3) + 17$$

$\Rightarrow \quad 3x - 12 > 10x - 15 + 17$ [remove the brackets]

$\Rightarrow \quad 3x - 10x > -15 + 17 + 12$ [letters to the left, numbers to the right]

$\Rightarrow \quad\quad -7x > 14$ [clear up both sides]

$\Rightarrow \quad\quad 7x < -14$ [change signs and reverse inequality sign]

$\Rightarrow \quad\quad x < -2$ [divide both sides by 7]

Note: A circle is put around –2 to indicate it is not part of the solution.

Example

Find the solution set E of $2x + 7 \leq 19$, $x \in R$.

Find the solution set H of $3 - 2x < 11$, $x \in R$.

Find $E \cap H$ and graph your solution on the number line.

Solution:

$E:$ $2x + 7 \le 19$

$\Rightarrow$ $2x \le 19 - 7$

$\Rightarrow$ $2x \le 12$

$\therefore$ $x \le 6$

$H:$ $3 - 2x < 11$

$\Rightarrow$ $-2x < 11 - 3$

$\Rightarrow$ $-2x < 8$

$\Rightarrow$ $2x > -8$

$\Rightarrow$ $x > -4$

$$E \cap H : -4 < x \le 6$$

Example

Solve $\frac{1}{2}x - 2 < x - \frac{1}{2}$, $x \in \mathbf{Z}$, and graph your solution on the number line.

Solution:

$\frac{1}{2}x - 2 < x - \frac{1}{2}$

$x - 4 < 2x - 1$ [multiply each part by 2]

$x - 2x < -1 + 4$ [letters to the left, numbers to the right]

$-x < 3$ [clear up both sides]

$x > -3$ [change signs and reverse inequality sign]

Indices

Fundamental Laws of Indices:

Law 1: $a^m . a^n = a^{m+n}$

           Multiplying powers of the same number, **add** the indices.

Law 2: $\dfrac{a^m}{a^n} = a^{m-n}$

           Dividing powers of the same number, **subtract** the index on the bottom from the index on the top.

Law 3: $(a^m)^n = a^{mn}$

Raising the power of a number to a power, **multiply** the indices.

Law 4: $(ab)^m = a^m b^m$

Raising a product to a power, **every** factor is raised to the power.

Law 5: $\left(\dfrac{a}{b}\right)^m = \dfrac{a^m}{b^m}$

Raising a quotient to a power, **both** top and bottom are raised to the power.

Law 6: $a^0 = 1$

Any number raised to the power zero has a value of 1.

Law 7: $a^{-m} = \dfrac{1}{a^m}$

A number with a negative index is equal to its reciprocal with a positive index.

Law 8: $a^{\frac{m}{n}} = \left(a^{\frac{1}{n}}\right)^m$

Take the root first and then raise to the power (or vice versa).

Note: Simplify $8^{\frac{1}{3}}$, means:

Find the number multiplied by itself three times that will equal 8.

Obviously, this is 2, i.e. $8^{\frac{1}{3}} = 2$.

Similarly, $81^{\frac{1}{4}} = 3$ and $25^{\frac{1}{2}} = 5$.

Note: $\sqrt{x} = x^{\frac{1}{2}}$

Example

Simplify each of the following:

(i) $32^{\frac{4}{5}}$ (ii) $27^{1\frac{2}{3}}$ (iii) $64^{-\frac{2}{3}}$ (iv) $27^{\frac{2}{3}} \cdot 16^{-\frac{3}{4}}$

Solution:

(i) $32^{\frac{4}{5}}$ $=$ $\left(32^{\frac{1}{5}}\right)^4$ $=$ $(2)^4$ $=$ 16

(ii) $27^{1\frac{2}{3}}$ $=$ $27^{\frac{5}{3}}$ $=$ $\left(27^{\frac{1}{3}}\right)^5$ $=$ $(3)^5 = 243$

39

(iii) $64^{-\frac{2}{3}} = \dfrac{1}{64^{\frac{2}{3}}} = \dfrac{1}{\left(64^{\frac{1}{3}}\right)^2} = \dfrac{1}{(4)^2} = \dfrac{1}{16}$

(iv) $27^{\frac{2}{3}} \cdot 16^{-\frac{3}{4}} = \dfrac{27^{\frac{2}{3}}}{16^{\frac{3}{4}}} = \dfrac{\left(27^{\frac{1}{3}}\right)^2}{\left(16^{\frac{1}{4}}\right)^3} = \dfrac{(3)^2}{(2)^3} = \dfrac{9}{8}$

Example

Express each of the following in the form: $\dfrac{a}{b}$, $a, b \in N$.

(i) $\left(2\dfrac{1}{4}\right)^{1\frac{1}{2}}$ **(ii)** $\left(\dfrac{25}{16}\right)^{-\frac{3}{2}}$ **(iii)** $\left(\dfrac{1}{27}\right)^{\frac{2}{3}}$

Solution:

(i) $\left(2\dfrac{1}{4}\right)^{1\frac{1}{2}} = \left(\dfrac{9}{4}\right)^{\frac{3}{2}} = \dfrac{9^{\frac{3}{2}}}{4^{\frac{3}{2}}} = \dfrac{\left(9^{\frac{1}{2}}\right)^3}{\left(4^{\frac{1}{2}}\right)^3} = \dfrac{(3)^3}{(2)^3} = \dfrac{27}{8}$

(ii) $\left(\dfrac{25}{16}\right)^{-\frac{3}{2}} = \dfrac{25^{-\frac{3}{2}}}{16^{-\frac{3}{2}}} = \dfrac{16^{\frac{3}{2}}}{25^{\frac{3}{2}}} = \dfrac{\left(16^{\frac{1}{2}}\right)^3}{\left(25^{\frac{1}{2}}\right)^3} = \dfrac{(4)^3}{(5)^3} = \dfrac{64}{125}$

(iii) $\left(\dfrac{1}{27}\right)^{\frac{2}{3}} = \dfrac{1^{\frac{2}{3}}}{27^{\frac{2}{3}}} = \dfrac{1}{\left(27^{\frac{1}{3}}\right)^2} = \dfrac{1}{(3)^2} = \dfrac{1}{9}$

Index Equations

Any equation involving the variable in the indices of the numbers is known as an index equation.

To solve an index equation do the following:

1. Write all the numbers as powers of the same number (usually a prime number).
2. Use the laws of indices, if necessary.
3. Equate the powers and solve this equation.

Example

(i) Find the value of x if $4^{x-1} = \frac{1}{32}$

(ii) Write $\frac{125}{\sqrt{5}}$ as a power of 5, and solve for x the equation $5^{2x+1} = \left(\frac{125}{\sqrt{5}}\right)^3$

Solution:

(i) $\quad 4^{x-1} = \frac{1}{32}$ $\qquad$ (both 4 and 32 can be written as powers of 2)

$\Rightarrow \quad (2^2)^{x-1} = \frac{1}{2^5}$ $\qquad$ (4 and 32 as powers of 2)

$\Rightarrow \quad 2^{2x-2} = 2^{-5}$ $\qquad$ (use the laws of indices)

$\Rightarrow \quad 2x - 2 = -5$ $\qquad$ (equate the powers)

$\Rightarrow \qquad 2x = -5 + 2$

$\Rightarrow \qquad 2x = -3$

$\Rightarrow \qquad x = -\frac{3}{2}$

(ii) $\quad \frac{125}{\sqrt{5}} = \frac{5^3}{5^{\frac{1}{2}}} = 5^{3-\frac{1}{2}} = 5^{2\frac{1}{2}}$

$5^{2x+1} = \left(\frac{125}{\sqrt{5}}\right)^3$

$\downarrow$

$\Rightarrow \quad 5^{2x+1} = \left(5^{2\frac{1}{2}}\right)^3$

$\Rightarrow \quad 5^{2x+1} = 5^{7\frac{1}{2}}$ $\qquad$ (multiply the indices on the right hand side)

$\Rightarrow \quad 2x + 1 = 7\frac{1}{2}$ $\qquad$ (equate the powers)

$\Rightarrow \quad 4x + 2 = 15$ $\qquad$ (multiply each part by 2)

$\Rightarrow \qquad 4x = 15 - 2$

$\Rightarrow \qquad 4x = 13$

$\Rightarrow \qquad x = \frac{13}{4}$

Finding the Equation of a Curve When Given Points on It

$f(x) = y$

$f(2) = 3$ means that when $x = 2$, $y = 3$ or the point $(2, 3)$ is on the curve.

$f(-1) = 0$ means that when $x = -1$, $y = 0$ or the point $(-1, 0)$ is on the curve.

Method for finding the equation of a curve.

> 1.   Let $y = f(x)$.
>
> 2.   Put in separately the given values of x and y to obtain two equations.
>
> 3.   Use simultaneous equations.

Example

The graph of the quadratic function $x \rightarrow f(x)$, $x \in \mathbf{R}$ is as shown.

Express $f(x)$ in the form $x^2 + bx + c$.

Solution:

For the graph, y is the same as $f(x)$.

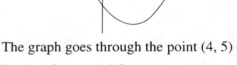

Let $y = f(x)$

$\therefore \qquad y = x^2 + bx + c$

The graph goes through the point $(-1, 0)$	The graph goes through the point $(4, 5)$
Put in -1 for x and 0 for y	Put in 4 for x and 5 for y
$y = x^2 + bx + c$	$y = x^2 + bx + c$
$0 = (-1)^2 + b(-1) + c$	$5 = (4)^2 + b(4) + c$
$0 = 1 - b + c$	$5 = 16 + 4b + c$
$\Rightarrow \quad b - c = 1 \qquad \textcircled{1}$	$\Rightarrow \quad 4b + c = -11 \qquad \textcircled{2}$

We now solve between equations $\textcircled{1}$ and $\textcircled{2}$:

$$
\begin{array}{ll}
b - c = 1 & \textcircled{1} \\
\underline{4b + c = -11} & \textcircled{2} \\
5b = -10 & \text{(add)} \\
b = -2 &
\end{array}
$$

put in $b = -2$ into $\textcircled{1}$ or $\textcircled{2}$

$$
\begin{array}{ll}
b - c = 1 & \textcircled{1} \\
\downarrow & \\
\Rightarrow -2 - c = 1 & \\
-c = 1 + 2 & \\
-c = 3 & \\
c = -3 &
\end{array}
$$

$$f(x) = x^2 + bx + c$$

$$\therefore \ f(x) = x^2 - 2x - 3$$

Sometimes we are not given a graph.

Example

$g : x \rightarrow ax^2 + bx + 1$ is a function defined on **R**.

If $g(1) = 0$ and $g(2) = 3$, write down two equations in a and b.

Hence, calculate the value of a and the value of b.

Solution:

$$\text{Let } y = g(x)$$
$$\therefore \ y = ax^2 + bx + 1$$

$g(1) = 0$	$g(2) = 3$
$\Rightarrow$ when $x = 1$, $y = 0$	$\Rightarrow$ when $x = 2$, $y = 3$
$\therefore$ put in 1 for x and 0 for y	$\therefore$ put in 2 for x and 3 for y
$y = ax^2 + bx + 1$	$y = ax^2 + bx + 1$
$0 = a(1)^2 + b(1) + 1$	$3 = a(2)^2 + b(2) + 1$
$0 = a + b + 1$	$3 = 4a + 2b + 1$
$\Rightarrow \quad a + b = -1 \qquad ①$	$\Rightarrow \quad 4a + 2b = 2$
	$\Rightarrow \quad 2a + b = 1 \qquad ②$

We now solve between the equations ① and ② :

$a + b = -1 \qquad ①$	$a + b = -1 \qquad ①$
$\underline{2a + b = 1 \qquad ②}$	$\downarrow$
$\quad -a = -2 \qquad$ (subtract)	$2 + b = -1$
$\quad a = 2$	$b = -1 - 2$
	$b = -3$

put in $a = 2$ into ① or ②

Thus, $a = 2$ and $b = -3$

Sometimes we are given points in disguise. For example, if we are given:

The solutions of $f(x) = 0$ are -3 and 1.

$\Rightarrow \ f(-3) = 0$, i.e. when $x = -3$, $y = 0$

$\Rightarrow \ f(-1) = 0$, i.e. when $x = -1$, $y = 0$

and we proceed as before.

3. COMPLEX NUMBERS

Addition, Subtraction and Multiplication by a Real Number

Example

If $z_1 = 2 + 3i$, $z_2 = 1 - 4i$ and $z_3 = -2i$, express

(i) $3z_1 - 2z_2$ **(ii)** $5z_2 - 4z_3$ in the form $a + bi$

Solution:

(i) $3z_1 - 2z_2$

$= 3(2 + 3i) - 2(1 - 4i)$

$= 6 + 9i - 2 + 8i$

$= 4 + 17i$

(ii) $5z_2 - 4z_3$

$= 5(1 - 4i) - 4(-2i)$

$= 5 - 20i + 8i$

$= 5 - 12i$

Multiplication

Multiplication of complex numbers is performed using the usual algebraic method except, i^2 **is replaced with –1.**

Example

Simplify $2 + 3i(4 + 5i) - 6i$ and express your answer in the form $p + qi$, $p, q \in R$.

Solution:

$2 + 3i (4 + 5i) - 6i$

$= 2 + 12i + 15i^2 - 6i$ (remove the brackets)

$= 2 + 12i + 15(-1) - 6i$ (replace i^2 with –1)

$= 2 + 12i - 15 - 6i$

$= -13 + 6i$

Example

If $z_1 = 2 - 5i$ and $z_2 = -1 - i$, express in the form $x + yi$:

(i) $z_1 \cdot z_2$ **(ii)** z_1^2 **(iii)** iz_1z_2

Solution:

(i) $z_1 \cdot z_2$

$= (2 - 5i)(-1 - i)$

$= -2 - 2i + 5i + 5i^2$

$= -2 - 2i + 5i + 5(-1)$

   (replace i^2 with -1)

$= -2 - 2i + 5i - 5$

$= -7 + 3i$

(ii) z_1^2

$= (2 - 5i)(2 - 5i)$

$= 4 - 10i - 10i + 25i^2$

$= 4 - 10i - 10i + 25\,(-1)$

   (replace i^2 with -1)

$= 4 - 10i - 10i - 25$

$= -21 - 20i$

(iii) iz_1z_2

$= i(2 - 5i)(-1 - i)$

First work out $i(2 - 5i)$ and then multiply your answer by $(-1 - i)$

$i\,(2 - 5i)$

$= 2i - 5i^2$

$= 2i - 5(-1)$

$= 2i + 5$

$= 5 + 2i$

$(5 + 2i)(-1 - i)$

$= -5 - 5i - 2i - 2i^2$

$= -5 - 5i - 2i - 2(-1)$

$= -5 - 5i - 2i + 2$

$= -3 - 7i$

Division

> **Multiply the top and bottom by the conjugate of the bottom**

This will convert the complex number on the bottom into a real number. The division is then performed by dividing the real number on the bottom into each part on the top.

If $z = a + bi$ then $\bar{z} = a - bi$,

i.e. simply change the sign of the imaginary part.

For example, if $z_1 = -3 + 2i$ then $\bar{z}_1 = -3 - 2i$ and

               if $z_2 = -5 + 4i$ then $\bar{z}_2 = -5 - 4i$

Example

Express $\dfrac{1 + 7i}{4 + 3i}$ in the form $a + bi$.

Solution:

$$\dfrac{1 + 7i}{4 + 3i} = \dfrac{1 + 7i}{4 + 3i} \cdot \dfrac{4 - 3i}{4 - 3i}$$ [Multiply top and bottom by the conjugate of the bottom]

Top by the Top	Bottom by the Bottom
$= (1 + 7i)(4 - 3i)$	$= (4 + 3i)(4 - 3i)$
$= 1(4 - 3i) + 7i(4 - 3i)$	$= 4(4 - 3i) + 3i(4 - 3i)$
$= 4 - 3i + 28i - 21i^2$	$= 16 - 12i + 12i - 9i^2$
$= 4 - 3i + 28i - 21(-1)$	$= 16 - 9(-1)$
$= 4 - 3i + 28i + 21$	$= 16 + 9$
$= 25 + 25i$	$= 25$

$$\therefore \dfrac{1 + 7i}{4 + 3i} = \dfrac{25 + 25i}{25} = \dfrac{25}{25} + \dfrac{25}{25}i = 1 + i$$

Example

If $\dfrac{2 - i}{1 - 2i} = p + qi,\ p,\ q \in \mathbf{R}$, evaluate $p^2 + q^2$.

Solution:

This is a division question in disguise.

$$\dfrac{2 - i}{1 - 2i} = \dfrac{2 - i}{1 - 2i} \cdot \dfrac{1 + 2i}{1 + 2i}$$ $\left(\begin{array}{l}\text{Multiply top and bottom by}\\ \text{the conjugate of the bottom}\end{array}\right)$

Top by the Top	Bottom by the Bottom
$(2 - i)(1 + 2i)$	$(1 + 2i)(1 - 2i)$
$= 2 + 4i - i - 2i^2$	$= 1 - 2i + 2i - 4i^2$
$= 2 + 4i - i - 2(-1)$	$= 1 - 2i + 2i - 4(-1)$
$= 2 + 4i - i + 2$	$= 1 - 2i + 2i + 4$
$= 4 + 3i$	$= 5$

$$\therefore \frac{2-i}{1-2i} = \frac{4+3i}{5} = \frac{4}{5} + \frac{3}{5}i$$

$$\therefore \frac{4}{5} + \frac{3}{5}i = p + qi$$

$$\therefore p = \frac{4}{5} \text{ and } q = \frac{3}{5}$$

$$p^2 + q^2$$
$$= \left(\frac{4}{5}\right)^2 + \left(\frac{3}{5}\right)^2$$
$$= \frac{16}{25} + \frac{9}{25}$$
$$= \frac{25}{25}$$
$$= 1$$

Equality of Complex Numbers

If two complex numbers are equal then:
their real parts are equal and their imaginary parts are also equal.

For example, if $a + bi = c + di$,

then $a = c$ and $b = d$.

This definition is very useful when dealing with equations involving complex numbers.
Equations involving complex numbers are usually solved with the following steps:

1. Remove the brackets.
2. Put an R under the real parts and an I under the imaginary parts to identify them.
3. Let the real parts equal the real parts and the imaginary parts equal the imaginary parts.
4. Solve these resultant equations (usually simultaneous equations).

Note: If one side of the equation does not contain a real part or an imaginary part it should be replaced with 0 or $0i$, respectively.

Example

Solve for real s and real t

$$s(2 - i) + ti(4 + 2i) = 1 + s + ti.$$

Solution:

$$s(2 - i) + ti(4 + 2i) = 1 + s + ti$$

1. $2s - si + 4ti + 2ti^2 = 1 + s + ti$ (remove the brackets)

$2s - si + 4ti + 2t(-1) = 1 + s + ti$ (replace i^2 with -1)

$2s - si + 4ti - 2t = 1 + s + ti$

2. R I I R R R I (identify real and imaginary parts)

3.   Real parts = Real parts   Imag. parts = Imag. parts

$$2s - 2t = 1 + s \qquad\qquad -s + 4t = t$$

$$\Rightarrow \qquad s - 2t = 1 \quad \text{①} \qquad\qquad \Rightarrow -s + 3t = 0 \quad \text{②}$$

4.   Solve between the equations ① and ②.

$$\begin{array}{ll} s - 2t = 1 \quad \text{①} & -s + 3t = 0 \quad \text{②} \\ \underline{-s + 3t = 0} \quad \text{②} & -s + 3(1) = 0 \\ t = 1 \quad \text{(add)} & -s + 3 = 0 \\ \text{put } t = 1 \text{ into ① or ②} & -s = -3 \\ & s = 3 \end{array}$$

Thus, $s = 3$, $t = 1$.

Example

$z = 4 - 2i$, if $\bar{z} - pz = qi$, $p, q \in \mathbf{R}$, find p and q.

Solution:

$$\bar{z} - pz = qi$$

The right hand side has no real part, hence a 0, representing the real part, should be placed on the right hand side.

$$\bar{z} - pz = 0 + qi \qquad \text{(put 0 in for real part)}$$

$$(4 + 2i) - p(4 - 2i) = 0 + qi \qquad \text{(sub. for } z \text{ and } \bar{z})$$

1. $4 + 2i - 4p + 2pi = 0 + qi$ (remove the brackets)

2. R I R I R I (identify real and imag. parts)

3.   Real Parts = Real Parts   Imag. parts = Imag. parts

$$4 - 4p = 0 \quad \text{(A)} \qquad\qquad 2 + 2p = q \quad \text{(B)}$$

4. Solve between the equations $\textcircled{A}$ and $\textcircled{B}$:

$$4 - 4p = 0 \qquad \textcircled{A}$$
$$\Rightarrow \qquad -4p = -4$$
$$\Rightarrow \qquad 4p = 4$$
$$\Rightarrow \qquad p = 1$$

put in $p = 1$ into $\textcircled{B}$

$$2 + 2p = q \qquad \textcircled{B}$$
$$2 + 2(1) = q$$
$$2 + 2 = q$$
$$4 = q$$

Solution: $p = 1$, $q = 4$

Example

Let $z = 3 - 2i$, solve for real s and real t

$$\frac{s + ti}{1 + 2i} = \bar{z}$$

Solution:

$$\frac{s + ti}{1 + 2i} = \bar{z}$$

$$\Rightarrow \quad \frac{s + ti}{1 + 2i} = 3 + 2i \qquad \text{[replace } \bar{z} \text{ with } (3 + 2i)\text{]}$$

$$\Rightarrow \quad s + ti = (1 + 2i)(3 + 2i) \qquad \text{[multiply both sides by } (1 + 2i)\text{]}$$

$$\Rightarrow \quad s + ti = 3 + 2i + 6i + 4i^2 \qquad \text{[remove brackets]}$$

$$\Rightarrow \quad s + ti = 3 + 2i + 6i + 4(-1) \qquad \text{[replace } i^2 \text{ with } -1\text{]}$$

$$\Rightarrow \quad s + ti = 3 + 2i + 6i - 4$$

$$\Rightarrow \quad s + ti = -1 + 8i$$

$$\quad R \quad I \quad R \quad I \qquad \text{[identify real and imaginary parts]}$$

$$\Rightarrow s = -1 \text{ and } t = 8 \qquad [R\text{'s} = R\text{'s and } I\text{'s} = I\text{'s}]$$

Argand Diagram

Each complex number must be written in the form $a + bi$ and then plot the point (a,b).
For example, the complex number $5 - 4i$ is represented by the point $(5, -4)$.

Example

$z = 2 + 3i$, plot z, iz and $\dfrac{13}{z}$ on an Argand diagram.

Solution:

First write each in the form $a + bi$.

$$z = 2 + 3i \qquad \text{(already in the form } a + bi\text{)}$$
$$= (2, 3)$$

iz

$= i(2 + 3i)$

$= 2i + 3i^2$

$= 2i + 3(-1)$

$= 2i - 3$

$= -3 + 2i$

$= (-3, 2)$

$\dfrac{13}{z}$

$= \dfrac{13}{2 + 3i} = \dfrac{13}{2 + 3i} \cdot \dfrac{2 - 3i}{2 - 3i}$

$= \dfrac{26 - 39i}{4 - 6i + 6i - 9i^2}$

$= \dfrac{26 - 39i}{13} = \dfrac{26}{13} - \dfrac{39}{13}i$

$= 2 - 3i$

$= (2, -3)$

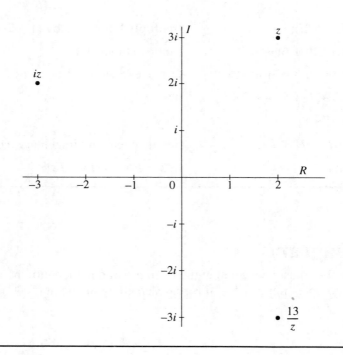

50

Transformations

Method:
Write each number as a point and continue as in coordinate geometry.

Example

$z_1 = 2 + 3i$, $z_2 = -1 + 5i$ and $z_3 = -4 + 7i$. Find:

(i) w, the image of z_1 under central symmetry in z_2.

(ii) s, the image of z_2 under the translation $z_3 \rightarrow z_1$.

Solution:

$z_1 = (2, 3)$ $z_2 = (-1, 5)$ $z_3 = (-4, 7)$ [points]

(i)   Find w

Rough diagram

(missing coordinates)

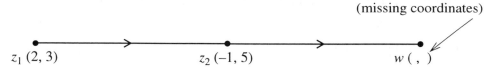

z_1 (2, 3) z_2 (-1, 5) w (,)

Translation from z_1 to z_2.

Rule: take 3 from real part, add 2 to imaginary part

Apply this translation to z_2 to find w.

z_2 (-1, 5) $\rightarrow$ (-1 - 3, 5 + 2) = w (-4, 7)

$\therefore$ $w = -4 + 7i$

(ii)   Find s

Rough diagram

z_3 (-4, 7) z_1 (2, 3)

(missing coordinates)

z_2 (-1, 5) s (,)

Translation from z_3 to z_1.

Rule: add 6 to real part, take 4 from imaginary part.

Apply this translation to z_2 to find s.

z_2 (-1, 5) $\rightarrow$ (-1 + 6, 5 - 4) = s (5, 1)

$\therefore$ $s = 5 + i$

Example

$u = 1 - 2i,$ $v = 2 + 5i,$ $x = 6 + 4i$ and $y = a + bi.$

If u, v, x and y are the vertices of the parallelogram $uvxy$, find the values of a and b.

Solution:

Make a rough diagram
(keep cyclic order).

$\overrightarrow{vx} = \overrightarrow{uy}$

(the movement from v to x is the same as u to y)

We find the rule that moves v to x.

Then apply this rule to u to find y.

$\overrightarrow{vx} : (2, 5) \rightarrow (6, 4)$

Rule: Add 4 to the real part and subtract 1 from the imag. part.

$\overrightarrow{uy} : (1, -2) \rightarrow (1 + 4, -2 - 1) = (5, -3)$

$\therefore$ the coordinates of y are $(5, -3)$

$\therefore$ $y = 5 - 3i$

$y = a + bi$

$\therefore$ $a = 5$ and $b = -3$

Note: By cyclic order we mean that the points are taken in either clockwise or anti-clockwise direction.

Modulus

The **modulus** of a complex number is the distance from the origin to the point representing the complex number on the Argand diagram.

If $z = a + bi$, then the modulus of z is written $|z|$ or $|a + bi|$.

The point z represents the complex number $a + bi$.

The modulus of z is the distance from the origin, o, to the complex number $a + bi$.

Using the theorem of Pythagoras

$|z| = \sqrt{a^2 + b^2}$

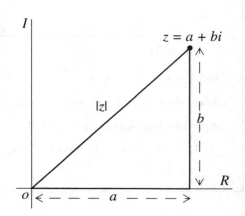

If $z = a + bi$, then

$$|z| = |a + bi| = \sqrt{a^2 + b^2}$$

Example

Find (i) $|3 + 4i|$ (ii) $|2 - 5i|$ (iii) $|3i|$

Solution:

(i) $|3 + 4i|$

$= \sqrt{3^2 + 4^2}$

$= \sqrt{9 + 16}$

$= \sqrt{25} = 5$

(ii) $|2 - 5i|$

$= \sqrt{2^2 + 5^2}$

$= \sqrt{4 + 25}$

$= \sqrt{29}$

(iii) $|3i| = 0 + 3i$

$= \sqrt{0^2 + 3^2}$

$= \sqrt{0 + 9}$

$= \sqrt{9} = 3$

Notes:

1. i **never** appears when the modulus formula is used.

2. The modulus of a complex number is **always positive**.

3. Before using the formula a complex number must be in the form $a + bi$.

Example

If $z_1 = 1 + 7i$ and $z_2 = 1 - 3i$, show that:

(i) $|z_1 . z_2| = |z_1| . |z_2|$ (ii) $\left|\dfrac{z_1}{z_2}\right| = \dfrac{|z_1|}{|z_2|}$

Solution:

(i)

$|z_1| = |1 + 7i| = \sqrt{1^2 + 7^2} = \sqrt{1 + 49} = \sqrt{50}$

$|z_2| = |1 - 3i| = \sqrt{1^2 + 3^2} = \sqrt{1 + 9} = \sqrt{10}$

$\therefore \quad |z_1| . |z_2| = \sqrt{50} . \sqrt{10} = \sqrt{50 . 10} = \sqrt{500}$

$|z_1 . z_2|$

First write $z_1 . z_2$ in the form $a + bi$.

$\quad z_1 . z_2 = (1 + 7i)(1 - 3i) = 1 - 3i + 7i - 21i^2 = 22 + 4i$

$\therefore \quad |z_1 . z_2| = |22 + 4i| = \sqrt{22^2 + 4^2} = \sqrt{484 + 16} = \sqrt{500}$

$\therefore \quad |z_1 . z_2| = |z_1| . |z_2|$

(ii) $\dfrac{|z_1|}{|z_2|} = \dfrac{\sqrt{50}}{\sqrt{10}} = \sqrt{\dfrac{50}{10}} = \sqrt{5}$

$$\left| \frac{z_1}{z_2} \right|$$

First write $\dfrac{z_1}{z_2}$ in the form $a + bi$

$$\frac{z_1}{z_2} = \frac{1 + 7i}{1 - 3i} = \frac{1 + 7i}{1 - 3i} \cdot \frac{1 + 3i}{1 + 3i} = \frac{1 + 3i + 7i + 21i^2}{1 + 3i - 3i - 9i^2}$$

$$= \frac{1 + 3i + 7i - 21}{1 + 9} = \frac{-20 + 10i}{10} = -2 + i$$

$\therefore \quad \left| \dfrac{z_1}{z_2} \right| = |-2 + i| = \sqrt{2^2 + 1^2} = \sqrt{4 + 1} = \sqrt{5}$

$$\therefore \quad \left| \frac{z_1}{z_2} \right| = \frac{|z_1|}{|z_2|}$$

The following results always hold (and can be very useful):

$$|z_1 . z_2| = |z_1| . |z_2| \qquad \left| \frac{z_1}{z_2} \right| = \frac{|z_1|}{|z_2|}$$

Example

Let $z_1 = 2 + 3i$.

Find $|z_1|$ and hence write down five other complex numbers whose modulus is the same as $|z_1|$.

If $z_2 = 2 + 3i$, find the value of $k \in \mathbf{R}$ such that $|z_1| = k \left| \dfrac{z_1}{z_2} \right|$.

Solution:

$|z_1| = |2 + 3i| = \sqrt{2^2 + 3^2} = \sqrt{4 + 9} = \sqrt{13}$

Five other complex numbers that have a modulus of $\sqrt{13}$ are:

$2 - 3i, \quad 3 + 2i, \quad 3 - 2i, \quad -3 - 2i, \quad -3 + 2i.$

$|z_2| = |2 - 3i| = \sqrt{2^2 + 3^2} = \sqrt{4 + 9} = \sqrt{13}$

$$\left| \frac{z_1}{z_2} \right| = \frac{|z_1|}{|z_2|} = \frac{\sqrt{13}}{\sqrt{13}} = 1$$

$$\text{Given:} \qquad |z_1| = k \left| \frac{z_1}{z_2} \right|$$

$$\downarrow \qquad \downarrow$$

$$\sqrt{13} = k\,(1)$$

$$\sqrt{13} = k$$

Example

If $z = 3 + 4i$, verify $\left|\dfrac{z}{|z|}\right| = 1$

Solution:

$|z| = |3 + 4i| = \sqrt{3^2 + 4^2} = \sqrt{9 + 16} = \sqrt{25} = 5$

$\dfrac{z}{|z|} = \dfrac{3 + 4i}{5} = \dfrac{3}{5} + \dfrac{4}{5}i$

$\left|\dfrac{z}{|z|}\right| = \left|\dfrac{3}{5} + \dfrac{4}{5}i\right| = \sqrt{\left(\dfrac{3}{5}\right)^2 + \left(\dfrac{4}{5}\right)^2} = \sqrt{\dfrac{9}{25} + \dfrac{16}{25}} = \sqrt{\dfrac{25}{25}} = \sqrt{1} = 1$

Example

$w = 4 + 6i$ and $z = 4 + 2i$. Calculate $|w - z|$.

Draw the set K of all complex numbers such that each is a distance of 4 from z. K intersects the imaginary axis at pi, find p.

Solution:

$$w - z = (4 + 6i) - (4 + 2i)$$
$$= 4 + 6i - 4 - 2i$$
$$= 0 + 4i$$
$$\therefore |w - z| = |0 + 4i|$$
$$= \sqrt{0^2 + 4^2}$$
$$= \sqrt{0 + 16} = \sqrt{16} = 4$$

Each complex number is a distance of 4 from z.

$z = 4 + 2i = (4, 2)$ [as a point]

$\therefore$ The set K is a circle of centre $(4, 2)$ and radius 4.

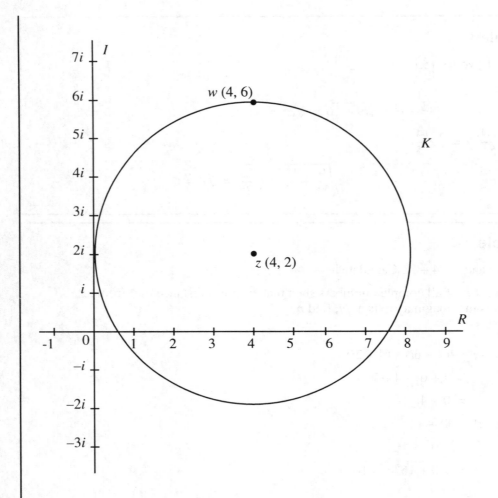

The circle intersects the imaginary axis at $2i$.

$\therefore \quad pi = 2i$

$\therefore \quad p = 2$

Note: When drawing a circle make sure the units on both axes are the same.

Quadratic Equations with Complex Roots

When a quadratic equation cannot be solved by factorisation the following formula can be used:

$$x = \frac{-b \pm \sqrt{b^2 - 4ac}}{2a}$$

Note: The whole of the top of the right hand side, including $-b$, is divided by $2a$.
It is often called the **quadratic** or $-b$ formula.

If $b^2 - 4ac < 0$, then the number under the square root sign will be negative, and so the solutions will be complex numbers.

Example

Solve the equation **(i)** $x^2 - 4x + 13 = 0$ **(ii)** $2x^2 + 2x + 1 = 0$.

Solution:

(i) $x^2 - 4x + 13 = 0$

     $ax^2 + bx + c = 0$

$a = 1, b = -4, c = 13$

$$x = \frac{-b \pm \sqrt{b^2 - 4ac}}{2a}$$

$$\Rightarrow x = \frac{4 \pm \sqrt{(-4)^2 - 4(1)(13)}}{2(1)}$$

$$\Rightarrow x = \frac{4 \pm \sqrt{16 - 52}}{2}$$

$$\Rightarrow x = \frac{4 \pm \sqrt{-36}}{2}$$

$$\Rightarrow x = \frac{4 \pm 6i}{2}$$

$$\Rightarrow x = 2 \pm 3i$$

$\therefore$ the roots are $2 + 3i$ and $2 - 3i$

(ii) $2x^2 + 2x + 1 = 0$

     $ax^2 + bx + c = 0$

$a = 2, b = 2, c = 1$

$$x = \frac{-b \pm \sqrt{b^2 - 4ac}}{2a}$$

$$\Rightarrow x = \frac{-2 \pm \sqrt{(2)^2 - 4(2)(1)}}{2(2)}$$

$$\Rightarrow x = \frac{-2 \pm \sqrt{4 - 8}}{4}$$

$$\Rightarrow x = \frac{-2 \pm \sqrt{-4}}{4}$$

$$\Rightarrow x = \frac{-2 \pm 2i}{4} = \frac{-1 \pm i}{2}$$

$$\Rightarrow x = -\frac{1}{2} \pm \frac{1}{2}i$$

$\therefore$ the roots are $-\frac{1}{2} + \frac{1}{2}i$ and $-\frac{1}{2} - \frac{1}{2}i$

Note: Notice in both solutions the roots occur in conjugate pairs. If one root of a quadratic equation, with real coefficients, is a complex number then the other root must also be complex and the conjugate of the first.

i.e.   if $3 - 4i$ is a root, then $3 + 4i$ is also a root.

     if $-2 - 5i$ is a root, then $-2 + 5i$ is also a root.

     if $a + bi$ is a root, then $a - bi$ is also a root.

Example

Verify that $-2 + 5i$ is a root of the equation $x^2 + 4x + 29 = 0$ and find the other root.

Solution:

Method 1:

If $-2 + 5i$ is a root, then when x is replaced by $-2 + 5i$ in the equation, the equation will be satisfied, i.e.

$$(-2 + 5i)^2 + 4(-2 + 5i) + 29 = 0$$

Method 2:

$$x^2 + 4x + 29 = 0$$

$a = 1, b = 4, c = 29$

$$x = \frac{-b \pm \sqrt{b^2 - 4ac}}{2a}$$

Check:

$(-2 + 5i)^2 + 4(-2 + 5i) + 29 = 0$

$= (-2 + 5i)(-2 + 5i) + 4(-2 + 5i) + 29$

$= 4 - 10i - 10i - 25 - 8 + 20i + 29$

$= 33 - 33 + 20i - 20i$

$= 0$

$\therefore \quad -2 + 5i$ is a root and

$-2 - 5i$ is the other root

(the conjugate of $-2 + 5i$)

$\Rightarrow x = \dfrac{-4 \pm \sqrt{(4)^2 - 4(1)(29)}}{2(1)}$

$\Rightarrow x = \dfrac{-4 \pm \sqrt{16 - 116}}{2}$

$\Rightarrow x = \dfrac{-4 \pm \sqrt{-100}}{2}$

$\Rightarrow x = \dfrac{-4 \pm 10i}{2}$

$\Rightarrow x = -2 \pm 5i$

$\therefore \quad -2 + 5i$ is a root and

$-2 - 5i$ is the other root

Sometimes we have to find unknown coefficients.

Example

If $3 - 4i$ is a root of $x^2 + ax + b = 0$, $a, b \in \mathbf{R}$, find a and b.

Solution:

If $3 - 4i$ is a root, then $3 + 4i$ is also a root.

Method 1:

$x^2 - (\text{add the roots})\, x + (\text{multiply the roots}) = 0$

$x^2 - (3 - 4i + 3 + 4i)x + (3 - 4i)(3 + 4i) = 0$

$x^2 - (6)x + 9 + 12i - 12i + 16 = 0$

$x^2 - 6x + 25 = 0$

Compare to: $x^2 + ax + b = 0$

$\therefore \qquad a = -6, \, b = 25$

Method 2:

Let $\qquad x = 3 - 4i \quad$ and $\quad x = 3 + 4i$

$\Rightarrow \quad x - 3 + 4i = 0$ and $x - 3 - 4i = 0$

$\Rightarrow (x - 3 + 4i)(x - 3 - 4i) = 0$

$\Rightarrow x^2 - 3x - 4xi - 3x + 9 + 12i + 4xi - 12i - 16i^2 = 0$

$\Rightarrow \qquad x^2 - 3x - 3x + 9 + 16 = 0$

$\Rightarrow \qquad\qquad x^2 - 6x + 25 = 0$

Compare to: $x^2 + ax + b = 0$

$\therefore \quad a = -6$ and $b = 25$

Cubic Equations

We could be given a cubic equation with one real root and two complex roots.

Example

Show that $x = 2$ is a root of $x^3 - 8x^2 + 46x - 68 = 0$ and find the other two roots, expressing your answers in the form $a + bi$.

Solution:

To show that $x = 2$ is a root, put in 2 for x.

$$x^3 - 8x^2 + 46x - 68 = 0$$

$$(2)^3 - 8(2)^2 + 46(2) - 68$$

$$= 8 - 8(4) + 46(2) - 68$$

$$= 8 - 32 + 92 - 68$$

$$= 100 - 100$$

$$= 0$$

$\therefore \quad x = 2$ is a root

$\Rightarrow (x - 2)$ is a factor.

Now divide $x^3 - 8x^2 + 46x - 68$ by $(x - 2)$

$$
\begin{array}{r}
x^2 - 6x + 34 \\
x - 2 \enclose{longdiv}{x^3 - 8x^2 + 46x - 68} \\
\underline{x^3 - 2x^2} \\
-6x^2 + 46x \\
\underline{-6x^2 + 12x} \\
34x - 68 \\
\underline{34x - 68} \\
0 + 0
\end{array}
$$

Now solve $x^2 - 6x + 34 = 0$.

We are told the roots are complex.

$\therefore \quad$ use the '$-b$' formula.

$x^2 - 6x + 34 = 0$

$a = 1, b = -6, c = 34$

$$x = \frac{-b \pm \sqrt{b^2 - 4ac}}{2a}$$

$$\Rightarrow x = \frac{6 \pm \sqrt{(-6)^2 - 4(1)(34)}}{2(1)}$$

$$\Rightarrow x = \frac{6 \pm \sqrt{36 - 136}}{2}$$

$$\Rightarrow x = \frac{6 \pm \sqrt{-100}}{2}$$

$$\Rightarrow x = \frac{6 \pm 10i}{2}$$

$$\Rightarrow x = 3 \pm 5i$$

$\therefore \quad 3 - 5i$ is a root and $3 + 5i$ is the other root.

4. SEQUENCES AND SERIES

A sequence is a list of numbers, e.g., 2, 5, 8, 11, 14, ...

A series is a sequence 'added up', e.g., 2 + 5 + 8 + 11 + 14 + ...

T_n is the nth term.

S_n is the sum of the first n terms.

Arithmetic Sequences and Series

$$a, a + d, a + 2d, a + 3d, ...$$

a = first term $\qquad\qquad\qquad$ d = common difference

1. $T_n = a + (n - 1)d$

2. $T_n - T_{n-1}$ = constant = common difference = d

$\quad$ (e.g. $T_3 - T_2 = T_2 - T_1 = d$)

3. $S_n = \dfrac{n}{2}\,[2a + (n - 1)d]$

Geometric Sequences and Series

$$a, ar, ar^2, ar^3, ...$$

a = first term $\qquad\qquad\qquad$ r = common ratio

1. $\quad T_n = ar^{n-1}$

2. $\quad \dfrac{T_n}{T_{n-1}}$ = constant = common ratio = r

$\quad$ (e.g. $\dfrac{T_3}{T_2} = \dfrac{T_2}{T_1} = r$)

3. $\quad$ **(a)** $S_n = \dfrac{a\,(r^n - 1)}{r - 1}$ $\qquad$ ($r > 1$ or $r < -1$)

$\quad\quad$ **(b)** $S_n = \dfrac{a\,(1 - r^n)}{1 - r}$ $\qquad$ ($-1 < r < 1$)

For all Series

$$\boxed{T_n = S_n - S_{n-1}} \quad \text{and} \quad \boxed{T_1 = S_1}$$

(e.g. $T_2 = S_2 - S_1$ $\qquad$ $T_8 = S_8 - S_7$ $\quad$ etc.)

We use this when given S_n of a series in terms of n and asked to find a, d, r or T_n (or any term).

Example

The first three terms of an arithmetic sequence are 3, 8, 13.

(i) Find the value of a, the first term, and d, the common difference.

(ii) Calculate the value of $T_{13} + S_{10}$.

(iii) Which term of the sequence is equal to 148?

Solution:

(i) $a = 3$ (given)

$d = T_2 - T_1 = 8 - 3 = 5$

Thus, $a = 3$ and $d = 5$

(ii) $T_n = a + (n - 1)d$

$\therefore T_{13} = 3 + 12(5)$

(put in $a = 3$, $d = 5$, $n = 13$)

$= 3 + 60$

$= 63$

$S_n = \dfrac{n}{2}[2a + (n-1)d]$

$\therefore S_{10} = \dfrac{10}{2}[2(3) + 9(5)]$

(put in $a = 3$, $d = 5$ and $n = 10$)

$= 5(6 + 45)$

$= 5(51)$

$= 255$

Thus, $T_{13} + S_{10} = 63 + 255 = 318$

(iii) Equation given in disguise:

$$T_n = 148$$

$\Rightarrow$ $a + (n - 1)d = 148$ (we know a and d, find n)

$\Rightarrow$ $3 + (n - 1)5 = 148$ (put in 3 for a and 5 for d)

$\Rightarrow$ $3 + 5n - 5 = 148$

$\Rightarrow$ $5n = 148 - 3 + 5$

$\Rightarrow$ $5n = 150$

$\Rightarrow$ $n = 30$

Thus, the 30th term is 148.

Example

In an arithmetic sequence, the first term, T_1, is 18, and the ninth term, T_9, is -14.

Express T_n in its simplest form and use this to find T_{30}.

Solution:

To find an expression for T_n we need to find the values of a and d.

Given: $T_1 = 18$

$\therefore \qquad a = 18$

Given: $T_9 = -14$

$\therefore \qquad a + 8d = -14$

$\Rightarrow \quad 18 + 8d = -14 \qquad [a = 18]$

$\Rightarrow \qquad 8d = -14 - 18$

$\Rightarrow \qquad 8d = -32$

$\Rightarrow \qquad d = -4$

Thus $a = 18$ and $d = -4$

$T_n = a + (n-1)d$

$T_n = 18 + (n-1)(-4) \quad [a = 18, d = -4]$

$T_n = 18 - 4n + 4$

$\qquad = 22 - 4n$

$\therefore \quad T_n = 22 - 4n$

$\Rightarrow T_{30} = 22 - 4(30) \qquad [n = 30]$

$\qquad = 22 - 120$

$\qquad = -98$

Thus, $T_n = 22 - 4n$ and $T_{30} = -98$

Example

The first three terms in an arithmetic sequence are $k + 6$, $2k + 1$, $k + 18$.

Calculate the value of k and write down the first three terms.

Solution:

We use the fact that in an arithmetic sequence the difference between any two consecutive terms is always the same. We are given the first three terms.

$\therefore \qquad T_3 - T_2 = T_2 - T_1 \qquad\qquad$ (common difference)

$(k + 18) - (2k + 1) = (2k + 1) - (k + 6) \qquad$ (put in given values)

$k + 18 - 2k - 1 = 2k + 1 - k - 6$

$k - 2k - 2k + k = 1 - 6 - 18 + 1$

$2k - 4k = 2 - 24$

$-2k = -22$

$2k = 22$

$k = 11$

$T_1 = k + 6 = 11 + 6 = 17$

$T_2 = 2k + 1 = 2(11) + 1 = 22 + 1 = 23$

$T_3 = k + 18 = 11 + 18 = 29$

Thus, the first three terms are 17, 23, 29.

Example

In an arithmetic sequence $T_6 = 20$ and $4T_2 = T_{10}$. Find a and d.

Solution:

We are given two equations in disguise and we use these to find a and d.

$$T_n = a + (n-1)d$$

Given: $T_6 = 20$

$\therefore$ $a + 5d = 20$ ①

Given: $4T_2 = T_{10}$

$\therefore$ $4(a + d) = a + 9d$

$\Rightarrow$ $4a + 4d = a + 9d$

$\Rightarrow$ $3a - 5d = 0$ ②

We now use the method of simultaneous equations to find a and d.

$a + 5d = 20$ ①

$\underline{3a - 5d = 0}$ ②

$4a = 20$ (add)

$a = 5$

Put in $a = 5$ into ① or ②

$a + 5d = 20$ ①

$5 + 5d = 20$

$5d = 20 - 5$

$5d = 15$

$d = 3$

Thus, $a = 5$ and $d = 3$.

Example

In an arithmetic series, the tenth term, T_{10}, is 19 and the sum to ten terms, S_{10}, is 55.
Find the first term and the common difference.

Show that
$$2S_n = 3n^2 - 19n.$$

Solution:

We are given two equations in disguise and we use them to find a and d.

$T_n = a + (n-1)d$

$T_{10} = 19$ (given)

$\therefore$ $a + 9d = 19$ ①

$S_n = \dfrac{n}{2}[2a + (n-1)d]$

$S_{10} = 55$ (given)

$\therefore$ $\dfrac{10}{2}(2a + 9d) = 55$

$\Rightarrow$ $5(2a + 9d) = 55$

$\Rightarrow$ $2a + 9d = 11$ ②

We now solve between equations $\textcircled{1}$ and $\textcircled{2}$:

$a + 9d = 19$	$\textcircled{1}$		$a + 9d = 19$	$\textcircled{1}$
$2a + 9d = 11$	$\textcircled{2}$		$-8 + 9d = 19$	
$-a = 8$	(subtract)		$9d = 19 + 8$	
$a = -8$			$9d = 27$	
			$d = 3$	

Put in $a = -8$ in $\textcircled{1}$ or $\textcircled{2}$.

Thus, the first term, a, is -8 and the common difference, d, is 3.

$S_n = \dfrac{n}{2} [2a + (n-1)d]$

$S_n = \dfrac{n}{2} [2(-8) + (n-1)3]$ (put in $a = -8$ and $d = 3$)

$S_n = \dfrac{n}{2} [-16 + 3n - 3]$

$S_n = \dfrac{n}{2} (3n - 19)$

$2S_n = n(3n - 19)$ (multiply both sides by 2)

$2S_n = 3n^2 - 19n$

Example

The general term, T_n, of an arithmetic sequence is given by $T_n = 2n + 5$. Find the first term, a, and the common difference, d. For what value of n is $S_n = 160$?
Show that $S_{n+3} - S_{n+1} = 4(n + 5)$.

Solution:

$T_n = 2n + 5$	$d = T_2 - T_1$
$T_1 = 2(1) + 5 = 2 + 5 = 7$	$= 9 - 7$
$T_2 = 2(2) + 5 = 4 + 5 = 9$	$= 2$

Thus, $a = 7$ and $d = 2$

Equation given in disguise:

$$S_n = 160$$

$\Rightarrow \qquad \dfrac{n}{2} [2a + (n-1)d] = 160$ (we know a and d, find n)

$\Rightarrow \qquad \dfrac{n}{2} [2(7) + (n-1)2] = 160$ (put in $a = 7$ and $d = 2$)

$\Rightarrow \qquad \dfrac{n}{2} (14 + 2n - 2) = 160$

$\Rightarrow \qquad \dfrac{n}{2} (2n + 12) = 160$

$\Rightarrow$ $\qquad n(n+6) = 160$

$\Rightarrow$ $\qquad n^2 + 6n = 160$

$\Rightarrow$ $\qquad n^2 + 6n - 160 = 0$

$\Rightarrow$ $\qquad (n-10)(n+16) = 0$

$\Rightarrow$ $\qquad n - 10 = 0 \quad \text{or} \quad n + 16 = 0$

$\Rightarrow$ $\qquad n = 10 \quad \text{or} \quad n = -16$

$\qquad$ (reject $n = -16$)

$\qquad$ Thus, $n = 10$

Note: If n is a fraction, or a negative number, ignore it.

$$S_n = \frac{n}{2}[2a + (n-1)d]$$

$$= \frac{n}{2}[2(7) + (n-1)2] = \frac{n}{2}(14 + 2n - 2) = \frac{n}{2}(2n + 12) = n(n+6)$$

$S_{n+3} = (n+3)(n+3+6)$	$S_{n+1} = (n+1)(n+1+6)$
[replace n with $(n+3)$ in S_n]	[replace n with $(n+1)$ in S_n]
$= (n+3)(n+9)$	$= (n+1)(n+7)$
$= n^2 + 12n + 27$	$= n^2 + 8n + 7$

$$\therefore \ S_{n+3} - S_{n+1} = (n^2 + 12n + 27) - (n^2 + 8n + 7)$$

$$= n^2 + 12n + 27 - n^2 - 8n - 7$$

$$= 4n + 20$$

$$= 4(n+5)$$

Example

T_n of a sequence is $5n + 3$. Verify that the sequence is arithmetic.

Solution:

To verify that a sequence is arithmetic we must show the following:

$$\boxed{T_n - T_{n-1} = \text{constant}}$$

$T_n = 5n + 3$ $\qquad\qquad$ $T_{n-1} = 5(n-1) + 3$ $\qquad$ [replace n with $(n-1)$]

$$= 5n - 5 + 3$$

$$= 5n - 2$$

$$T_n - T_{n-1}$$

$$= (5n + 3) - (5n - 2)$$

$$= 5n + 3 - 5n + 2$$

$$= 5 \qquad \text{(a constant, i.e. does not contain } n\text{)}$$

$T_n - T_{n-1} = $ a constant

Thus, the sequence is arithmetic.

Note: To show that a sequence is **arithmetic**, it is necessary to show that $T_n - T_{n-1}$ is constant.

To show that a sequence is **not arithmetic**, it is only necessary to show that the difference between any two consecutive terms is not the same. In practice, this usually involves showing that $T_3 - T_2 \neq T_2 - T_1$ or similar.

Consider the next example.

Example

T_n of a sequence is $n^2 + 3n + 2$. Verify that the sequence is not arithmetic.

Solution:

$T_n = n^2 + 3n + 2$

$T_1 = (1)^2 + 3(1) + 2$	$T_2 = (2)^2 + 3(2) + 2$	$T_3 = (3)^2 + 3(3) + 2$
$= 1 + 3 + 2$	$= 4 + 6 + 2$	$= 9 + 9 + 2$
$= 6$	$= 12$	$= 20$

$$T_3 - T_2 = 20 - 12 = 8 \qquad\qquad T_2 - T_1 = 12 - 6 = 6$$

$$T_3 - T_2 \neq T_2 - T_1$$

Thus, the sequence is not arithmetic.

Note: We could also have shown $T_n - T_{n-1} \neq$ a constant to show that the sequence is not arithmetic.

Example

In an arithmetic series, $S_n = 2n^2 - 3n$.

Find the first term, a, and the common difference, d.

Solution:

In this type of problem we use the fact that:

$$\boxed{T_n = S_n - S_{n-1} \text{ and } T_1 = S_1}$$

(e.g. $T_2 = S_2 - S_1,$ $\qquad$ $T_3 = S_3 - S_2,$ $\qquad$ $T_4 = S_4 - S_3$ etc.)

$$S_n = 2n^2 - 3n$$

$$S_1 = 2(1)^2 - 3(1)$$
$$= 2 - 3$$
$$= -1$$

$$S_2 = 2(2)^2 - 3(2)$$
$$= 2(4) - 3(2)$$
$$= 8 - 6$$
$$= 2$$

$$a = T_1 = S_1 = -1$$
$$T_2 = S_2 - S_1 = (2) - (-1) = 2 + 1 = 3$$
$$d = T_2 - T_1 = (3) - (-1) = 3 + 1 = 4$$

Example

The first three terms of a geometric sequence are 5, 15, 45.

(i) Find the values of a and r.

(ii) Write down an expression for T_n and, hence, calculate T_9.

(iii) Calculate S_6, the sum to six terms.

(iv) Which term of the sequence is equal to 10 935?

Solution:

(i) $a = 5$ (given) $\qquad$ $r = \dfrac{T_2}{T_1} = \dfrac{15}{5} = 3$

Thus, $a = 5$ and $r = 3$

(ii) $T_n = ar^{n-1} = 5(3)^{n-1}$

$T_9 = 5(3)^{9-1} = 5(3)^8 = 5(6\,561) = 32\,805$

(iii) $S_n = \dfrac{a(r^n - 1)}{r - 1}$

$\therefore\; S_6 = \dfrac{5(3^6 - 1)}{3 - 1} = \dfrac{5(729 - 1)}{2} = \dfrac{5(728)}{2} = \dfrac{3\,640}{2} = 1\,820$

(iv) Equation given in disguise:

$T_n = 10\,935$

$\Rightarrow \quad ar^{n-1} = 10\,935$ $\qquad$ (we know a and r, find n)

$\Rightarrow 5(3)^{n-1} = 10\,935$ $\qquad$ (put in $a = 5$ and $r = 3$)

$\Rightarrow \quad 3^{n-1} = 2\,187$ $\qquad$ (divide both sides by 5)

$\Rightarrow \quad 3^{n-1} = 3^7$ $\qquad$ (both as powers of 3)

$\Rightarrow \quad n - 1 = 7$ $\qquad$ (equate the powers)

$\Rightarrow \quad n = 7 + 1 = 8$

Thus the 8th term of the sequence is 10 935.

Example

The first two terms of a geometric series are 32 + 16 + ...

Find:

(i) r, the common ratio

(ii) T_n, the nth term

(iii) S_n, the sum to n terms

(iv)   the value of $S_6 + T_8$.

Solution:

(i) $r = \dfrac{T_2}{T_1} = \dfrac{16}{32} = \dfrac{1}{2}$

(ii) $T_n = ar^{n-1} = 32\left(\dfrac{1}{2}\right)^{n-1}$

(iii) $S_n = \dfrac{a(1 - r^n)}{1 - r} = \dfrac{32\left[1 - \left(\frac{1}{2}\right)^n\right]}{1 - \frac{1}{2}} = \dfrac{32\left[1 - \left(\frac{1}{2}\right)^n\right]}{\frac{1}{2}} = 64\left[1 - \left(\dfrac{1}{2}\right)^n\right]$

(iv)

$S_6 = 64\left[1 - \left(\dfrac{1}{2}\right)^6\right]$

$\quad = 64\left(1 - \dfrac{1}{64}\right)$

$\quad = 64 - 1$

$\quad = 63$

$T_8 = 32\left(\dfrac{1}{2}\right)^7$

$\quad = 32\left(\dfrac{1}{128}\right)$

$\quad = \dfrac{32}{128}$

$\quad = \dfrac{1}{4}$

$\therefore \quad S_6 + T_8 = 63 + \dfrac{1}{4} = 63\dfrac{1}{4}$

Example

The first three terms of a geometric sequence are $3x - 5$, $x - 1$ and $x - 2$.
Find the values of x.

Solution:

We use the fact that in a geometric sequence, any term divided by the previous term is always a constant.

$\therefore \qquad \dfrac{T_3}{T_2} = \dfrac{T_2}{T_1}$ (common ratio)

$\Rightarrow \qquad \dfrac{x - 2}{x - 1} = \dfrac{x - 1}{3x - 5}$ (put in given values)

$\Rightarrow \qquad (x - 2)(3x - 5) = (x - 1)(x - 1)$ (cross multiply)

$\Rightarrow \qquad 3x^2 - 11x + 10 = x^2 - 2x + 1$ (remove brackets)

$$\Rightarrow \qquad 2x^2 - 9x + 9 = 0 \qquad\qquad\qquad \text{(everything to the left)}$$

$$\Rightarrow \qquad (2x - 3)(x - 3) = 0 \qquad\qquad\qquad \text{(factorise)}$$

$$\Rightarrow \qquad 2x - 3 = 0 \quad \text{or} \quad x - 3 = 0 \qquad\qquad \text{(let each factor = 0)}$$

$$\Rightarrow \qquad 2x = 3 \qquad\qquad \text{or} \qquad x = 3$$

$$\Rightarrow \qquad x = \frac{3}{2} \qquad\qquad \text{or} \qquad x = 3$$

Thus, the values of x are $\frac{3}{2}$ or 3.

Example

In a geometric sequence $T_2 = -6$ and $T_5 = 48$.

Find, the first term, a, the common ratio, r, T_n and T_{10}.

Solution:

$$T_n = ar^{n-1}$$

Given: $\quad T_2 = -6$ $\qquad\qquad\qquad\qquad$ | $\qquad$ **Given:** $\quad T_5 = 48$

$\Rightarrow \qquad ar = -6 \qquad\qquad$ ① $\qquad$ | $\qquad \Rightarrow \qquad ar^4 = 48 \qquad\qquad$ ②

We now divide ② by ① to eliminate a and find r.

$\dfrac{②}{①}$ $\qquad\qquad\qquad\qquad\qquad\qquad$ | $\qquad$ Now put $r = -2$ into ① or ②:

$\qquad\qquad\qquad\qquad\qquad\qquad\qquad$ | $\qquad\qquad\qquad ar = -6 \qquad\qquad$ ①

$\Rightarrow \qquad \dfrac{ar^4}{ar} = \dfrac{48}{-6}$ $\qquad\qquad$ | $\qquad\qquad\qquad\qquad \downarrow$

$\qquad\qquad\qquad\qquad\qquad\qquad\qquad$ | $\qquad\qquad\qquad a\,(-2) = -6$

$\Rightarrow \qquad r^3 = -8$ $\qquad\qquad\qquad$ | $\qquad\qquad\qquad -2a = -6$

$\Rightarrow \qquad r = -2$ $\qquad\qquad\qquad$ | $\qquad\qquad\qquad\quad 2a = 6$

$\qquad\qquad\qquad\qquad\qquad\qquad\qquad$ | $\qquad\qquad\qquad\qquad a = 3$

Thus, $a = 3$, $r = -2$

$T_n = ar^{n-1} = 3\,(-2)^{n-1}$

$T_{10} = 3\,(-2)^9 = 3(-512) = -1\,536$

Note: If the index of r is even, we get two values for r, positive and negative.

Example

T_n of a sequence is $3 \cdot 5^n$. Verify that the sequence is geometric.

Solution:

To verify that a sequence is geometric we must show the following:

$$\boxed{\frac{T_n}{T_{n-1}} = \text{constant}}$$

$T_n = 3 \cdot 5^n$ $\qquad\qquad$ $T_{n-1} = 3 \cdot 5^{n-1}$ $\qquad\qquad$ [replace n with $(n-1)$]

$$\frac{T_n}{T_{n-1}} = \frac{3 \cdot 5^n}{3 \cdot 5^{n-1}}$$

$$= \frac{5^n}{5^{n-1}}$$

$= 5^{n-n+1}$ $\qquad$ (subtract index on the bottom from the index on top)

$= 5^1$

$= 5$ $\qquad$ (a constant, i.e. does not contain n)

$\dfrac{T_n}{T_{n-1}}$ is a constant, thus the sequence is geometric.

Note: To show that a sequence is **geometric**, it is necessary to show that $T_n \div T_{n-1}$ is a constant. To show that a sequence is **not geometric**, it is only necessary to show that the ratio of any two consecutive terms is not the same. In practice, this usually involves showing that $T_3 \div T_2 \ne T_2 \div T_1$ or similar.

Example

The first three terms of a geometric series are $1 + 2 + 4 + \ldots.$

(i) Write down the values of a and r.

(ii) How many terms of the series must be added together to get a total of $2\,047$?

(iii) Show that $S_{33} < 2^{33}$.

Solution:

(i) $a = 1$ (given) $\qquad\qquad$ $r = \dfrac{T_2}{T_1} = \dfrac{2}{1} = 2$

(ii) Equation given in disguise:

$$S_n = 2\,047$$

$\Rightarrow \qquad \dfrac{a\,(r^n - 1)}{r - 1} = 2\,047$ $\qquad$ (we know a and r, find n)

$\Rightarrow \qquad \dfrac{1\,(2^n - 1)}{2 - 1} = 2\,047$ $\qquad$ (put in $a = 1$ and $r = 2$)

$\Rightarrow \qquad \dfrac{2^n - 1}{1} = 2\,047$

$\Rightarrow \qquad 2^n - 1 = 2\,047$

$\Rightarrow \qquad 2^n = 2\,048$

$\Rightarrow \qquad 2^n = 2^{11}$ $\qquad$ (both as power of 2)

$\Rightarrow \qquad n = 11$ $\qquad$ (equate the powers)

Thus, the sum of the first 11 items will give 2 048.

(iii)

$$S_n = \frac{a(r^n - 1)}{r - 1}$$

$$\therefore \qquad S_{33} = \frac{1(2^{33} - 1)}{2 - 1} \quad \text{(put in } n = 33, \, a = 1 \text{ and } r = 2\text{)}$$

$$= \frac{2^{33} - 1}{1}$$

$$= 2^{33} - 1 < 2^{33}$$

$$\therefore \ S_{33} < 2^{33}$$

Example

In a geometric series, $S_n = 5(3^n - 1)$. Find a, r and T_n.

Solution:

In this type of problem we use the fact that:

$$\boxed{T_n = S_n - S_{n-1} \text{ and } T_1 = S_1}$$

(e.g., $T_2 = S_2 - S_1$, $\qquad T_3 = S_3 - S_2$, $\qquad T_4 = S_4 - S_3$ $\qquad$ etc.)

Given: $\qquad S_n = 5(3^n - 1)$

$$\begin{array}{ll}
S_1 = 5(3^1 - 1) & \qquad\qquad S_2 = 5(3^2 - 1) \\
\quad = 5(3 - 1) & \qquad\qquad\quad = 5(9 - 1) \\
\quad = 5(2) & \qquad\qquad\quad = 5(8) \\
\quad = 10 & \qquad\qquad\quad = 40
\end{array}$$

$a = T_1 = S_1 = 10$ $\qquad\qquad$ Thus, $\qquad a = 10$

$T_2 = S_2 - S_1 = 40 - 10 = 30$ $\qquad\qquad\qquad\quad r = 3$

$r = \dfrac{T_2}{T_1} = \dfrac{30}{10} = 3$ $\qquad\qquad\qquad\qquad T_n = 10 . 3^{n-1}$

$T_n = ar^{n-1} = 10 . 3^{n-1}$

5. CALCULUS AND FUNCTIONS

Notation:

$$y = f(x)$$
$$\frac{dy}{dx} = f'(x)$$

Differentiation from First Principles

To differentiate from first principles, do the following:

Step 1: Let $y = f(x)$ (i.e. y = what is to be differentiated).

Step 2: Replace y with $(y + \Delta y)$ and replace every x with $(x + \Delta x)$.

Step 3: Multiply out the right hand side until there are no brackets left.

Step 4: Subtract $y = f(x)$ to get Δy in terms of x and Δx.

Step 5: Divide across by Δx to get $\dfrac{\Delta y}{\Delta x}$.

Step 6: Find $\lim\limits_{\Delta x \to 0} \dfrac{\Delta y}{\Delta x}$ by replacing Δx by 0 everywhere it occurs.

   i.e. discard any terms on the right hand side which contain Δx.

Note: We divide Δx into Δy before putting $\Delta x = 0$.

Example

Differentiate from first principles $x^2 - 5x + 3$, with respect to x.

Solution:

1. $\qquad\qquad y = x^2 - 5x + 3$

2. $\qquad y + \Delta y = (x + \Delta x)^2 - 5(x + \Delta x) + 3$

3. $\qquad y + \Delta y = x^2 + 2x\Delta x + (\Delta x^2) - 5x - 5\Delta x + 3$

4. $\qquad y \qquad = x^2 \qquad\qquad - 5x \qquad + 3$

   $\overline{\qquad\qquad\qquad\qquad\qquad\qquad\qquad\qquad\qquad}$

   $\qquad \Delta y = 2x\Delta x + (\Delta x)^2 - 5\Delta x \qquad\qquad$ (subtract)

5. $\qquad \dfrac{\Delta y}{\Delta x} = 2x + \Delta x - 5$

6. $\lim\limits_{\Delta x \to 0} \dfrac{\Delta y}{\Delta x} = \dfrac{dy}{dx} = 2x + 0 - 5 = 2x - 5$

The Four Rules

1. General Rule:

$$y = x^n$$
$$\frac{dy}{dx} = nx^{n-1}$$

Words: Multiply by the power and reduce the power by 1

2. Product Rule:

$$y = uv$$
$$\frac{dy}{dx} = u\frac{dv}{dx} + v\frac{du}{dx}$$

Words: First by the derivative of the second + second by the derivative of the first

3. Quotient Rule:

$$y = \frac{u}{v}$$
$$\frac{dy}{dx} = \frac{v\dfrac{du}{dx} - u\dfrac{dv}{dx}}{v^2}$$

Words: $\dfrac{\text{Bottom by the derivative of the top} - \text{Top by the derivative of the bottom}}{(\text{Bottom})^2}$

4. Chain Rule:

$$y = (\text{function})^{\text{power}}$$
$$\frac{dy}{dx} = \text{power}\,(\text{function})^{\text{power}-1}\,(\text{function differentiated})$$

Words:
1. Multiply by the power and reduce the power by 1.
2. Multiply this by the derivative of what is inside the bracket.

Example

Differentiate each of the following:

(i) $\quad 5x^3 - 4x^2 - 3x + 2$ **(ii)** $\quad (x^3 - 4)(5x^2 - 2)$ **(iii)** $\quad (2x^2 - 1)^7$

(iv) $\quad \dfrac{x^3 - 4x}{x^2 - 1}$ **(v)** $\quad \dfrac{5}{x^3}$ **(vi)** $\quad \sqrt{x}$

Solution:

(i) $\qquad y = 5x^3 - 4x^2 - 3x + 2$

$\qquad \dfrac{dy}{dx} = 15x^2 - 8x - 3$

(ii) $\qquad y = (x^3 - 4)(5x^2 - 2)$ (product rule)

$\qquad \dfrac{dy}{dx} = u\dfrac{dv}{dx} + v\dfrac{du}{dx}$ $u = x^3 - 4$ $v = 5x^2 - 2$

$\qquad\qquad = (x^3 - 4)(10x) + (5x^2 - 2)(3x^2)$ $\dfrac{du}{dx} = 3x^2$ $\dfrac{dv}{dx} = 10x$

$\qquad\qquad = 10x^4 - 40x + 15x^4 - 6x^2$

$\qquad\qquad = 25x^4 - 6x^2 - 40x$

(iii) $\qquad y = (2x^2 - 1)^7$ (chain rule)

$\qquad \dfrac{dy}{dx} = 7(2x^2 - 1)^6(4x) = 28x(2x^2 - 1)^6$

(iv) $y = \dfrac{x^3 - 4x}{x^2 - 1}$ (quotient rule)

$\dfrac{dy}{dx} = \dfrac{v\dfrac{du}{dx} - u\dfrac{dv}{dx}}{v^2}$ $u = x^3 - 4x$ $v = x^2 - 1$

$\qquad = \dfrac{(x^2 - 1)(3x^2 - 4) - (x^3 - 4x)(2x)}{(x^2 - 1)^2}$ $\dfrac{du}{dx} = 3x^2 - 4$ $\dfrac{dv}{dx} = 2x$

$\qquad = \dfrac{3x^4 - 4x^2 - 3x^2 + 4 - 2x^4 + 8x^2}{(x^2 - 1)^2}$

$\qquad = \dfrac{x^4 + x^2 + 4}{(x^2 - 1)^2}$

Note: It is usual practice to multiply out and simplify the top but **not** the bottom.

(v)

$$y = \frac{5}{x^3}$$

$$y = 5x^{-3}$$

$$\frac{dy}{dx} = -3 \cdot 5\, x^{-3-1}$$

$$= -15x^{-4}$$

$$\frac{dy}{dx} = -\frac{15}{x^4}$$

(vi)

$$y = \sqrt{x}$$

$$y = x^{\frac{1}{2}}$$

$$\frac{dy}{dx} = \frac{1}{2}\, x^{\frac{1}{2}-1}$$

$$= \frac{1}{2}\, x^{-\frac{1}{2}}$$

$$= \frac{1}{2} \cdot \frac{1}{x^{\frac{1}{2}}}$$

$$= \frac{1}{2} \cdot \frac{1}{\sqrt{x}}$$

$$= \frac{1}{2\sqrt{x}}$$

Evaluating Derivatives

It is good practice **not** to simplify before you put in the given values.

Example

(i) Find the value of $\frac{dy}{dx}$ at $x = 2$ when $y = (1 - x^2)^3$.

(ii) If $h = 20t - 5t^2$, find $\frac{dh}{dt}$ when $t - 4 = 0$.

(iii) Find the value of $\frac{dy}{dx}$ at $x = -1$ when $y = \frac{2x^2 + 3}{2x - 1}$

Solution:

(i)

$$y = (1 - x^2)^3 \quad \text{(use chain rule)}$$

$$\frac{dy}{dx} = 3(1 - x^2)^2(-2x)$$

$$\left.\frac{dy}{dx}\right|_{x=2} = 3(1 - 2^2)^2[-2(2)]$$

$$= 3(1 - 4)^2(-4)$$

$$= 3\,(-3)^2(-4)$$

$$= 3(9)(-4)$$

$$= -108$$

(ii)

$$h = 20t - 5t^2$$

$$\frac{dh}{dt} = 20 - 10t$$

$$t - 4 = 0 \quad \Rightarrow \quad t = 4$$

$$\left.\frac{dh}{dt}\right|_{t=4} = 20 - 10(4)$$

$$= 20 - 40$$

$$= -20$$

(iii) $\qquad y = \dfrac{2x^2 + 3}{2x - 1}$ $\hspace{2cm}$ (use quotient rule)

$$\frac{dy}{dx} = \frac{(2x-1)(4x) - (2x^2+3)(2)}{(2x-1)^2}$$

$$\left[\frac{v\dfrac{du}{dx} - u\dfrac{dv}{dx}}{v^2}\right]$$

$$\left.\frac{dy}{dx}\right|_{x=-1} = \frac{(-2-1)(-4) - (2+3)(2)}{(-2-1)^2}$$

$$= \frac{(-3)(-4) - (5)(2)}{(-3)^2}$$

$$= \frac{12 - 10}{9}$$

$$= \frac{2}{9}$$

Given $\frac{dy}{dx}$, to Find the Coordinates of the Corresponding Points on a Curve

Sometimes the value of $\dfrac{dy}{dx}$ (slope of the curve at any point on it) is given and we need to find the coordinates of the point, or points, corresponding to this slope.

When this happens we do the following:

Step 1: Find $\dfrac{dy}{dx}$.

Step 2: Let $\dfrac{dy}{dx}$ equal the given value of the slope and solve this equation for x.

Step 3: Substitute the x values obtained in Step 2 into the original function to get the corresponding values for y.

Example

Find the coordinates of the points on the curve $y = x^3 - 3x^2 - 22x + 5$ at which the tangents to the curve have a slope of 2.

Solution:

1. $\qquad y = x^3 - 3x^2 - 22x + 5$

$$\frac{dy}{dx} = 3x^2 - 6x - 22$$

2. Given: Slope $= 2$

$$\therefore \qquad \frac{dy}{dx} = 2$$

$$\Rightarrow \qquad 3x^2 - 6x - 22 = 2$$

$$\Rightarrow \qquad 3x^2 - 6x - 24 = 0$$

$$\Rightarrow \qquad x^2 - 2x - 8 = 0$$

$$\Rightarrow \qquad (x - 4)(x + 2) = 0$$

$$\Rightarrow \qquad x - 4 = 0 \quad \text{or} \quad x + 2 = 0$$

$$\Rightarrow \qquad x = 4 \quad \text{or} \quad x = -2$$

3. Find the y values.

$y = x^3 - 3x^2 - 22x + 5$	$y = x^3 - 3x^2 - 22x + 5$
$x = 4$	$x = -2$
$\Rightarrow \quad y = (4)^3 - 3(4)^2 - 22(4) + 5$	$\Rightarrow \quad y = (-2)^3 - 3(-2)^2 - 22(-2) + 5$
$= 64 - 48 - 88 + 5$	$= -8 - 12 + 44 + 5$
$= -67$	$= 29$
point $(4, -67)$	point $(-2, 29)$

Thus, the required points are $(4, -67)$ and $(-2, 29)$.

Note: If a fraction $= 0$, then the top of the fraction must equal 0.

e.g. if $\dfrac{3x - 6}{x - 1} = 0 \qquad \Rightarrow \quad 3x - 6 = 0$

Consider the next example where the slope is given in disguise.

Example

Let $f(x) = \dfrac{x^2 + 5}{2 - x}$, $x \neq 2$.

Find the values of x for which tangents to the curve of $f(x)$ are parallel to the X axis.

Solution:

$$f(x) = \frac{x^2 + 5}{2 - x} \qquad\qquad \text{(use quotient rule)}$$

$$f'(x) = \frac{(2 - x)(2x) - (x^2 + 5)(-1)}{(2 - x)^2} \qquad \left[\frac{v\dfrac{du}{dx} - u\dfrac{dv}{dx}}{v^2} \right]$$

$$= \frac{4x - 2x^2 + x^2 + 5}{(2 - x)^2}$$

$$= \frac{-x^2 + 4x + 5}{(2 - x)^2}$$

Equation given in disguise:

Slope = 0   (because parallel to X axis)

$\therefore$ $f'(x) = 0$

$\Rightarrow$ $\dfrac{-x^2 + 4x + 5}{(2-x)^2} = 0$

$\Rightarrow$ $-x^2 + 4x + 5 = 0$ (fraction = 0, $\Rightarrow$ top = 0)

$\Rightarrow$ $x^2 - 4x - 5 = 0$

$\Rightarrow$ $(x-5)(x+1) = 0$

$\Rightarrow$ $x - 5 = 0$ or $x + 1 = 0$

$\Rightarrow$ $x = 5$ or $x = -1$

Thus, the values of x are 5 and -1.

Applications of Differentiation

$\dfrac{dy}{dx}$ = the slope of a tangent to a curve at any point on the curve.

When considering increasing and decreasing functions we always examine their graphs from left to right.

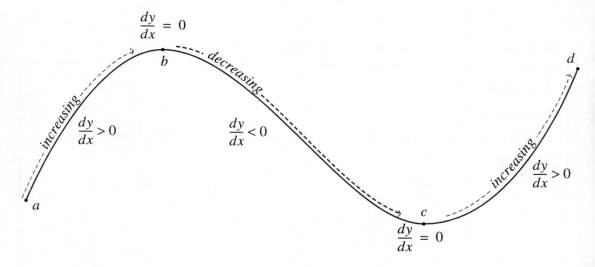

Consider the graph above:

1.   From a to b and from c to d the graph is increasing,

i.e. the slopes of the tangents are positive $\Rightarrow \dfrac{dy}{dx} > 0$.

2. From b to c the graph is decreasing,

i.e. the slopes of the tangents are negative $\Rightarrow \dfrac{dy}{dx} < 0$.

3. At b and c the graph is neither increasing or decreasing,

i.e. the slopes of the tangents are zero $\Rightarrow \dfrac{dy}{dx} = 0$.

We consider the following applications:

1. Finding the slope and equation of a tangent.
2. Maximum and minimum points.
3. Rates of change.
4. Increasing and decreasing functions.
5. Sketching curves.

1. Slope and Equation of a Tangent

To find the slope and equation of a tangent to a curve at a given point, (x_1, y_1), on the curve, do the following:

Step 1: Find $\dfrac{dy}{dx}$.

Step 2: Evaluate $\dfrac{dy}{dx}\bigg|_{x = x_1}$ (this gives the slope of the tangent, m)

[If the angle the curve makes with the X axis is required use the tan tables or calculator]

Step 3: Use m (from Step 2) and the given point (x_1, y_1) in the equation:

$$(y - y_1) = m(x - x_1)$$

Note: Sometimes only the value of x is given. When this happens, substitute the value of x into the original function to find y for Step 3.

Example

Find the equation of the tangent to the curve $f(x) = \dfrac{x - 1}{x + 2}$ at the point $(-1, -2)$.

Solution:

For the curve, $y = f(x)$.

1.
$$y = \frac{x-1}{x+2}$$

(use quotient rule)

$$\frac{dy}{dx} = \frac{(x+2)(1)-(x-1)(1)}{(x+2)^2}$$

2. At the point $(-1, -2)$, $x = -1$

$$\left.\frac{dy}{dx}\right|_{x=-1} = \frac{(-1+2)(1)-(-1-1)(1)}{(-1+2)^2}$$

$$= \frac{(1)(1)-(-2)(1)}{(1)^2}$$

$$= \frac{1+2}{1} = \frac{3}{1} = 3$$

3. $m = 3$, $\quad x_1 = -1$, $\quad y_1 = -2$

$$(y - y_1) = m(x - x_1)$$

$\Rightarrow \qquad (y + 2) = 3(x + 1)$

$\Rightarrow \qquad y + 2 = 3x + 3$

$\Rightarrow \quad -3x + y + 2 - 3 = 0$

$\Rightarrow \qquad -3x + y - 1 = 0$

$\Rightarrow \qquad 3x - y + 1 = 0$

Example

$f(x) = 2x^3 - 3x^2 - 13x + 2$, $x \in \mathbf{R}$.

Find the derivative of $f(x)$.

Find the coordinates of the points on the curve $f(x)$ at which the tangents to the curve are parallel to the line $y = 5 - x$. Find the equations of the tangents at these points.

Solution:

For the graph, $y = f(x)$.

Curve: $\quad y = 2x^3 - 3x^2 - 13x + 2$ $\qquad\qquad$ Line: $y = 5 - x$

$$\frac{dy}{dx} = 6x^2 - 6x - 13 \qquad\qquad\qquad \frac{dy}{dx} = -1$$

Given: Slope of curve = Slope of line

$\Rightarrow \qquad 6x^2 - 6x - 13 = -1$

$\Rightarrow \qquad 6x^2 - 6x - 12 = 0$

$\Rightarrow \qquad\quad x^2 - x - 2 = 0$

$\Rightarrow \qquad (x-2)(x+1) = 0$

$\Rightarrow \qquad x - 2 = 0 \qquad \text{or} \qquad x + 1 = 0$

$\Rightarrow \qquad\quad x = 2 \qquad \text{or} \qquad x = -1$

We have the x coordinates, now we need the y coordinates.

$$y = 2x^3 - 3x^2 - 13x + 2$$

$x = 2$	$x = -1$
$y = 2(2)^3 - 3(2)^2 - 13(2) + 2$	$y = 2(-1)^3 - 3(-1)^2 - 13(-1) + 2$
$\quad = 2(8) - 3(4) - 13(2) + 2$	$\quad = 2(-1) - 3(1) - 13(-1) + 2$
$\quad = 16 - 12 - 26 + 2$	$\quad = -2 - 3 + 13 + 2$
$\quad = 18 - 38$	$\quad = 15 - 5$
$\quad = -20$	$\quad = 10$
$\therefore \quad x = 2, y = -20$	$\therefore \quad x = -1, y = 10$

Thus, $(2, -20)$ and $(-1, 10)$ are the required points.

At both of these points the slope of the tangents are equal to -1.

$m = -1, \quad x_1 = 2, \quad y = -20$	$m = -1, \quad x_1 = -1, \quad y_1 = 10$
$(y - y_1) = m(x - x_1)$	$(y - y_1) = m(x - x_1)$
$(y + 20) = -1(x - 2)$	$(y - 10) = -1(x + 1)$
$y + 20 = -x + 2$	$y - 10 = -x - 1$
$x + y + 20 - 2 = 0$	$x + y - 10 + 1 = 0$
$x + y + 18 = 0$	$x + y - 9 = 0$

Thus, the equations of the tangents are $x + y + 18 = 0$ and $x + y - 9 = 0$

Example

Let $y = x^2 - 5x + 6, x \in \mathbf{R}$.

Find the slopes of the tangents to the graph of y at the points $(2, 0)$ and $(3, 0)$, and investigate if these two tangents are at right angles to each other.

Solution:

$$y = x^2 - 5x + 6$$
$$\frac{dy}{dx} = 2x - 5 \qquad \text{(Slope at any point)}$$

at $(2, 0)$, $x = 2$	at $(3,0)$, $x = 3$
$\left.\dfrac{dy}{dx}\right|_{x=2} = 2(2) - 5$	$\left.\dfrac{dy}{dx}\right|_{x=3} = 2(3) - 5$
$\qquad = 4 - 5$	$\qquad = 6 - 5$
$\qquad = -1$	$\qquad = 1$
$\therefore \quad$ Slope at $x = 2$ is -1	$\therefore \quad$ Slope at $x = 3$ is 1

(Slope at $x = 2$)(Slope at $x = 3$) = $(-1)(1) = -1$

$\therefore$ the tangents are at right angles to each other.

2. Maximum and Minimum Points

To find the maximum or minimum points on a curve do the following:

Step 1: Find $\dfrac{dy}{dx}$.

Step 2: Let $\dfrac{dy}{dx} = 0$ and solve this equation for x.

Step 3: Substitute x values obtained in Step 2 into the original function to get the corresponding values of y.

Step 4: By comparing the y values we can determine which point is the local maximum or minimum point. The point with the greater y value is the local maximum point and the point with the smaller y value is the local minimum point.

Example

Find the coordinates of the local maximum and minimum points of the curve $y = 5 + 18x + 6x^2 - 2x^3$.

Solution:

1.
$$y = 5 + 18x + 6x^2 - 2x^3$$

$$\frac{dy}{dx} = 18 + 12x - 6x^2$$

2. Let $\dfrac{dy}{dx} = 0$ and solve for x.

$\Rightarrow 18 + 12x - 6x^2 = 0$

$\Rightarrow -6x^2 + 12x + 18 = 0$

$\Rightarrow 6x^2 - 12x - 18 = 0$

$\Rightarrow \quad x^2 - 2x - 3 = 0$

$\Rightarrow \quad (x - 3)(x + 1) = 0$

$\Rightarrow \quad x - 3 = 0 \quad$ or $\quad x + 1 = 0$

$\Rightarrow \quad\quad x = 3 \quad$ or $\quad x = -1$

3. Now find the y values:

$y = 5 + 18x + 6x^2 - 2x^3$	$y = 5 + 18x + 6x^2 - 2x^3$
$x = 3$	$x = -1$
$\Rightarrow \quad y = 5 + 18(3) + 6(3)^2 - 2(3)^3$	$y = 5 + 18(-1) + 6(-1)^2 - 2(-1)^3$
$= 5 + 18(3) + 6(9) - 2(27)$	$= 5 + 18(-1) + 6(1) - 2(-1)$
$= 5 + 54 + 54 - 54$	$= 5 - 18 + 6 + 2$
$= 59$	$= -5$
point $(3, 59)$	point $(-1, -5)$

4. $59 > -5$

Thus, the local maximum point is $(3, 59)$ and the local minimum point is $(-1, -5)$.

3. Rates of Change

$\dfrac{dV}{dp}$ = rate of change of V with respect to p.

$\dfrac{dR}{dt}$ = rate of change of R with respect to t.

Example

The volume, V, of a certain gas is given by $V = \dfrac{20}{p}$, where p is the pressure.

Find **(i)** $\dfrac{dV}{dp}$, the rate of change of V with respect to p.

      (ii) the value of $\dfrac{dV}{dp}$ when $p = 10$.

Solution:

(i)
$$V = \frac{20}{p} = \frac{20}{p^1}$$

$\therefore$
$$V = 20p^{-1}$$
$$\frac{dV}{dp} = -20p^{-2}$$
$$= -\frac{20}{p^2}$$

Thus, $\dfrac{dV}{dp} = -\dfrac{20}{p^2}$

(ii) value of $\dfrac{dV}{dp}$ when $p = 10$

$$\frac{dV}{dp} = -\frac{20}{p^2}$$

$$\left.\frac{dV}{dp}\right|_{p=10} = -\frac{20}{10^2}$$

$$= -\frac{20}{100}$$

$$= -\frac{1}{5}$$

Example

The rate at which oil is flowing in a value in an experiment is R cm³/s. The flow of oil varies with the time, t seconds, as given by the equation $R = 8t - t^2$.

Find **(i)** $\dfrac{dR}{dt}$, the rate of change of R with respect of t.

      (ii) the value of $\dfrac{dR}{dt}$ after 6 seconds.

      (iii) the time when the rate of flow is a maximum and calculate this m~

Solution:

(i) $R = 8t - t^2$

$$\frac{dR}{dt} = 8 - 2t$$

(ii) after 6 ~

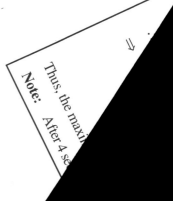

(iii) Maximum flow occurs when $\dfrac{dR}{dt} = 0$

$\dfrac{dR}{dt} = 0$

$\Rightarrow \quad 8 - 2t = 0$

$\Rightarrow \quad -2t = -8$

$\Rightarrow \quad 2t = 8$

$\Rightarrow \quad t = 4$

We now evaluate the flow of oil, R, when $t = 4$

$$R = 8t - t^2$$

$$t = 4$$

$\Rightarrow \quad R = 8(4) - (4)^2$

$$= 32 - 16$$

$$= 16$$

Thus, the maximum flow of 16 cm^3/s occurs after 4 seconds.

Example

The height h metres of a balloon is related to the time t seconds by $h = 120t - 15t^2$

Find

(i) its height after 2 seconds

(ii) the maximum height reached by the balloon.

Solution:

(i) after 2 seconds, $t = 2$

$$h = 120t - 15t^2$$

$$t = 2$$

$\Rightarrow \quad h = 120(2) - 15(2)^2$

$$= 120(2) - 15(4)$$

$$= 240 - 60$$

$$= 180 \text{ m}$$

Thus, after 2 seconds, the height of the balloon is 180 m.

(ii) Maximum height occurs when $\dfrac{dh}{dt} = 0$

$$h = 120t - 15t^2$$

$\dfrac{dh}{dt} = 120 - 30t = 0 \qquad$ (max.)

$$-30t = -120$$

$$30t = 120$$

$$t = 4$$

We now evaluate the height, h, when $t = 4$

$$h = 120t - 15t^2$$

$$t = 4$$

$\Rightarrow \quad h = 120(4) - 15(4)^2$

$$= 120(4) - 15(16)$$

$$= 480 - 240$$

$$= 240$$

num height reached by the balloon is 240 m (this occurs after 4 seconds).

conds, the balloon is momentarily at rest (it stops rising and begins to fall).

Suppose s represents the distance an object travelled and t represents the time,

then $\dfrac{ds}{dt}$ represents the speed at any time (rate of change of distance)

and $\dfrac{d^2s}{dt^2}$ represents the acceleration at any time (rate of change of speed).

Example

A body moves along a straight line and its distance, s metres, from a fixed point on the line is given by $s = 4t(8 - t)$, where t is the time in seconds.

Find:

(i)   the distance travelled after 3 seconds

(ii)   its speed after t seconds

(iii)   its speed after 2 seconds

(iv)   the time at which the body is at rest

(v)   its acceleration.

Solution:

(i) $\quad s = 4t(8 - t)$

$\qquad s = 32t - 4t^2 \qquad$ (first multiply out)

After 3 seconds, $t = 3$

$\Rightarrow \qquad s = 32(3) - 4(3)^2 \qquad$ (put in 3 for t)

$\qquad\qquad = 96 - 36$

$\qquad\qquad = 60$

Thus, after 3 seconds, it has travelled a distance of 60 m.

(ii)   Speed $= \dfrac{ds}{dt}$

$\qquad s = 32t - 4t^2$

$\qquad \dfrac{ds}{dt} = 32 - 8t$

After t seconds, its speed is $(32 - 8t)$ m/s

(iii)   After 2 seconds, $t = 2$

$\qquad \dfrac{ds}{dt}\bigg|_{t=2} = 32 - 8(2)$

$\qquad\qquad\quad = 32 - 16$

$\qquad\qquad\quad = 16$

After 2 seconds, its speed is 16 m/s

(iv)   Body is at rest when speed $= 0$

$\qquad$ Speed $= 0$

$\Rightarrow \quad 32 - 8t = 0$

$\Rightarrow \qquad -8t = -32$

$\Rightarrow \qquad\quad 8t = 32$

$\Rightarrow \qquad\qquad t = 4$

It is at rest after 4 seconds

(v)   Acceleration

$\qquad \dfrac{ds}{dt} = 32 - 8t$

$\qquad \dfrac{d^2s}{dt^2} = -8 \qquad$ (differentiate again)

Its acceleration is -8 m/s^2

4. Increasing and Decreasing Functions

We use the following rules when dealing with increasing and decreasing functions:

Curve increasing: $\dfrac{dy}{dx} > 0$	Curve decreasing: $\dfrac{dy}{dx} < 0$

Example

Let $y = 6x^2 - 12x + 7$, $x \in \mathbf{R}$.

Find the range of values of x for which the graph of y is increasing.

Solution:

$$y = 6x^2 - 12x + 7$$

$$\frac{dy}{dx} = 12x - 12$$

Increasing: $\dfrac{dy}{dx} > 0$

$$\Rightarrow \quad 12x - 12 > 0$$

$$\Rightarrow \quad\quad\quad 12x > 12$$

$$\Rightarrow \quad\quad\quad\quad x > 1$$

Thus, the graph of y is increasing for all $x > 1$

Example

If $y = \dfrac{4x + 1}{x - 3}$, $x \in \mathbf{R}$, show that $\dfrac{dy}{dx} < 0$ for all $x \neq 3$.

Solution:

$$y = \frac{4x + 1}{x - 3}$$

(quotient, $\therefore$ use quotient rule)

$$\frac{dy}{dx} = \frac{(x - 3)(4) - (4x + 1)(1)}{(x - 3)^2}$$

$$\left[\frac{v\dfrac{du}{dx} - u\dfrac{dv}{dx}}{v^2} \right]$$

$$= \frac{4x - 12 - 4x - 1}{(x - 3)^2}$$

$$= \frac{-13}{(x - 3)^2}$$

$$\frac{dy}{dx} = \frac{-13}{(x - 3)^2}$$

Top: -13 is always negative   Bottom: $(x - 3)^2 > 0$, always positive, for $x \neq 3$.

i.e. the top is always negative and the bottom is always positive

$\therefore$ this fraction is always negative

i.e. $\quad \dfrac{-13}{(x - 3)^2} < 0$, for all $x \neq 3$

$\therefore \quad\quad \dfrac{dy}{dx} < 0$, for all $x \neq 3$

5. Sketching Curves

When drawing a rough sketch of quadratic or cubic functions, when given limited information, the following is useful to remember:

1.	$\dfrac{dy}{dx} = 0$	turning points (max. or min. points)
2.	$\dfrac{dy}{dx} > 0$	curve is increasing
3.	$\dfrac{dy}{dx} < 0$	curve is decreasing
4.	$y = 3$ at $x = -2$	the point $(-2, 3)$ is on the curve

Example

Draw a rough graph of a function $y = f(x)$ which satisfies the following conditions:

(i) $y = 6$ at $x = -2$

         $y = -2$ at $x = 1$

(ii) $\dfrac{dy}{dx} = 0$ at $x = -2$ and $x = 1$

(iii) $\dfrac{dy}{dx} < 0$ for $-2 < x < 1$

(iv) $\dfrac{dy}{dx} > 0$ for $x < -2$ and $x > 1$

Solution:

(i)   Given two points on the curve $(-2, 6)$ and $(1, -2)$.

(ii)   These two points are turning points (local maximum or minimum points).

(iii)   The curve is decreasing between $x = -2$ and $x = 1$.

(iv)   The curve is increasing before $x = -2$ and after $x = 1$.

Below is a rough sketch of the curve:

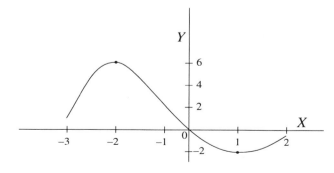

Functions

Example

The function f is defined by $f : x \rightarrow 7 - 3x$.

Find $f(-2)$ and find a number k such that $kf(-2) = f(24)$.

Solution:

$$f(-2) = 7 - 3(-2) = 7 + 6 = 13$$
$$f(24) = 7 - 3(24) = 7 - 72 = -65$$
$$kf(-2) = f(24)$$

$$\Rightarrow \quad k(13) = -65$$
$$\Rightarrow \quad 13k = -65$$
$$\Rightarrow \quad k = -5$$

Example

$f : x \rightarrow x^2 - 1$ and $g : x \rightarrow 1 - 2x$.

Find the values of x for which $3f(x) = 5g(x)$.

Solution:

$$3f(x) = 5g(x)$$

$$\Rightarrow \quad 3(x^2 - 1) = 5(1 - 2x)$$
$$\Rightarrow \quad 3x^2 - 3 = 5 - 10x$$
$$\Rightarrow 3x^2 - 3 - 5 + 10x = 0$$
$$\Rightarrow \quad 3x^2 + 10x - 8 = 0$$
$$\Rightarrow \quad (3x - 2)(x + 4) = 0$$
$$\Rightarrow \quad 3x - 2 = 0 \quad \text{or} \quad x + 4 = 0$$
$$\Rightarrow \quad 3x = 2 \quad \text{or} \quad x = -4$$
$$\Rightarrow \quad x = \frac{2}{3} \quad \text{or} \quad x = -4$$

Example

Let $g(x) = x(x - 2)$ for $x \in \mathbf{R}$.

Find $g(0)$, $g(4)$, $g(-2)$.

Show that $g(1 + t) = g(1 - t)$ for $t \in \mathbf{R}$.

Find the derivative, $g'(x)$, and show that $g'(x) > 0$ for $x > 1$.

Solve the equation $g(x) - g'(x) + 1 = 0$.

Solution:

$g(x) = x(x - 2) = x^2 - 2x$

$g(0)$	$g(4)$	$g(-2)$
$= (0)^2 - 2(0)$	$= (4)^2 - 2(4)$	$= (-2)^2 - 2(-2)$
$= 0 - 0$	$= 16 - 8$	$= 4 + 4$
$= 0$	$= 8$	$= 8$

$g(1 + t)$	$g(1 - t)$
$= (1 + t)^2 - 2(1 + t)$	$= (1 - t)^2 - 2(1 - t)$
$= 1 + 2t + t^2 - 2 - 2t$	$= 1 - 2t + t^2 - 2 + 2t$
$= t^2 - 1$	$= t^2 - 1$

$$\therefore \ g(1 + t) = g(1 - t)$$

$g(x) = x^2 - 2x$	$g'(x) > 0$
$g'(x) = 2x - 2$ $\quad \Rightarrow$	$2x - 2 > 0$
$\Rightarrow$	$2x > 2$
$\Rightarrow$	$x > 1$

$$\therefore \ g'(x) > 0 \text{ for } x > 1$$

$g(x) - g'(x) + 1 = 0$

$(x^2 - 2x) - (2x - 2) + 1 = 0$

$x^2 - 2x - 2x + 2 + 1 = 0$

$x^2 - 4x + 3 = 0$

$(x - 3)(x - 1) = 0$

$x - 3 = 0 \quad \text{or} \quad x - 1 = 0$

$x = 3 \quad \text{or} \quad x = 1$

Example

On the right is part of the graph of the function

$f : x \rightarrow -x^2 - 2x + 8, \; x \in \mathbf{R}.$

Find the coordinates of p, q, r and s,

where q is the turning point of the curve.

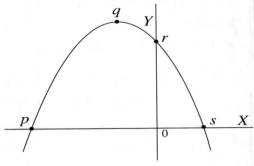

Solution:

For the graph $y = -x^2 - 2x + 8$.

On the X axis $y = 0$. Therefore to find p and s we let $y = 0$ and solve.

$$y = -x^2 - 2x + 8$$
$$0 = -x^2 - 2x + 8 \qquad \text{(let } y = 0)$$
$$\Rightarrow \quad x^2 + 2x - 8 = 0 \qquad \text{(everything to the left)}$$
$$\Rightarrow \quad (x + 4)(x - 2) = 0$$
$$\Rightarrow \quad x + 4 = 0 \quad \text{or} \quad x - 2 = 0$$
$$\Rightarrow \quad x = -4 \quad \text{or} \quad x = 2$$

$\therefore$ the curve cuts the X axis at -4 and 2.

Thus, the coordinates of p are $(-4, 0)$ and the coordinates of s are $(2, 0)$.

On the Y axis $x = 0$. Therefore to find r we let $x = 0$ and solve.

$$y = -x^2 - 2x + 8$$
$$y = -(0)^2 - 2(0) + 8 \qquad \text{(let } x = 0)$$
$$y = 0 + 0 + 8$$
$$y = 8$$

$\therefore$ the curve cuts the Y axis at 8.

Thus, the coordinates of r are $(0, 8)$.

For a turning point (maximum point here) $\dfrac{dy}{dx} = 0$

$y = -x^2 - 2x + 8$	Now we find y
$\dfrac{dy}{dx} = -2x - 2 = 0 \quad \text{(max. / min.)}$	$y = -x^2 - 2x + 8$
$\Rightarrow \quad -2x - 2 = 0$	$x = -1$
$\Rightarrow \quad -2x = 2$	$\Rightarrow \quad y = -(-1)^2 - 2(-1) + 8$
$\Rightarrow \quad 2x = -2$	$= -(1) - 2(-1) + 8$
$\Rightarrow \quad x = -1$	$= -1 + 2 + 8$
	$= 9$

Thus, the coordinates of the turning point q are $(-1, 9)$

The coordinates are $p(-4, 0)$, $q(-1, 9)$, $r(0, 8)$ and $s(2, 0)$.

Periodic Functions

We will be given a graph of a periodic, or repeating, function, and asked to find its period and range.

Example

The graph shows a portion of a periodic function $f : x \rightarrow f(x)$. Write down the period and range of the function.

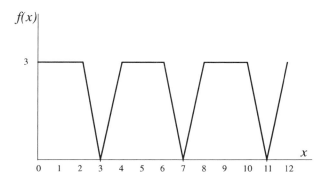

Solution:

The period is the smallest interval on the x axis which the graph takes to complete one full cycle.

From the graph, the period $= 4$

Range $=$ [lowest y value, highest y value] $= [0, 3]$

Example

The graph shows a portion of a periodic function $f : x \rightarrow f(x)$.

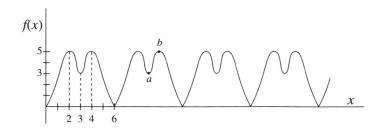

(i)   Write down the period and range of the function.

(ii) Evaluate, $f(2), f(3), f(4), f(26), f(27)$.

(iii) Write down the coordinates of a and b.

(iv) State one value of x in the range $72 \leq x \leq 78$ for which $f(x) = 3$.

Solution:

(i) Period = 6 and range = [0, 5]

(ii) Evaluate $f(2)$ means 'when $x = 2$ what is the value of $f(x)$'

From the graph:

$f(2) = 5$ $\qquad$ $f(3) = 3$ $\qquad\qquad$ $f(4) = 5$

$f(26)$ and $f(27)$

The section of the graph for $24 \leq x \leq 30$ is shown below:

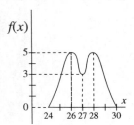

$\therefore$ $\quad$ $f(26) = 5$ and

$\qquad$ $f(27) = 3$

Alternative method:

As the period is 6 (we can keep subtracting 6):

$f(26) = f(20) = f(14) = f(8) = f(2) = 5$

$f(27) = f(21) = f(15) = f(9) = f(3) = 3$

(iii) The section of the graph for $6 \leq x \leq 12$ is shown below:

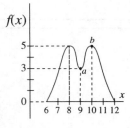

The coordinates of a are (9, 3) and the coordinates of b are (10, 5).

(iv) The section of the graph for $72 \leq x \leq 78$ is shown below:

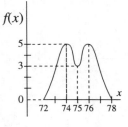

one value for $f(x) = 3$ is 75

Graphing and Using Functions

Notes:

(i) Never give answers outside the given domain of x.

(ii) $y = f(x)$, so $f(x)$ can be replaced by y.

(iii) In general, if given x find y or if given y find x.

Main Problems:

1. Find the values of x for which $f(x) = 0$ (or $y = 0$).

This question is asking 'where does the curve meet the X axis?'

Solution: Write down the values of x where the graph meets the X axis.

2. Find the values of x for which $f(x) = 3$ (or $f(x) - 3 = 0$ or $y - 3 = 0$).

This question is asking 'when $y = 3$, what are the values of x?'

Solution: Draw the line $y = 3$. Where this line meets the curve draw broken perpendicular lines onto the X axis. Write down the values of x where these broken lines meet the X axis.

3. Find the value of $f(2\frac{1}{2})$.

This question is asking 'when $x = 2\frac{1}{2}$, what is the value of y?'

Solution: From $x = 2\frac{1}{2}$ on the X axis draw a broken perpendicular line until it meets the curve. Then draw a broken horizontal line until it meets the Y axis. The position where this line meets the Y axis is the value of $f(2\frac{1}{2})$.

4. **Positive**: Find the range of values of x for which $f(x) > 0$.

This question is asking 'for what values of x is the graph **above** the X axis?'

Solution: Write down the values of x for which the graph is above the X axis.

5. **Negative:** Find the range of values of x for which $f(x) < 0$.

This question is asking 'for what values of x is the graph below the X axis?'

Solution: Write down the values of x for which the graph is below the X axis.

Note: If the question uses $f(x) \geq 0$ or $f(x) \leq 0$, then where the graph meets the X axis must also included.

6. **Increasing:** Find the range of values of x for which $f(x)$ is increasing.

This question is asking 'for what values of x is the graph **rising** as we go from left to right?'

Solution: Write down the values of x for which the graph is rising.

7. **Decreasing:** Find the range of values of x for which $f(x)$ is decreasing.

This question is asking 'for what values of x is the graph **falling** as we go from left to right?'

Solution: Write down the values of x for which the graph is falling.

Note: A range is usually given in the form $a \leq x \leq b$.

If the end points are not included the range is written $a < x < b$.

Be guided by the question, e.g.

$f(x) \geq 0$ or $f(x) \leq 0$ use $a \leq x \leq b$.

$f(x) > 0$ or $f(x) < 0$ use $a < x < b$.

8. Two functions graphed on the same axes and scales:

Often we have to use two graphs to answer certain questions.

For example, $f(x) = 2x^3 - 3x^2 - 6x + 2$, $\quad g(x) = x - 3$

$f(x)$ is a curve, $g(x)$ is a line

(a) Find the values of x for which $f(x) = g(x)$ [or $f(x) - g(x) = 0$].

$f(x) = g(x) \Rightarrow$ curve = line

This question is asking 'for what values of x does the curve and line intersect?'

Solution: Where the curve and line meet draw broken perpendicular lines onto the X axis.

Write down the values of x where these broken lines meet the X axis.

(b) Find the range of values of x for which $f(x) > g(x)$ [or $f(x) - g(x) > 0$]

$f(x) > g(x) \Rightarrow$ curve **above** the line

This question is asking 'for what values of x is the curve above the line?'

Solution: Write down the values of x for which the curve is above the line.

(c) Problems involving **8(a)** and **8(b)** above can arise in disguise when using the graph to solve a **new** equation or **new** inequality.

Use your graph to find the values of x for which $2x^3 - 3x^2 - 5x + 5 < 0$.

Solution:

This inequality is a combination of the curve and the line in disguise.

Let $f(x) =$ Old function and $2x^3 - 3x^2 - 5x + 5 =$ New function.

Old: $2x^3 - 3x^2 - 5x + 2 < 0$
$\qquad \downarrow \qquad \downarrow \qquad \downarrow \quad \downarrow$
New: $2x^3 - 3x^2 - 6x + 5 < 0$

$\Rightarrow$ New function = Old function $- x + 3 < 0$

$\qquad \Rightarrow \qquad$ Old function $< x - 3$

$\qquad \Rightarrow \qquad f(x) < g(x)$

$\qquad \Rightarrow \qquad$ curve is **below** the line

In disguise, this question is asking 'for what values of x is the curve below the line?'

Solution: Write down the values of x for which the curve is below the line.

9. **Using two graphs to evaluate square roots and cube roots:**

Suppose the functions $f : x \rightarrow x^3 + x^2 + x - 3$ and $g : x \rightarrow x^2 + x + 2$ are graphed on the same axes and scales.

Use both graphs to estimate $\sqrt[3]{5}$.

Solution: Let $f(x) = g(x)$ [Where the curves are equal]

Where the curves intersect is the most common way to use graphs to evaluate roots.

$$\Rightarrow \quad x^3 + x^2 + x - 3 = x^2 + x + 2$$
$$\Rightarrow \quad x^3 - 3 = 2$$
$$\Rightarrow \quad x^3 = 5$$
$$\Rightarrow \quad x = \sqrt[3]{5}$$

Hence, where the two curves intersect can be used to estimate $\sqrt[3]{5}$.

Find where the two curves intersect. From this point draw a broken perpendicular line onto the X axis. Write down this value of x. It is a good approximation for $\sqrt[3]{5}$.

10. **Number of Roots:**

The number of times a graph meets the X axis gives the number of roots it has. Often we need to find a range of values of a constant, which shifts a graph up or down, giving a graph a certain number of roots, e.g.

For what values of k does the equation $f(x) = k$ have three roots?

Solution:

The equation $f(x) = k$ will have **three** roots if the line $y = k$ cuts the graph three times.

So we have to draw lines parallel to the X axis that cut the graph three times.

The range of values of k will be in between the lowest and highest values on the Y axis so that the line $y = k$ cuts the graph three times.

11. **Local maximum and minimum points or the local maximum and minimum values:**

Often we are asked to find the local maximum and minimum points or the local maximum and minimum values. Consider the graph on the right. The local maximum and minimum points are where the graph turns, $(-1, 2)$ and $(1, -3)$, respectively. The local maximum and minimum values are found by drawing a line from the turning points to the Y axis and reading the values where these lines meet the Y axis. The maximum and minimum values are 2 and -3, respectively.

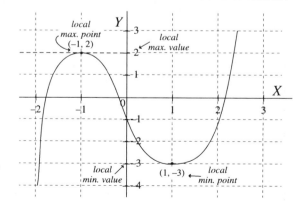

95

Example

The function $f: x \rightarrow x^3 - 2x^2 - 6x + 4$ is defined on the domain $-2 \leq x \leq 4$ for $x \in \mathbf{R}$.

Noting that $f(-2) = 0$ and $f(2) = -8$, draw the graph of the function.

Use your graph to find, as accurately as possible:

(i) the values of x for which $f(x) = 0$.

(ii) the range of values of $x > 0$ for which $f(x) < 0$.

Using the same axes and scales draw the graph of the function

$g : x \rightarrow 2x - 5$, for $x \in \mathbf{R}$.

Find (iii) the range of values of x for which $g(x) > f(x)$.

(iv) the two roots of the equation

$$x^3 - 2x^2 - 8x + 9 = 0.$$

Solution:

Let $y = f(x)$

x	x^3		$2x^2$		$6x$		4	y
-2	-8	$-$	8	$+$	12	$+$	4	0
-1	-1	$-$	2	$+$	6	$+$	4	7
0	0	$-$	0	$+$	0	$+$	4	4
1	1	$-$	2	$-$	6	$+$	4	-3
2	8	$-$	8	$-$	12	$+$	4	-8
3	27	$-$	18	$-$	18	$+$	4	-5
4	64	$-$	32	$-$	24	$+$	4	12

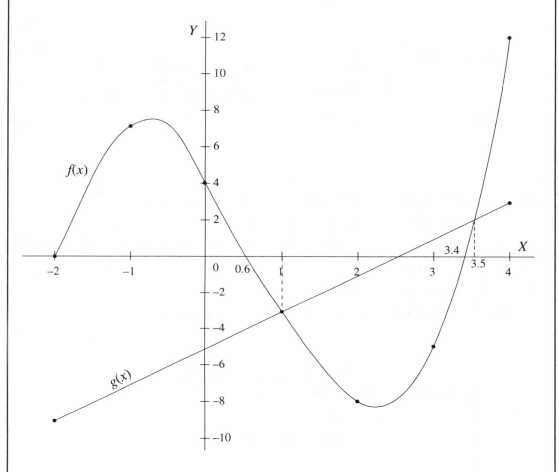

(i) The values of x for which $f(x) = 0$.

$f(x) = 0$ is where the graph cuts the X axis.

The graph cuts the X axis at -2, 0.6 and 3.4, approximately.

$\therefore$ $f(x) = 0$ for $x = -2$, $x = 0.6$ and $x = 3.4$

(ii) The range of values of $x > 0$ for which $f(x) < 0$.

This is the set of values of $x > 0$ for which the graph of $f(x)$ is below the X axis.

The graph of $f(x)$ is below the X axis, and $x > 0$, for values of x between 0.6 and 3.4.

$\therefore$ $f(x) < 0$, for $x > 0$, for $0.6 < x < 3.4$

The graph of $g(x) = 2x - 5$ (or $y = 2x - 5$) is a straight line.

Hence, two points are all that are needed to graph it.

Choose two suitable values of x (usually the two extreme values) and find the corresponding values of y.

$$y = 2x - 5$$

$x = -2$	$x = 4$
$y = 2(-2) - 5$	$y = 2(4) - 5$
$y = -4 - 5$	$y = 8 - 5$
$y = -9$	$y = 3$
$(-2, -9)$	$(4, 3)$

By drawing a line between the points $(-2, -9)$ and $(4, 3)$ the graph of $g(x)$ is obtained

(iii) The range of values of x for which $g(x) > f(x)$ (i.e. line > curve).

$g(x) > f(x)$ is where the line lies above the curve.

From the graph, the line is above the curve for values of x between 1 and 3·5.

$\therefore$ $g(x) > f(x)$ for $1 < x < 3 \cdot 5$

(iv) The roots of the equation $x^3 - 2x^2 - 8x + 9 = 0$

Let $f(x) =$ Old function and $x^3 - 2x^2 - 8x + 9 =$ New function.

$$\text{Old: } x^3 - 2x^2 - 6x + 4 = 0$$
$$\downarrow \quad \downarrow \quad \downarrow \quad \downarrow$$
$$\text{New: } x^3 - 2x^2 - 8x + 9 = 0$$

$\Rightarrow$ New function = Old function $- 2x + 5 = 0$

$\Rightarrow$ Old function $- 2x + 5 = 0$

$\Rightarrow$ Old function $= 2x - 5$

$\Rightarrow$ $f(x) = g(x)$

$\Rightarrow$ curve = line

$f(x) = g(x)$ is where the curve and the line intersect. Where the curve and the line intersect, draw perpendiculars onto the X axis and read off the x values. These values of x will be the approximate roots of the equation $x^3 - 2x^2 - 8x + 9 = 0$

From the graph, the curve and the line intersect at 1 and 3·5 approximately.

$\therefore$ $x^3 - 2x^2 - 8x + 9 = 0$ for $x = 1$ and $x = 3 \cdot 5$

Example

Let $g(x) = x(4 - x)$, $x \in \mathbf{R}$.

Find: $g(0)$, $g(3)$, $g(\frac{1}{4})$, $g(-1)$, $g'(0)$, $g'(-\frac{1}{2})$

On the same axes and scales graph the functions:

$g(x)$ and $g'(x)$ in the domain $-1 \le x \le 5$, $x \in \mathbf{R}$.

Find, using calculus, the coordinates of the local maximum of the curve $g(x) = x(4 - x)$.

Compare this point to the turning point on the graph of $g(x)$.

Solution:

$g(x) = x(4 - x) = 4x - x^2$

$g(0)$	$g(3)$	$g(\frac{1}{4})$
$= 4(0) - (0)^2$	$= 4(3) - (3)^2$	$= 4(\frac{1}{4}) - (\frac{1}{4})^2$
$= 0 - 0$	$= 12 - 9$	$= 1 - \frac{1}{16}$
$= 0$	$= 3$	$= \frac{15}{16}$

$g(x) = 4x - x^2$

$g'(x) = 4 - 2x$

$g'(-1)$	$g'(0)$	$g'(-\frac{1}{2})$
$= 4 - 2(-1)$	$= 4 - 2(0)$	$= 4 - 2(-\frac{1}{2})$
$= 4 + 2$	$= 4 - 0$	$= 4 + 1$
$= 6$	$= 4$	$= 5$

$$g(x) = 4x - x^2$$
$$y = 4x - x^2$$

x	$4x$	$-$	x^2	y
−1	−4	−	1	−5
0	0	−	0	0
1	4	−	1	3
2	8	−	4	4
3	12	−	9	3
4	16	−	16	0
5	20	−	25	−5

$$g'(x) = 4 - 2x$$
$$y = 4 - 2x \text{ (a line)}$$

$x = -1$	$x = 5$
$y = 4 - 2(-1)$	$y = 4 - 2(5)$
$y = 4 + 2$	$y = 4 - 10$
$y = 6$	$y = -6$
$(-1, 6)$	$(5, -6)$

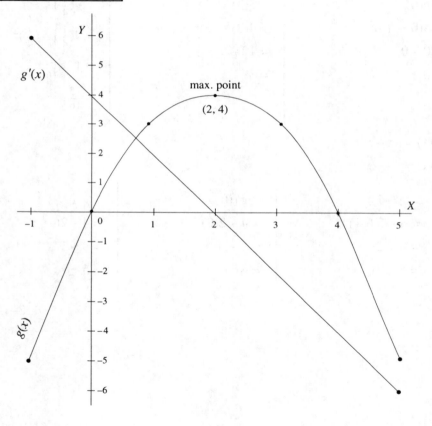

max. point
(2, 4)

$g'(x)$

$g(x)$

Maximum point using calculus:

$$g(x) = 4x - x^2$$
$$\Rightarrow \quad y = 4x - x^2$$
$$\Rightarrow \quad \frac{dy}{dx} = 4 - 2x$$

$$\frac{dy}{dx} = 0 \text{ (for max. / min.)}$$
$$\Rightarrow 4 - 2x = 0$$
$$\Rightarrow \quad -2x = -4$$
$$\Rightarrow \quad 2x = 4$$
$$\Rightarrow \quad x = 2$$

$x = 2$

$y = 4x - x^2 = 4(2) - (2)^2 = 8 - 4 = 4$

Using calculus, the local maximum point is (2, 4).

From the graph, the local maximum point is also (2, 4).

Both give the same result.

Example

Let $f(x) = \dfrac{1}{x - 3}$, $x \neq 3$ and $g(x) = x - 3$, $x \in \mathbf{R}$.

Find $f(2\frac{1}{2})$, $f(2\frac{3}{4})$, $f(3\frac{1}{4})$ and $f(3\frac{1}{2})$

Complete the following tables:

x	-1	0	1	2	$2\frac{1}{2}$	$2\frac{3}{4}$	3	$3\frac{1}{4}$	$3\frac{1}{2}$	4	5	6	7
$f(x)$	$-\frac{1}{4}$			-1			undefined					$\frac{1}{3}$	

x	-1	4	7
$g(x)$			4

Using the same axes and scales, and in the same domain, graph the functions $f(x)$ and $g(x)$.

Draw the vertical asymptote to $f(x)$ with a broken line.

Write down the equations of both asymptotes to the graph of $f(x)$.

Using your graph:

(i) Find the values of $x > 3$ for which $f(x) < g(x)$

(ii) Solve the equation $\dfrac{1}{x - 3} = x - 3$

Solution:

$$f(x) = \frac{1}{x-3}$$

$$f(2\tfrac{1}{2}) = \frac{1}{2\tfrac{1}{2}-3} = \frac{1}{-\tfrac{1}{2}} = \frac{2}{-1} = -2$$

$$f(3\tfrac{1}{4}) = \frac{1}{3\tfrac{1}{4}-3} = \frac{1}{\tfrac{1}{4}} = \frac{4}{1} = 4$$

$$f(3\tfrac{1}{2}) = \frac{1}{3\tfrac{1}{2}-3} = \frac{1}{\tfrac{1}{2}} = \frac{2}{1} = 2$$

$$f(2\tfrac{3}{4}) = \frac{1}{2\tfrac{3}{4}-3} = \frac{1}{-\tfrac{1}{4}} = \frac{4}{-1} = -4$$

Completed tables:

x	-1	0	1	2	$2\tfrac{1}{2}$	$2\tfrac{3}{4}$	3	$3\tfrac{1}{4}$	$3\tfrac{1}{2}$	4	5	6	7
$f(x)$	$-\tfrac{1}{4}$	$-\tfrac{1}{3}$	$-\tfrac{1}{2}$	-1	-2	-4	undefined	4	2	1	$\tfrac{1}{2}$	$\tfrac{1}{3}$	$\tfrac{1}{4}$

x	-1	4	7
$g(x)$	-4	1	4

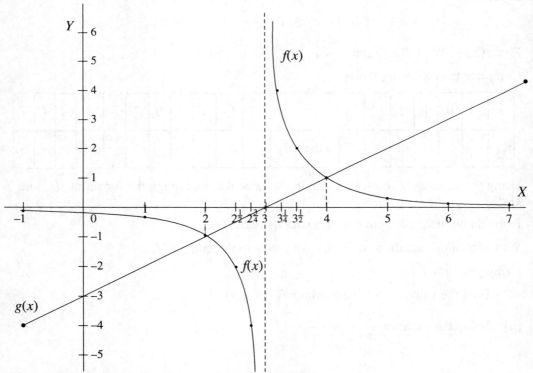

The equation of the vertical asymptote to $f(x)$ is $x = 3$ (broken line on the graph).

The equation of the horizontal asymptote to $f(x)$ is $y = 0$ (the X axis).

(i) Find the values of $x > 3$ for which $f(x) < g(x)$ (i.e. curve $<$ line)

$f(x) < g(x)$ is where the curve lies below the line and $x > 3$.

From the graph, the curve is below the line for values of x between 4 and 7.

∴ $x > 3$ and $f(x) < g(x)$ for $4 < x \leq 7$

[4 is not included because at $x = 4$, $f(x) = g(x)$]

(ii) Solve the equation $\quad \dfrac{1}{x-3} = x - 3$

$$\dfrac{1}{x-3} = x - 3$$

$\Rightarrow \qquad f(x) = g(x)$

$\Rightarrow \qquad$ curve = line

$f(x) = g(x)$ is where the curve and the line intersect.

The curve and the line intersect at $x = 2$ and $x = 4$ (broken lines on graph)

∴ $\dfrac{1}{x-3} = x - 3$ for $x = 2$ and $x = 4$

6. AREA AND VOLUME

Distances and Area

1. Rectangle

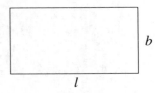

Area = lb

Perimeter = $2l + 2b = 2(l + b)$

2. Square

Area = l^2

Perimeter = $4l$

3. Triangle

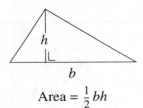

Area = $\frac{1}{2}bh$

4. Parallelogram

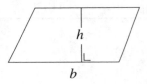

Area = bh

5. Circle (Disc)

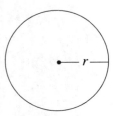

Area = πr^2

Circumference = $2\pi r$

6. Sector of a circle

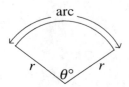

Area = $\frac{\theta}{360} \times \pi r^2$

Length of arc = $\frac{\theta}{360} \times 2\pi r$

(Similar to circle with $\frac{\theta}{360}$ in front of formulae)

Example

The figure on the right is made up of a semi-circle, a rectangle and a triangle.

Find the area of the figure in cm².

(Take $\pi = \frac{22}{7}$)

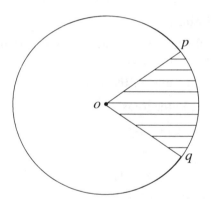

|←40 cm→|

84 cm

|←————— 212 cm —————→|

Solution:

The radius of the semi-circle = $\frac{84}{2}$ = 42

∴ the length of the rectangle = 212 – 42 – 40 = 130 cm

1. Area of semi-circle = $\frac{1}{2}\pi r^2 = \frac{1}{2} \times \frac{22}{7} \times \frac{42}{1} \times \frac{42}{1} = 2\,772$ cm²

2. Area of rectangle = $l \times b = 130 \times 84 = 10\,920$ cm²

3. Area of triangle = $\frac{1}{2}bh = \frac{1}{2} \times 84 \times 40 = 1\,680$ cm²

Thus, the area of the figure = 2772 + 10 920 + 1 680 = 15 372 cm²

Example

In the diagram, o is the centre of the circle of radius length 15 cm.

$|\angle poq| = 72°$

Find in terms of π:

(i) the length of the minor arc pq

(ii) the area of the shaded sector.

Solution:

(i) length of minor arc pq

$= \dfrac{|\angle poq|}{360} \times 2\pi r$

$= \dfrac{72}{360} \times 2 \times \pi \times 15$

$= \dfrac{1}{5} \times 2 \times \pi \times 15$

$= 6\pi$ cm

(ii) Area of shaded sector

$= \dfrac{|\angle poq|}{360} \times \pi r^2$

$= \dfrac{72}{360} \times \pi \times 15 \times 15$

$= \dfrac{1}{5} \times \pi \times 15 \times 15$

$= 45\pi$ cm²

Example

The area of a circle is $81\pi\,\text{cm}^2$. It's length is $k\pi\,\text{cm}$. Calculate k.

Solution:

Equation given in disguise:

$$\text{Area} = 81\pi\,\text{cm}^2$$
$$\downarrow$$
$$\Rightarrow \quad \pi r^2 = 81\pi$$
$$\Rightarrow \quad r^2 = 81$$
$$\Rightarrow \quad r = 9\,\text{cm}$$

length of a circle

$$= 2\pi r$$
$$\downarrow$$
$$= 2\pi(9)$$
$$= 18\pi\,\text{cm}$$

Comparing : $k\pi = 18\pi$

$$\therefore \qquad k = 18$$

Example

A square is inscribed in a circle. The diameter of the circle is 5 cm in length. Find the area of the square.

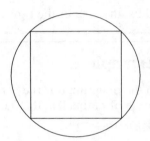

Solution:

Let the length of a side of the square be x cm, its diagonal is 5 cm.

$\therefore$ the area of the square is x^2 cm^2.

Using Pythagoras' theorem:

$$x^2 + x^2 = 5^2$$
$$\Rightarrow \quad 2x^2 = 25$$
$$\Rightarrow \quad x^2 = 12\cdot5$$

Thus, the area of the square is $12\cdot5$ cm^2

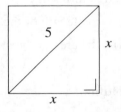

Areas of Irregular Shapes, Simpson's Rule

Simpson's rule gives a concise formula to enable us to make a very good approximation of the area of an irregular shape.

Consider the diagram below:

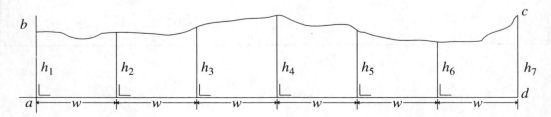

To find the area of the figure *abcd* do the following:

1. Divide the figure into an **even** number of strips of **equal** width, w.
2. Number and measure each height, h. There will be an **odd** number of heights.
3. Use the following formula:

$$\text{Area} = \frac{w}{3}\,[(h_1 + h_7) + 4(h_2 + h_4 + h_6) + 2(h_3 + h_5)]$$

   i.e. $\text{Area} = \dfrac{w}{3}\,[(F + L) + 4(E) + 2(R)]$

   where, w = width of strip

   $F + L$ = first and last heights

   $4(E)$ = 4 times the sum of the even-numbered heights

   $2(R)$ = 2 times the sum of the remaining odd-numbered heights

Example

The outline of a plot of land is shown in the sketch below.

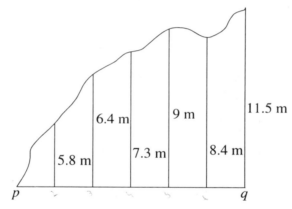

At intervals of 12 m along *pq*, perpendicular measurements 5·8m, 6·4m, 7·3m, 9m, 8·4m, 11·5m are made to the top boundary. Use Simpson's Rule to estimate the area of the plot, correct the nearest square metre.

Solution:

1. We divide the figure into 6 strips (given) each of 12 m width (given).

2. From the diagram:

   $w = 12$, $h_1 = 0$, $h_2 = 5{\cdot}8$, $h_3 = 6{\cdot}4$,

   $h_4 = 7{\cdot}3$, $h_5 = 9$, $h_6 = 8{\cdot}4$, $h_7 = 11{\cdot}5$

3.

$$\text{Area} = \frac{w}{3}[(F + L) + 4(E) + 2(R)]$$

$$= \frac{w}{3}[(h_1 + h_7) + 4(h_2 + h_4 + h_6) + 2(h_3 + h_5)]$$

$$= \frac{12}{3}[(0 + 11 \cdot 5) + 4(5 \cdot 8 + 7 \cdot 3 + 8 \cdot 4) + 2(6 \cdot 4 + 9)]$$

$$= 4[11 \cdot 5 + 4(21 \cdot 5) + 2(15 \cdot 4)]$$

$$= 4[11 \cdot 5 + 86 + 30 \cdot 8]$$

$$= 4[128 \cdot 3]$$

$$= 513 \cdot 2$$

$$= 513 \text{ m}^2 \text{ (correct to the nearest m}^2)$$

Sometimes we are given an equation in disguise.

Example

Surveyors make the following sketch in estimating the area of a building site, where k is the length shown. Using Simpson's Rule, they estimate the area of the site to be 100 square units. Find k.

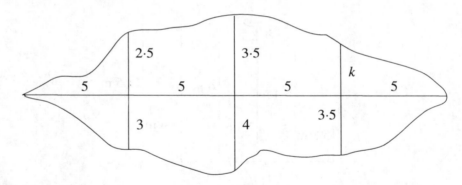

Solution:

Equation given in disguise: Given values

$$\text{Area} = 100$$

$$\therefore \quad \frac{w}{3}[(F + L) + 4(E) + 2(R)] = 100$$

$$\Rightarrow \quad \frac{w}{3}[(h_1 + h_5) + 4(h_2 + h_4) + 2(h_3)] = 100$$

$$\Rightarrow \quad \frac{5}{3}[(0 + 0) + 4(5 \cdot 5 + k + 3 \cdot 5) + 2(7 \cdot 5)] = 100$$

$$\Rightarrow \quad \frac{5}{3}(22 + 4k + 14 + 15) = 100 \quad \text{(remove internal brackets)}$$

$$\Rightarrow \quad \frac{5}{3}(4k + 51) = 100$$

$$\Rightarrow \quad 5(4k + 51) = 300 \quad \text{(multiply both sides by 3)}$$

Given values:
$w = 5$
$h_1 = 0$
$h_2 = 5 \cdot 5$
$h_3 = 7 \cdot 5$
$h_4 = (k + 3 \cdot 5)$
$h_5 = 0$

$$\Rightarrow \qquad 20\,k + 255 = 300 \qquad \text{(remove brackets)}$$
$$\Rightarrow \qquad 20k = 300 - 255$$
$$\Rightarrow \qquad 20k = 45$$
$$\Rightarrow \qquad k = 2\cdot25 \qquad \text{(divide both sides by 20)}$$

Volume

Rectangular Objects

1. Rectangular Solid

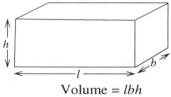

Volume = *lbh*
Surface Area = 2*lb* + 2*lh* + 2*bh*

2. Cube

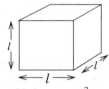

Volume = l^3
Surface Area = $6l^2$

Example

An open rectangular tank (no top) is full of water.
The volume of water in the tank is 2·4 litres.
If its length is 20 cm and its breadth is 15 cm, find
(i) its height and **(ii)** its surface area.

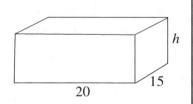

Solution:

1 litre = 1 000 cm³, $\qquad \therefore$ 2·4 litres = 2·4(1 000) = 2 400 cm³

(i) Equation given in disguise:

$\qquad$ Volume = 2 400 cm³

$\Rightarrow \quad l \times b \times h = 2\,400$

$\Rightarrow \quad (20)(15)h = 2\,400$

$\Rightarrow \qquad 300\,h = 2\,400$

$\Rightarrow \qquad\qquad h = 8$ cm

(ii) Surface area

$\qquad = lb + 2lh + 2bh$ (no top)

$\qquad = (20)(15) + 2(20)(8) + 2(15)(8)$

$\qquad = 300 + 320 + 240$

$\qquad = 860$ cm²

Example

The surface area of a cube is 54 cm^2.

Calculate its volume.

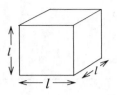

Solution:

Let the length of one side of the cube be l cm.

Equation given in disguise:

Surface area = 54 cm^2	Volume = l^3
$\Rightarrow$ $6l^2 = 54$	$= 3^3$
$\Rightarrow$ $l^2 = 9$	$= 27$ cm^3
$\Rightarrow$ $l = 3$ cm	Thus, the volume of the cube is 27 cm^3

Example

The surface area of a solid rectangular block is 258 cm^2. If its breadth is 6 cm and height is 5 cm, calculate its **(i)** length and **(ii)** volume.

Solution:

(i)   Equation given in disguise:

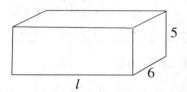

Surface area = 258

$\Rightarrow$ $2lb + 2lh + 2bh = 258$

$\Rightarrow$ $2l(6) + 2l(5) + 2(6)(5) = 258$

$\Rightarrow$ $12l + 10l + 60 = 258$

$\Rightarrow$ $22l + 60 = 258$

$\Rightarrow$ $22l = 258 - 60$

$\Rightarrow$ $22l = 198$

$\Rightarrow$ $l = \dfrac{198}{22} = 9$ cm

(ii)   Volume = lbh

$= (9)(6)(5)$

$= 270$

$\therefore$ Volume = 270 cm^3

Uniform Cross-Section

Many solid objects have the same cross-section throughout their length.

Here are some examples:

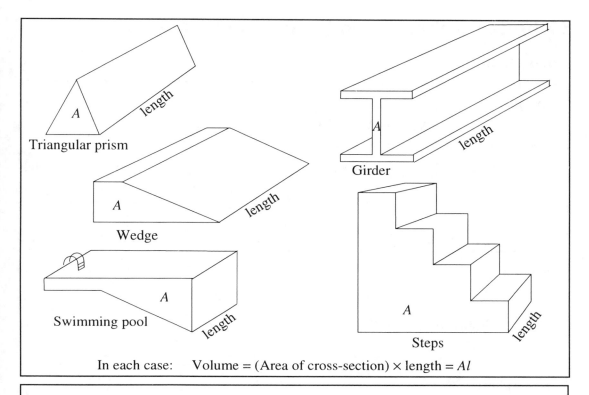

Triangular prism

Wedge

Girder

Swimming pool

Steps

In each case: Volume = (Area of cross-section) × length = Al

Example

Five rectangular shaped concrete steps
are constructed as shown.

Each step measures 1·2 m by 0·4 m and
the total height is 1·0 m with each step
having the same height of 0·2 m.

Calculate the volume of the solid concrete
construction.

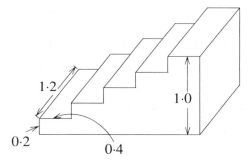

Solution:

The cross-section of the steps is made up of 5 rectangles, each of width 0·4 m.

The smallest rectangle has a height of 0·2 and the height of each rectangle after this
increases by 0·2 m.

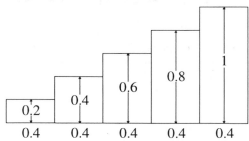

    Area of cross-section

= Area of 5 rectangles

= $(0·4)(0·2) + (0·4)(0·4) + (0·4)(0·6) +$
   $(0·4)(0·8) + (0·4)(1)$

= $0·08 + 0·16 + 0·24 + 0·32 + 0·4$

= $1·2 \text{ m}^2$

Volume = (Area of cross-section) × length

       = $1·2 × 1·2$

       = $1·44 \text{ m}^3$

Thus, the volume of concrete used in the construction of the steps in 1·44 m^3

Cylinder, Sphere, Hemisphere and Cone

Formulae:

Cylinder:

$$\text{Volume, } V = \pi r^2 h$$

$$\text{Curved Surface Area (C.S.A.)} = 2\pi rh$$

$$\text{Total Surface Area (T.S.A.)} = 2\pi rh + 2\pi r^2$$

$$= 2\pi r(h + r)$$

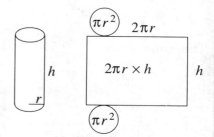

Sphere:

$$\text{Volume, } V = \frac{4}{3}\pi r^3$$

$$\text{Curved Surface Area (C.S.A.)} = 4\pi r^2$$

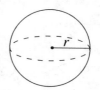

Hemisphere:

$$\text{Volume, } V = \frac{2}{3}\pi r^3$$

$$\text{Curved Surface Area (C.S.A.)} = 2\pi r^2$$

$$\text{Total Surface Area (T.S.A.)} = 2\pi r^2 + \pi r^2$$

$$= 3\pi r^2$$

Cone:

$$\text{Volume, } V = \frac{1}{3}\pi r^2 h$$

$$\text{Curved Surface Area (C.S.A.)} = \pi rl$$

$$\text{Total Surface Area (T.S.A.)} = \pi rl + \pi r^2$$

$$= \pi r(l + r)$$

$$\text{Pythagoras' Theorem: } l^2 = r^2 + h^2$$

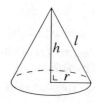

Combinations of Different Objects

Example

A solid metal ornament consists of a hemisphere of radius length 4 cm surmounted by a solid cone.

The cone's volume is twice the hemisphere's.

Find, h, the height of the cone.

Solution:

Equation given in disguise:

Volume of cone = twice the volume of the hemisphere

$\Rightarrow \qquad \frac{1}{3}\pi r^2 h = 2(\frac{2}{3}\pi r^3)$

$\Rightarrow \qquad \frac{1}{3}\pi r^2 h = \frac{4}{3}\pi r^3$

$\Rightarrow \qquad \pi r^2 h = 4\pi r^3 \qquad$ (multiply both sides by 3)

$\Rightarrow \qquad r^2 h = 4r^3 \qquad$ (divide both sides by π)

$\Rightarrow \qquad (4)(4)h = 4(4)(4)(4) \qquad$ (put in $r = 4$)

$\Rightarrow \qquad 16h = 256$

$\Rightarrow \qquad h = 16$

Thus, the height of the cone is 16 cm.

Example

A solid block, as shown, has a height of 12 cm and a base measuring 30 cm by 15·7 cm.

A solid cylinder is cut out of the block from top to bottom, as in the diagram. If the volume of the cylinder is $\frac{1}{6}$ of the volume of the block, calculate the radius of the cylinder.

(Take $\pi = 3\cdot14$)

Solution:

Equation given in disguise:

Volume of cylinder = $\frac{1}{6}$ (Volume of block)

$\Rightarrow \qquad \pi r^2 h = \frac{1}{6} lbh \qquad$ (we know π, h, l and b, find r)

$\Rightarrow$ $(3\cdot14)r^2(12) = \frac{1}{6}(30)(15\cdot7)(12)$ (put in $\pi = 3\cdot14$, $h = 12$, $l = 30$, $b = 15\cdot7$)

$\Rightarrow$ $37\cdot68\,r^2 = 942$

$\Rightarrow$ $r^2 = 25$ (divide both sides by $37\cdot68$)

$\Rightarrow$ $r = 5$

Thus, the radius of the cylinder is 5 cm

Example

A small candle is in the shape of a cone which fits exactly on top of a cylinder as shown. The cylinder has a radius of length 2 cm. The slant length of the cone is 2·5 cm.

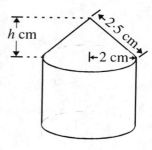

Calculate

(i) the height, h, of the cone

(ii) the volume of the cone in terms of π.

The volume of the cylinder is 5 times the volume of the cone.

Calculate the total height and surface area of the candle, in terms of π.

Solution:

(i) Using Pythagoras' theorem:

$r^2 + h^2 = l^2$ (we know r and l, find h)

$\Rightarrow$ $2^2 + h^2 = 2\cdot5^2$ (put in $r = 2$ and $l = 2\cdot5$)

$\Rightarrow$ $4 + h^2 = 6\cdot25$

$\Rightarrow$ $h^2 = 6\cdot25 - 4$

$\Rightarrow$ $h^2 = 2\cdot25$

$\Rightarrow$ $h = \sqrt{2\cdot25}$

$\Rightarrow$ $h = 1\cdot5$ cm

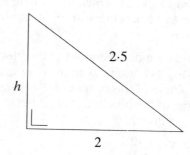

(ii) Volume of cone $= \frac{1}{3}\pi r^2 h$

$= \frac{1}{3}\pi(2)(2)(1\cdot5)$

$= 2\pi\,\text{cm}^3$

Equation given in disguise:

Volume of cylinder = 5 (Volume of cone)

Diagram:

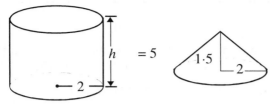

$\Rightarrow$ $\qquad$ $\pi r^2 h = 5\,(2\pi)$ $\qquad$ (volume of cone $= 2\pi$)

$\Rightarrow$ $\qquad$ $\pi r^2 h = 10\pi$ $\qquad$ (we know r, find h)

$\Rightarrow$ $\qquad$ $r^2 h = 10$ $\qquad$ (divide both sides by π)

$\Rightarrow$ $\qquad$ $4h = 10$ $\qquad$ (put in $r = 2$)

$\Rightarrow$ $\qquad$ $h = 2\cdot5$

$\therefore$ $\qquad$ height of the candle = height of cylinder + height of cone
$$= 2\cdot5 + 1\cdot5 = 4 \text{ cm}$$

Surface area = area of base of the candle + curved surface of cylinder
+ curved surface of area of cone.

$= \pi r^2 + 2\pi rh + \pi rl$

$= \pi(2)^2 + 2\pi(2)(2\cdot5) + \pi(2)(2\cdot5)$

$= 4\pi + 10\pi + 5\pi$

$= 19\pi$

Thus, the surface area of the candle is $19\pi \text{ cm}^2$

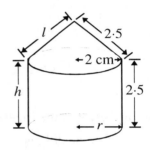

Example

A cone has a base radius of 9 cm and a height of 12 cm. A smaller cone is cut from the top of this cone. If the radius of the smaller cone is 6 cm, find its height.

Calculate the ratio, Volume of larger cone : Volume of smaller cone.

Solution:

The height of the smaller cone is missing.

We can find it using similar triangles.

Diagram of the situation:

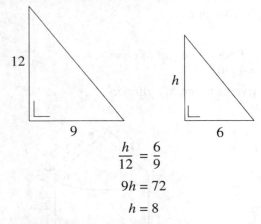

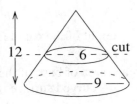

$$\frac{h}{12} = \frac{6}{9}$$

$$9h = 72$$

$$h = 8$$

Thus, the height of the smaller cone is 8 cm.

Volume of larger cone : Volume of smaller cone

$\Rightarrow \qquad \frac{1}{3}\pi R^2 H : \frac{1}{3}\pi r^2 h$

$\Rightarrow \qquad \pi R^2 H : \pi r^2 h \qquad$ (multiply both sides by 3)

$\Rightarrow \qquad R^2 H : r^2 h \qquad$ (divide both sides by π)

$\Rightarrow \qquad (9)(9)(12) : (6)(6)(8) \qquad$ (put in $R = 9$, $H = 12$, $r = 6$ and $h = 8$)

$\Rightarrow \qquad 972 : 288$

$\Rightarrow \qquad 27 : 8 \qquad$ (divide both sides by 36)

Thus, the ratio, Volume of larger cone : Volume of smaller cone = 27 : 8

Example

The lower portion (A) of a test-tube is hemispherical and the upper portion (B) is cylindrical.

The length of the test-tube is 14·5 cm and the diameter is 3 cm.

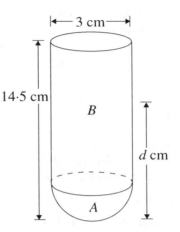

Calculate:

(i)   the length of B

(ii) the volume of the test-tube, in terms of π.

(iii) If water is poured into the test-tube find the depth, d, of the water when its volume is half the volume of the test-tube.

Solution:

(i)   The radius of the hemisphere = 1·5 cm ($\frac{1}{2}$ the diameter of the cylinder)

∴ the length of the cylinder B = 14·5 − 1·5 = 13 cm

(ii) Volume of test-tube = Volume of cylinder B + Volume of hemisphere A

$\Rightarrow$ $\qquad\qquad\qquad = \pi r^2 h + \frac{2}{3} \pi r^3$

$\Rightarrow$ $\qquad\qquad\qquad = \pi(1\cdot5)(1\cdot5)(13) + \frac{2}{3} \pi(1\cdot5)(1\cdot5)(1\cdot5)$

$\Rightarrow$ $\qquad\qquad\qquad = 29\cdot25\pi + 2\cdot25\pi$

$\Rightarrow$ $\qquad\qquad\qquad = 31\cdot5\pi \text{ cm}^3$

Thus, the volume of the test-tube is $31\cdot5\pi \text{ cm}^3$

(iii) The best way to approach this is to think of the test-tube turned upside down and imagine the water only going into the cylinder and find the height by which it would rise and subtract this from 14·5 to find d.

Equation given in disguise:

Volume of water in cylinder = $\frac{1}{2}$ (Volume of test-tube)

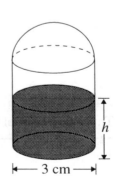

$\Rightarrow$ $\qquad\qquad \pi r^2 h = \frac{1}{2}(31\cdot5\pi)$ (we know r, find h)

$\Rightarrow$ $\qquad\qquad \pi r^2 h = 15\cdot75\pi$

$\Rightarrow$ $\qquad\qquad r^2 h = 15\cdot75$ $\qquad$ (divide both sides by π)

$\Rightarrow$ $\qquad\qquad (1\cdot5)^2 h = 15\cdot75$ $\qquad$ (put in r = 1·5)

$\Rightarrow$ $\qquad\qquad 2\cdot25h = 15\cdot75$

$\Rightarrow$ $\qquad\qquad h = 7$

Thus, the depth, d, the water would rise to in the test-tube = 14·5 − 7 = 7·5 cm

Recasting

Many of the questions we meet require us to solve a recasting problem. What happens is that a certain solid object is melted down and its shape is changed. We use the following fact:

> The volume remains the same after it is melted down

Example

A sphere of radius 15 cm is made of lead. The sphere is melted down. Some of the lead is used to form a solid cone of radius 10 cm and height 27 cm. The rest of the lead is used to form a cylinder of base radius 12 cm. Calculate the height of the cylinder.

Solution:

Equation given in disguise:

Volume of cylinder + Volume of cone   = Volume of sphere

(diagram of the situation)

$$\Rightarrow \quad \pi r^2 h \quad + \quad \tfrac{1}{3}\pi r^2 h \quad = \tfrac{4}{3}\pi r^3$$

$$\Rightarrow \quad r^2 h \quad + \quad \tfrac{1}{3}r^2 h \quad = \tfrac{4}{3}r^3 \qquad \text{(divide each part by } \pi)$$

$$\Rightarrow \quad (12)(12)(h) \quad + \quad \tfrac{1}{3}(10)(10)(27) = \tfrac{4}{3}(15)(15)(15) \quad \text{(put in given values)}$$

$$\Rightarrow \quad 144h \ + \ 900 \qquad = 4\,500$$

$$\Rightarrow \qquad\qquad\qquad 144h = 4\,500 - 900$$

$$\Rightarrow \qquad\qquad\qquad 144h = 3\,600$$

$$\Rightarrow \qquad\qquad\qquad\qquad h = 25$$

Thus, the height of the cylinder is 25 cm.

Moving Liquids

In many questions we have to deal with moving liquid from one container to another container of different dimensions or shape. Again to help us solve the problem we use the fact that:

> The volume of the moved liquid does not change

Example

The base of a right circular cone has a radius of length 5 cm. The height of the cone is 12 cm. Calculate the volume in terms of π.

The inverted cone is filled with water. The water then drips from the vertex at the rate $\frac{\pi}{5}$ cm^3/s.

Calculate the time in seconds until the cone is empty, assuming the volume of water to be the same as the volume of the cone.

If all the water dripped into a dry cylindrical can of diameter 10 cm in length, calculate the height of water in the can.

Solution:

$$\text{Volume of cone} = \tfrac{1}{3}\pi r^2 h$$

$$= \tfrac{1}{3}\pi(5)(5)(12)$$

$$= 100\pi \text{ cm}^3 \qquad \text{(multiply top and bottom by 5)}$$

$$\text{Time to empty cone} = \frac{\text{Volume of cone}}{\text{Rate of flow}} = \frac{100\pi}{\dfrac{\pi}{5}} = \frac{500\pi}{\pi} = 500 \text{ seconds}$$

Equation given in disguise:

Volume of cylinder = Volume of cone

$$\Rightarrow \qquad \pi r^2 h = 100\pi$$

$$\Rightarrow \qquad r^2 h = 100 \qquad \text{(divide both sides by } \pi\text{)}$$

$$\Rightarrow \qquad 25h = 100 \qquad \text{(put in } r = 5\text{)}$$

$$\Rightarrow \qquad h = 4$$

Thus, the water will rise to a height of 4 cm in the cylinder.

Diagram

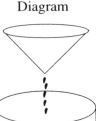

Displaced Liquid

In many questions we have to deal with situations where liquid is displaced by immersing, or removing, a solid object. In all cases the following principle helps us to solve these problems:

> Volume of displaced liquid = Volume of immersed solid object

Example

(i) Find, in terms of π, the volume of a solid metal sphere of radius 6 cm.

(ii) Five such identical spheres are completely submerged in a cylinder containing water.

If the radius of the cylinder is 8 cm, by how much will the level of the water drop if the spheres are removed from the cylinder?

Solution:

(i) Volume of sphere $= \frac{4}{3}\pi r^3 = \frac{4}{3}\pi(6)(6)(6) = 288\pi \text{ cm}^3$

(ii) Diagram: Old situation   New situation

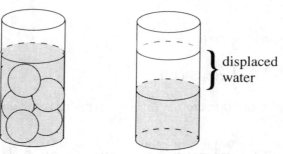

displaced water

Equation given in disguise:

Volume of displaced water = Volume of five spheres

Diagram:

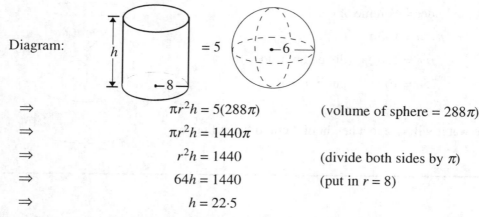

$\Rightarrow$ $\pi r^2 h = 5(288\pi)$ (volume of sphere $= 288\pi$)

$\Rightarrow$ $\pi r^2 h = 1440\pi$

$\Rightarrow$ $r^2 h = 1440$ (divide both sides by π)

$\Rightarrow$ $64h = 1440$ (put in $r = 8$)

$\Rightarrow$ $h = 22 \cdot 5$

Thus, the level of water in the cylinder would fall by 22·5 cm.

Flow of Liquid

Example

Water flows through a circular pipe of internal base diameter 6 cm at a speed of 10 cm/s. Calculate, in terms of π, the rate of flow of water from the pipe. The water flows into a cylindrical container of base diameter 36 cm and height 100 cm. How long will it take to fill the container?

Solution:

Rate of flow $= \dfrac{\text{Volume}}{\text{Time}} = $ Volume of water in 10 cm of the pipe per second

$= \pi r^2 h$

$= \pi(3)(3)(10)$

$= 90\pi \text{ cm}^3/\text{s}$

Volume of cylindrical container $= \pi r^2 h$

$= \pi(18)(18)(100)$

$= 32\,400\pi \text{ cm}^3$

Time $= \dfrac{\text{Volume}}{\text{Rate of flow}} = \dfrac{32\,400\,\pi}{90\,\pi}$

$= 360$ seconds

$= 6$ minutes

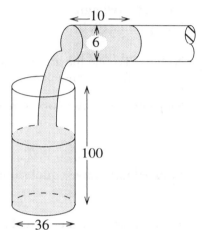

7. THE LINE

In all cases (x_1, y_1) and (x_2, y_2) represent points.

1. **Distance between two points.**

$$\sqrt{(x_2 - x_1)^2 + (y_2 - y_1)^2}$$

2. **Midpoint of a line segment.**

$$\left(\frac{x_1 + x_2}{2}, \frac{y_1 + y_2}{2}\right)$$

3. **Area of a triangle.**
   [one point at (0, 0)]

$$\frac{1}{2}|x_1 y_2 - x_2 y_1|$$

Note: To find the area of a quadrilateral (4 sided figure), divide it into two triangles, find the area of each triangle separately and add the results.

4. **Slope of line, given two points.**

$$m = \frac{y_2 - y_1}{x_2 - x_1}$$

5. **Parallel lines have equal slopes.**

$$\text{If } L \parallel K \Leftrightarrow m_L = m_K$$

6. **If two lines are perpendicular, then the product of their slopes equals –1.**

$$\text{If } L \perp K \Leftrightarrow m_L \cdot m_K = -1$$

(In 5 and 6 above, m_L and m_K are the slopes of the lines L and K, respectively.)

Note: If we know the slope of a line and we need to find the slope of a line perpendicular to it, simply do the following:
Turn the known slope upside down and change sign.

e.g. if a line has a slope of $\frac{3}{5}$, then a line perpendicular to it has a slope of $-\frac{5}{3}$, because $\frac{3}{5} \times -\frac{5}{3} = -1$.

7. **Equation of a line.**

$$(y - y_1) = m(x - x_1)$$

We need:

1. The slope of the line, m.
2. A point on the line, (x_1, y_1).

8. **Slope of a line when given its equation.**

To find the slope of a line when given its equation, we do the following:

Method 1:

> Get y on its own and the number in front of x is the slope.

Note: The number in front of x is called the **coefficient** of x.

In short, write the line in the form:

$y = mx \qquad + c$

$y = (\text{slope})x \; + \; (\text{where the line cuts the } Y \text{ axis})$

Method 2:

> If the line is in the form $ax + by + c = 0$, then $-\dfrac{a}{b}$ is the slope.

In words: slope $= -\dfrac{\text{number in front of } x}{\text{number in front of } y}$

Note: When using this method, make sure every term is on the left hand side in the given equation of the line.

9. **Proving lines are parallel or perpendicular.**

To prove whether or not two lines are parallel, do the following:

> 1. Find the slope of each line.
> 2. (a) If the slopes are the same, the lines are parallel.
>   (b) If the slopes are different, the lines are **not** parallel.

To prove whether or not two lines are perpendicular, do the following:

> 1. Find the slope of each line.
> 2. Multiply both slopes.
> 3. (a) If the answer in Step 2 is –1, the lines are perpendicular.
>   (b) If the answer in Step 2 is **not** –1, the lines are **not** perpendicular.

10. **Verify that a point belongs to a line.**

Substitute the coordinates of the point into the equation of the line. If the coordinates satisfy the equation, then the point is on the line. Otherwise, the point is not on the line.

11. **Point of intersection of two lines.**

Use the method of solving simultaneous equations to find the point of intersection of two lines.

12. Graphing lines.

To draw a line only two points are needed. The easiest points to find are where lines cut the X and Y axes. This is known as the **intercept method**.

Note: | On the X axis $y = 0$.   On the Y axis $x = 0$.

To draw a line do the following:

1. Let $y = 0$ and find x.
2. Let $x = 0$ and find y.
3. Plot these two points.
4. Draw the line through these points.

If the constant in the equation of a line is zero, e.g. $3x - 5y = 0$, or $4x = 3y$, then the line will pass through the origin, $(0, 0)$. In this case the **intercept method** will not work.

To draw a line that contains the origin, $(0, 0)$, do the following:

1. Choose a suitable value for x and find the corresponding value for y (or vice versa).
2. Plot this point.
3. A line drawn through this point and the origin is the required line.

Note: A very suitable value is to let x equal the number in front of y and then find the corresponding value for y (or vice versa).

13. Lines parallel to the axes.

$x = 2$ is a line parallel to the Y axis through 2 on the X axis.

$y = -1$ is a line parallel to the X axis through -1 on the Y axis.

Note: | $y = 0$ is the equation of the X axis.
$x = 0$ is the equation of the Y axis.

14. Axial symmetry in the axes or central symmetry in the origin.

The following three patterns emerge and it is worth memorising them:

1. Axial symmetry in the X axis $\rightarrow$ **change the sign of y.**
2. Axial symmetry in the Y axis $\rightarrow$ **change the sign of x.**
3. Central symmetry in the origin $\rightarrow$ **change the sign of both x and y.**

15. **Image of a line under an axial symmetry in the axes or central symmetry in the origin.**

To find the image of a line under axial symmetry in the axes or central symmetry in the origin, use either of the following two methods:

> **1.** Select any two points on the given line. Find the image of each of these points under whichever transformation is asked. Then find the equation of the line through these two image points.
>
> **2.** Use the results of the previous section:
>
> **(a)** Axial symmetry in the X axis, 'change the sign of y in the equation'.
>
> **(b)** Axial symmetry in the Y axis, 'change the sign of x in the equation'.
>
> **(c)** Central symmetry in the origin, $(0, 0)$, 'change the sign of both x and y in the equation'.

16. **Image of a line under a translation or a central symmetry.**

The image of a line under a translation or central symmetry is a line parallel to the original line. To find the image of a line under a translation or a central symmetry, use any of the following three methods:

> **1.** Select any two points on the given line. Find the image of each point under the translation or central symmetry. Find the equation of the line through these two image points.
>
> **2.** Select one point on the given line. Find the image of this point under the translation or central symmetry. Find the slope of the given line. Use this slope and the image point to find the equation of the image line.
>
> **3.** Say the line is $5x + 4y - 7 = 0$. Then a parallel line will be of the form $5x + 4y + k = 0$. All that is needed is to find the constant k. To find k, select one point on the given line. Find the image of this point under the translation or central symmetry. Substitute this image point into the second equation to find k, hence, the equation of the line under the translation or central symmetry is found.

Example

$a(-2, 4)$, $b(2, 2)$ and $c(5, 3)$ are three points.

(i) Find $|ab|$
(ii) Find the midpoint of $[bc]$
(iii) Find the area of $\triangle abc$
(iv) Find the slope of ab
(v) Find the equation of the line ab
(vi) Find the equation of the line, L, through the point c where $L \perp ab$
(vii) $L \cap ab = \{p\}$, find the coordinates of p
(viii) Find the image of c under the axial symmetry in the line ab.

Solution:

(i) $|ab|$

$a(-2, 4)$ and $b(2, 2)$

$x_1 = -2 \qquad x_2 = 2$

$y_1 = 4 \qquad y_2 = 2$

$|ab| = \sqrt{(x_2 - x_1)^2 + (y_2 - y_1)^2}$

$= \sqrt{(2 + 2)^2 + (2 - 4)^2}$

$= \sqrt{(4)^2 + (-2)^2}$

$= \sqrt{16 + 4}$

$= \sqrt{20}$

$\therefore \quad |ab| = \sqrt{20}$

(ii) Midpoint of $[bc]$

$b(2, 2)$ and $c(5, 3)$

$x_1 = 2 \qquad x_2 = 5$

$y_1 = 2 \qquad y_2 = 3$

$\text{Midpoint} = \left(\dfrac{x_1 + x_2}{2}, \dfrac{y_1 + y_2}{2} \right)$

$= \left(\dfrac{2 + 5}{2}, \dfrac{2 + 3}{2} \right)$

$= \left(\dfrac{7}{2}, \dfrac{5}{2} \right)$

$\therefore \quad \left(\dfrac{7}{2}, \dfrac{5}{2} \right)$ is the midpoint of $[bc]$

(iii) $a(-2, 4)$, $b(2, 2)$ and $c(5, 3)$

Map (move) the point $a(-2, 4)$ to $(0, 0)$

$(-2, 4) \qquad (2, 2) \qquad (5, 3)$

$\downarrow \qquad\qquad \downarrow \qquad\qquad \downarrow$

$(0, 0) \qquad (4, -2) \qquad (7, -1)$

$\qquad\qquad \downarrow \qquad\qquad \downarrow$

$\qquad\qquad (x_1, y_1) \qquad (x_2, y_2)$

Rule: 'add 2 to x, take 4 from y'

$x_1 = 4 \qquad x_2 = 7$

$y_1 = -2 \qquad y_2 = -1$

$\text{Area of } \triangle abc = \dfrac{1}{2} |x_1 y_2 - x_2 y_1|$

$= \dfrac{1}{2} |(4)(-1) - (7)(-2)|$

$= \dfrac{1}{2} |-4 + 14|$

$= \dfrac{1}{2} |10|$

$= 5$

(iv) Slope of ab

$a(-2, 4)$ and $b(2, 2)$

$x_1 = -2 \qquad x_2 = 2$

$y_1 = 4 \qquad y_2 = 2$

$m = \dfrac{y_2 - y_1}{x_2 - x_1}$

$= \dfrac{2 - 4}{2 + 2}$

$= \dfrac{-2}{4}$

$= -\dfrac{1}{2}$

(v) Equation of ab

containing $(-2, 4)$ with slope $= -\dfrac{1}{2}$

$x_1 = -2 \qquad y_1 = 4 \qquad m = -\dfrac{1}{2}$

$(y - y_1) = m(x - x_1)$

$(y - 4) = -\dfrac{1}{2}(x + 2)$

$\Rightarrow \qquad 2(y - 4) = -1(x + 2)$

$\Rightarrow \qquad 2y - 8 = -x - 2$

$\Rightarrow \quad x + 2y - 8 + 2 = 0$

$\Rightarrow \qquad x + 2y - 6 = 0$

(vi) Through $c(5, 3)$ and $L \perp ab$

Slope of $ab = -\frac{1}{2}$

$\therefore$ perpendicular slope $= \frac{2}{1} = 2$

(turn upside down and change sign)

containing $(5, 3)$ with slope $= 2$

$$x_1 = 5 \quad y_1 = 3 \quad m = 2$$
$$(y - y_1) = m(x - x_1)$$
$$(y - 3) = 2(x - 5)$$
$$\Rightarrow \qquad y - 3 = 2x - 10$$
$$\Rightarrow \quad -2x + y - 3 + 10 = 0$$
$$\Rightarrow \qquad -2x + y + 7 = 0$$
$$\Rightarrow \qquad 2x - y - 7 = 0$$

(vii) $L \cap ab$, use simultaneous equations

$x + 2y = 6$	(ab)
$2x - y = 7$	(L)
$x + 2y = 6$	(ab)
$4x - 2y = 14$	$(L \times 2)$
$5x = 20$	(add)
$x = 4$	

put $x = 4$ into L or (ab)

$x + 2y = 6 \quad (ab)$
$\downarrow$
$\Rightarrow \quad 4 + 2y = 6$
$\Rightarrow \qquad 2y = 6 - 4$
$\Rightarrow \qquad 2y = 2$
$\Rightarrow \qquad y = 1$

$$\therefore \quad L \cap ab = \{p\} = (4, 1)$$

(viii) A diagram is very useful.

c is on L, $L \perp ab$ and $L \cap ab = (4, 1) = \{p\}$.

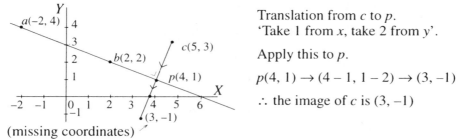

(missing coordinates)

Translation from c to p.
'Take 1 from x, take 2 from y'.

Apply this to p.

$p(4, 1) \rightarrow (4 - 1, 1 - 2) \rightarrow (3, -1)$

$\therefore$ the image of c is $(3, -1)$

Example

If $m(4, 5)$ is the midpoint of $[pq]$, and $p = (-2, 8)$, find the coordinates of q.

Solution:

Step 1. Rough diagram **(missing coordinates)**

$p(-2, 8) \qquad m(4, 5) \qquad q(\ ,\ )$

Step 2. Translation from p to m. Rule: 'add 6 to x, take 3 from y'.

Step 3. Apply this translation to m.

$m(4, 5) \rightarrow (4 + 6, 5 - 3) = (10, 2)$

$\therefore$ the coordinates of q are $(10, 2)$.

Example

$p(-2, -1)$, $q(2, -2)$, $r(a,b)$ and $s(2, -4)$ are the vertices of the parallelogram $pqrs$.

Find the coordinates of r.

Solution:

Make a rough diagram (keep cyclic order).

Since $pqrs$ is a parallelogram, $\overrightarrow{qr} = \overrightarrow{ps}$

(i.e. the movement from q to r is the same as the movement from p to s).

We find the rule that moves p to s.

Then apply this rule to q to find r.

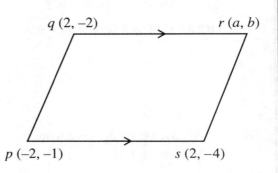

$\overrightarrow{ps} : (-2, -1) \rightarrow (2, -4)$

Rule: add 4 to x, take 3 from y

$\overrightarrow{qr} : (2, -2) \rightarrow (2 + 4, -2 - 3) = (6, -5)$.

Thus, the coordinates of r are $(6, -5)$

Note: By cyclic order we mean that the points are taken in either clockwise, or anti-clockwise, order.

Example

M is the line $3x + ky = 11$ which contains $(1, 2)$.

Find the value of k and the coordinates of the point where M cuts the Y axis.

Solution:

$(1, 2)$

$3x + ky = 11$

Substitute $x = 1$ and $y = 2$

$3(1) + k(2) = 11$

$\Rightarrow \qquad 3 + 2k = 11$

$\Rightarrow \qquad 2k = 11 - 3$

$\Rightarrow \qquad 2k = 8$

$\Rightarrow \qquad k = 4$

$M: 3x + 4y = 11$

On the Y axis, $x = 0$

Substitute $x = 0$

$3(0) + 4y = 11$

$\Rightarrow \qquad 4y = 11$

$\Rightarrow \qquad y = \frac{11}{4}$

Thus, the line cuts the Y axis at $(0, \frac{11}{4})$.

Example

$L: 2x - 3y - 15 = 0$ and $K: 5x - y - 5 = 0$ are two lines.

If $L \cap K = \{q\}$, find the coordinates of q.

Solution:

Point of intersection, $\therefore$ use simultaneous equations.

First write both lines in the form $ax + by = k$.

$$2x - 3y = 15 \qquad (L)$$
$$\underline{5x - y = 5} \qquad (K)$$
$$\overline{10x - 15y = 75} \qquad (L) \text{ x } 5$$
$$\underline{10x - 2y = 10} \qquad (K) \text{ x } 2$$
$$\overline{-13y = 65} \qquad \text{(subtract)}$$
$$13y = -65$$
$$y = -5$$

Put $y = -5$ into equation (L) or (K).

$$2x - 3y = 15 \qquad (L)$$
$$\downarrow$$
$$\Rightarrow 2x - 3(-5) = 15$$
$$\Rightarrow \quad 2x + 15 = 15$$
$$\Rightarrow \quad 2x = 15 - 15$$
$$\Rightarrow \quad 2x = 0$$
$$\Rightarrow \quad x = 0$$

Thus, the coordinates of q are $(0, -5)$

If the point of intersection contains fractions, a very useful method is to:

Step 1:	Remove the x's and get a value for y.
Step 2:	Remove the y's and get a value for x.

Note: This method can be used even if the point of intersection contains whole numbers only.

Example

$L: 6x + 3y - 11 = 0$ and $K: 5x + 2y - 8 = 0$ are two lines. $L \cap K = \{p\}$.
Find the coordinates of p.

Solution:

Remove the x's

$$6x + 3y = 11 \quad (L)$$
$$\underline{5x + 2y = \ 8} \quad (K)$$
$$\overline{30x + 15y = 55} \quad (L) \times 5$$
$$\underline{30x + 12y = 48} \quad (K) \times 6$$
$$\overline{3y = 7} \qquad \text{subtract}$$
$$\Rightarrow \quad y = \frac{7}{3}$$

Remove the y's

$$6x + 3y = 11 \quad (L)$$
$$\underline{5x + 2y = \ 8} \quad (K)$$
$$\overline{12x + 6y = 22} \quad (L) \times 2$$
$$\underline{15x + 6y = 24} \quad (K) \times 3$$
$$\overline{-3x = -2} \qquad \text{subtract}$$
$$\Rightarrow \quad 3x = 2$$
$$x = \frac{2}{3}$$

$\therefore$ the coordinates of p are $(\frac{2}{3}, \frac{7}{3})$

Example

L: $5x + 2y - 10 = 0$ and K: $2x - 5y + 20 = 0$ are two lines. Prove $L \perp K$.

Solution:

Find slope of L

$$5x + 2y - 10 = 0$$
$$2y = -5x + 10$$
$$y = -\frac{5}{2}x + 5$$
$$\therefore \quad \text{slope of } L = -\frac{5}{2}$$

Find slope of K

$$2x - 5y + 20 = 0$$
$$-5y = -2x - 20$$
$$5y = 2x + 20$$
$$y = \frac{2}{5}x + 4$$
$$\therefore \quad \text{slope of } K = \frac{2}{5}$$

$$(\text{slope of } L) \times (\text{slope of } K) = -\frac{5}{2} \times \frac{2}{5} = -1$$
$$\therefore \ L \perp K$$

Note: To get the slopes we could have used $m = -\frac{a}{b}$ in each case (as in the next example).

Example

The line $4x + ty = 12$ is perpendicular to the line $8x - y = 8$.

Find the value of t.

Solution:

$$4x + ty = 12$$
$$\text{Slope} = m_1 = -\frac{a}{b} = -\frac{4}{t}$$

$$8x - y = 8$$
$$\text{Slope} = m_2 = -\frac{a}{b} = -\frac{8}{-1} = \frac{8}{1}$$

lines are perpendicular

$$\therefore \ m_1 \cdot m_2 = -1$$

$$\Rightarrow \qquad -\frac{4}{t} \times \frac{8}{1} = -1$$

$$\Rightarrow \qquad -\frac{32}{t} = -1$$

$$\Rightarrow \qquad -32 = -t \quad \text{(multiply both sides by } t\text{)}$$

$$\Rightarrow \qquad 32 = t$$

Example

Find the equation of the following lines:

(i) containing the point $(-1, 4)$ with slope 2.

(ii) containing the point $(-3, -1)$ with slope $-\frac{3}{4}$.

Solution:

(i) containing $(-1, 4)$ with slope 2

$$x_1 = -1, \qquad y_1 = 4, \qquad m = 2$$

$$(y - y_1) = m(x - x_1)$$

$$\Rightarrow \qquad (y - 4) = 2(x + 1)$$

$$\Rightarrow \qquad y - 4 = 2x + 2$$

$$\Rightarrow -2x + y - 4 - 2 = 0$$

$$\Rightarrow \qquad -2x + y - 6 = 0$$

$$\Rightarrow \qquad 2x - y + 6 = 0$$

(ii) containing the point $(-3, -1)$ with slope $-\frac{3}{4}$

$$x_1 = -3, \qquad y_1 = -1, \qquad m = -\frac{3}{4}$$

$$(y - y_1) = m(x - x_1)$$

$$\Rightarrow \qquad (y + 1) = -\frac{3}{4}(x + 3)$$

$$\Rightarrow \qquad 4(y + 1) = -3(x + 3)$$

(multiply both sides by 4)

$$\Rightarrow \qquad 4y + 4 = -3x - 9$$

$$\Rightarrow 3x + 4y + 4 + 9 = 0$$

$$\Rightarrow \qquad 3x + 4y + 13 = 0$$

Example

$a(-6, -1)$ and $b(-1, 2)$ are two points. Find the equation of the line ab.

Solution:

The slope is missing. We first find the slope and use **either** point to find the equation.

$$(-6, -1) \qquad (-1, 2)$$
$$(x_1, y_1) \qquad (x_2, y_2)$$

$$m = \frac{y_2 - y_1}{x_2 - x_1}$$

$$m = \frac{2 + 1}{-1 + 6}$$

$$= \frac{3}{5}$$

$\therefore$ slope of line ab is $\frac{3}{5}$

containing $(-6, -1)$ with slope $\frac{3}{5}$

$$x_1 = -6, \qquad y_1 = -1, \qquad m = -\frac{3}{5}$$

$$(y - y_1) = m(x - x_1)$$

$$(y + 1) = \frac{3}{5}(x + 6)$$

$$5(y + 1) = 3(x + 6)$$

(multiply both sides by 5)

$$5y + 5 = 3x + 18$$

$$-3x + 5y + 5 - 18 = 0$$

$$-3x + 5y - 13 = 0$$

$$3x - 5y + 13 = 0$$

Example

The equation of the line L is $2x - y + 1 = 0$. The line K contains the point $(1, 3)$.

If $K \perp L$, find the equation of K.

Solution:

We have a point $(1, 3)$. The slope is missing.

Step 1: Find the slope of L

$$2x - y + 1 = 0$$

$$\Rightarrow \qquad -y = -2x - 1$$

$$\Rightarrow \qquad y = 2x + 1$$

$\therefore$ slope of $L = 2$

Step 2: Find the slope of K

Slope of $L = 2 = \dfrac{2}{1}$

$$L \perp K$$

$\therefore$ slope of $K = -\dfrac{1}{2}$

(turn upside down and change sign)

Step 3: containing $(1, 3)$ with slope $-\dfrac{1}{2}$

$$x_1 = 1, \qquad y_1 = 3, \qquad m = -\dfrac{1}{2}$$

$$(y - y_1) = m(x - x_1)$$

$$\Rightarrow \qquad (y - 3) = -\dfrac{1}{2}(x - 1)$$

$$\Rightarrow \qquad 2(y - 3) = -1(x - 1)$$

(multiply both sides by 2)

$$\Rightarrow \qquad 2y - 6 = -x + 1$$

$$\Rightarrow \qquad x + 2y - 6 - 1 = 0$$

$$\Rightarrow \qquad x + 2y - 7 = 0$$

Thus, the equation of the line K is $x + 2y - 7 = 0$

Example

The equation of the line L is $x - 2y - 4 = 0$. L intersects the X axis at p and the Y axis at q.

Find the coordinates of p and the coordinates of q. Show L on a diagram.

Solution:

We make use of the fact:

> On the X axis, $y = 0$
>
> On the Y axis, $x = 0$

$x - 2y = 4$	
$y = 0$	$x = 0$
$x = 4$	$-2y = 4$
$p(4,0)$	$2y = -4$
	$y = -2$
	$q(0, -2)$

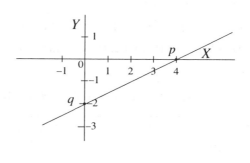

Plot the points $p(4,0)$ and $q(0, -2)$.

Draw the line through these points.

Example

Find the image of the line $2x + 5y - 8 = 0$ by **(i)** S_X **(ii)** S_Y and **(iii)** S_o.

(i) S_X, axial symmetry in the X axis, simply 'change the sign of y'.

∴ $S_X(2x + 5y - 8 = 0)$ is: $2x - 5y - 8 = 0$

(ii) S_Y, axial symmetry in the Y axis, simply 'change the sign of x'.

∴ $S_Y(2x + 5y - 8 = 0)$ is: $-2x + 5y - 8 = 0$ or $2x - 5y + 8 = 0$

(iii) S_o, central symmetry in the origin, simply 'change the sign of both x and y'.

∴ $S_o (2x + 5y - 8 = 0)$ is: $-2x - 5y - 8 = 0$ or $2x + 5y + 8 = 0$.

As can be seen in **(iii)**, the result is simply to change the sign of the constant.

Example

L is the line $y = 1$, M is the line $x = 2$.

Find the image of $p(3,2)$ under S_L o S_M

i.e. axial symmetry in L after M.

Name the single transformation which is equivalent to S_L o S_M.

Solution:

Draw a diagram of the situation.

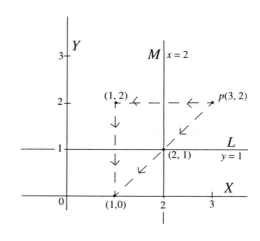

$S_M (3, 2) = (1, 2)$ $S_L (1, 2) = (1, 0)$

∴ the image of (3, 2) under $S_L \circ S_M = (1, 0)$

$S_L \circ S_M$ is equal to a central symmetry in the point of intersection of L and M.

$$L \cap M = (2, 1)$$

∴ $S_L \circ S_M = S_{(2, 1)}$, i.e. a central symmetry in the point (2, 1).

Example

Verify that the point (3, −4) is on the line $7x - 2y - 29 = 0$. Find the image of the line under the central symmetry in the point (1, 1).

Solution:

$7x - 2y - 29 = 0$

    ↓   ↘

$7(3) - 2(-4) - 29$ (put in $x = 3$ and $y = -4$)

$= 21 + 8 - 29$

$= 29 - 29 = 0$

∴   (3, −4) is on the line $7x - 2y - 29 = 0$

Translation : $(3, -4) \rightarrow (1,1)$ **Rule:** Take 2 from x, add 5 to y

The image of (1, 1) under this translation will be a point on the image line.

$(1, 1) \rightarrow (1 - 2, 1 + 5) = (-1, 6)$

Thus, the point (−1, 6) will be on the image line.

Slope of the image line will have the same slope as the line $7x - 2y - 29 = 0$

$7x - 2y - 29 = 0$	or	$m = -\dfrac{a}{b}$
$-2y = -7x + 29$		
$2y = 7x - 29$		$= -\dfrac{7}{-2}$
$y = \dfrac{7}{2}x - \dfrac{29}{2}$		$= \dfrac{7}{2}$

∴ Slope $= \dfrac{7}{2} \Rightarrow$ slope of image line $= \dfrac{7}{2}$

Equation of image line: containing (−1, 6) with slope $= \dfrac{7}{2}$

$x_1 = -1,$ $y_1 = 6,$ $m = \dfrac{7}{2}$

$$(y - y_1) = m(x - x_1)$$

$$(y - 6) = \frac{7}{2}(x + 1)$$

$$2(y - 6) = 7(x + 1) \qquad \text{[multiply both sides by 2]}$$

$$2y - 12 = 7x + 7$$

$$-7x + 2y - 12 - 7 = 0$$

$$-7x + 2y - 19 = 0$$

$$7x - 2y + 19 = 0$$

$\therefore$ the image line is $7x - 2y + 19 = 0$

Example

The slope of the line through the points $(2,1)$ and $(6, k)$ is $\frac{7}{2}$. Find the value of k.

Solution:

$(2, 1)$ and $(6, k)$

$(x_1, y_1) \quad (x_2, y_2)$

$$m = \frac{y_2 - y_1}{x_2 - x_1}$$

$$= \frac{k - 1}{6 - 2}$$

$$= \frac{k - 1}{4}$$

$\therefore$ Slope $= \dfrac{k - 1}{4}$

Given: Slope $= \dfrac{7}{2}$

$$\therefore \quad \frac{k - 1}{4} = \frac{7}{2}$$

$$2k - 2 = 28$$

(cross multiply)

$$2k = 28 + 2$$

$$2k = 30$$

$$k = 15$$

Thus, the value of k is 15.

Example

$a(2, k)$, $b(3, -1)$ and $c(-1, -3)$ are the vertices of $\Delta\ abc$.

If the area of $\Delta\ abc = 13$, find the two possible values of k.

Solution:

Map (move) the point $(-1, -3)$ to $(0, 0)$ [always map a known point]

$(2,\ k) \qquad (3, -1) \qquad (-1, -3)$
  $\downarrow$ $\qquad\qquad \downarrow$ $\qquad\qquad\quad \downarrow$
$(3, k + 3) \quad (4, 2) \qquad\ (0, 0)$
  $\downarrow$ $\qquad\qquad \downarrow$
$(x_1, y_1) \qquad (x_2, y_2)$

Rule: add 1 to x, add 3 to y

$x_1 = 3 \qquad\qquad y_1 = k + 3$

$x_2 = 4 \qquad\qquad y_2 = 2$

Given: area of $\Delta\,abc = 13$

$\therefore$ $\frac{1}{2}|x_1y_2 - x_2y_1| = 13$

$\Rightarrow$ $\frac{1}{2}|(3)(2) - 4(k+3)| = 13$ (put in values for x_1, y_1, x_2, y_2)

$\Rightarrow$ $|(3)(2) - 4(k + 3)| = 26$ (multiply both sides by 2)

$\Rightarrow$ $|6 - 4k - 12| = 26$ (remove brackets inside)

$|-4k - 6| = 26$

$(-4k - 6) = \pm\,26$ (must include positive and negative solutions)

$-4k - 6 = 26$	or	$-4k - 6 = -26$
$-4k = 26 + 6$		$-4k = -26 + 6$
$-4k = 32$		$-4k = -20$
$4k = -32$		$4k = 20$
$k = -8$		$k = 5$

$\therefore$ $k = -8$ or $k = 5$

Example

$c(1, 6)$ and $d(-3, -1)$ are two points. The point r has coordinates $(2, y)$ such that
$$|cd| = |cr|.$$

Find the two possible values of y.

Solution:

$|cd|$	$|cr|$
$c(1,6)$ and $d(-3, -1)$	$c(1, 6)$ and $r(2, y)$
$(x_1, y_1)\qquad(x_2, y_2)$	$(x_1, y_1)\qquad(x_2, y_2)$
$x_1 = 1,\ y_1 = 6\qquad x_2 = -3,\ y_2 = -1$	$x_1 = 1,\ y_1 = 6\qquad x_2 = 2,\ y_2 = y$
$|cd| = \sqrt{(x_2 - x_1)^2 + (y_2 - y_1)^2}$	$|cr| = \sqrt{(x_2 - x_1)^2 + (y_2 - y_1)^2}$
$= \sqrt{(-3 - 1)^2 + (-1 - 6)^2}$	$= \sqrt{(2 - 1)^2 + (y - 6)^2}$
$= \sqrt{(-4)^2 + (-7)^2}$	$= \sqrt{(1)^2 + (y - 6)^2}$
$= \sqrt{16 + 49}$	$= \sqrt{1 + y^2 - 12y + 36}$
$= \sqrt{65}$	$= \sqrt{y^2 - 12y + 37}$

$$\text{Given: } |cd| = |cr|$$
$$\Rightarrow \qquad \sqrt{65} = \sqrt{y^2 - 12y + 37}$$
$$\Rightarrow \qquad \sqrt{y^2 - 12y + 37} = \sqrt{65} \qquad \text{(swap sides)}$$
$$\Rightarrow \qquad y^2 - 12y + 37 = 65 \qquad \text{(square both sides)}$$
$$\Rightarrow \qquad y^2 - 12y - 28 = 0$$
$$\Rightarrow \qquad (y - 14)(y + 2) = 0$$
$$\Rightarrow \qquad y - 14 = 0 \quad \text{or} \quad y + 2 = 0$$
$$\Rightarrow \qquad y = 14 \quad \text{or} \qquad y = -2$$
$$\therefore \qquad y = 14 \quad \text{or} \qquad y = -2$$

8. THE CIRCLE

Equation of a Circle

Note: Two quantities are needed to find the equation of a circle:

1. Centre   2. Radius

The equation of a circle, centre $(0, 0)$ and radius r, is

$$x^2 + y^2 = r^2$$

The equation of a circle, centre (h, k) and radius r, is

$$(x - h)^2 + (y - k)^2 = r^2$$

Note: When drawing a circle always make sure the scales are the same on both the X and Y axes.

Points Inside, On or Outside a Circle

If the coordinates of a point satisfy the equation of a circle then that point is **on** the circle. Otherwise, the point is either **inside** or **outside** the circle.

The following method is used to decide whether a point is inside, on or outside a circle:

1. Substitute the coordinates of the given point into the equation of the circle.
2. One of the following three situations will arise:
   - (i)   LHS < RHS,   the point is **inside** the circle
   - (ii)   LHS = RHS,   the point is **on** the circle
   - (iii) LHS > RHS,   the point is **outside** the circle

Note: Finding the distance between the centre of a circle and the given point and comparing this distance to the radius can also be used to determine if a point is inside, on or outside a circle.

Equation of a Tangent to a Circle at a Given Point

A tangent is perpendicular to the radius that joins the
centre of a circle to the point of tangency. This fact
is used to find the slope of the tangent. In the
diagram on the right, the radius, R, is perpendicular
to the tangent, T, at the point of tangency, p.

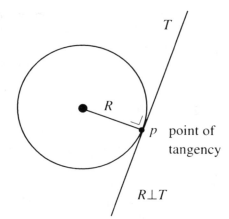

The equation of a tangent to a circle at a given point is found with the following steps:

Step 1: Find the slope of the radius to the point of tangency.

Step 2: Turn this slope upside down and change its sign.

This gives the slope of the tangent.

Step 3: Use the coordinates of the point of contact and the slope of the
tangent at this point in the formula:

$$(y - y_1) = m(x - x_1)$$

This gives the equation of the tangent.

Circle Intersecting the Axes

To find where a circle intersects the axes we use the following:

The circle intersects the X axis at $y = 0$

The circle intersects the Y axis at $x = 0$

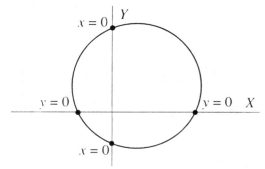

Intersection of a Line and a Circle

To find the points where a line and a circle meet, the 'method of substitution' between their equations is used. The method involves the following three steps:

> 1. Get x or y on its own from the line.
>
>   (Look carefully and select the variable which will make the working easier.)
>
> 2. Substitute for this same variable into the equation of the circle and solve the resultant quadratic equation.
>
> 3. Substitute **separately** the value(s) obtained in Step 2 into the linear equation in Step 1 to find the corresponding value(s) of the other variable.

Note: If there is only one **point of intersection** between a line and a circle, then the line is a **tangent** to the circle.

Transformations on Circles

Under a central symmetry, axial symmetry, translation or rotation a circle will keep the **same** radius. Hence, all that is needed is to find the image of the centre under the particular transformation. The equation of a circle under a transformation is found with the following steps:

> 1. Find the **centre** and **radius** of the given circle.
>
> 2. Find the image of the centre under the given transformation.
>
> 3. Use this new centre and the radius of the original circle in the equation:
>
> $$(x - h)^2 + (y - k)^2 = r^2$$
>
> to find the equation of the circle.

Equation of a Circle in the Form: $x^2 + y^2 + 2hx + 2ky + c = 0$

When the equation of a circle is given in this form we use the following method to find its centre and radius:

1. Make sure every term is on the left hand side and the coefficients of x^2 and y^2 are equal to 1.

2. Centre $= (-h, -k) = (-\frac{1}{2}$ coefficient of x, $-\frac{1}{2}$ coefficient of $y)$

3. Radius $= \sqrt{h^2 + k^2 - c}$

Note: c is the constant in the equation when every term is on the left hand side and the coefficients of x^2 and y^2 are 1.

Example

C is a circle centre $(0, 0)$ and passing through the point $(3, 1)$.

Find the radius length and the equation of C.

Solution:

Centre $(0, 0)$, therefore C is of the form $x^2 + y^2 = r^2$.

The radius of C needs to be found.

The radius is the distance from $(0, 0)$ to $(3, 1)$.

Using the distance formula,

$$\begin{aligned} r &= \sqrt{(3-0)^2 + (1-0)^2} \\ &= \sqrt{3^2 + (1)^2} \\ &= \sqrt{9+1} = \sqrt{10} \\ x^2 + y^2 &= (\sqrt{10})^2 \\ \Rightarrow \quad x^2 + y^2 &= 10 \end{aligned}$$

$\therefore$ C is the circle $x^2 + y^2 = 10$

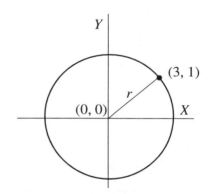

Example

K_1: $x^2 + y^2 = 25$ and K_2: $x^2 + y^2 = 13$ are the equations of two circles. Find the radius of each.

Solution:

$$K_1: x^2 + y^2 = 25$$
$$\text{Compare to: } x^2 + y^2 = r^2$$
$$\Rightarrow \qquad r^2 = 25$$
$$\Rightarrow \qquad r = 5$$
$\therefore$ radius of K_1 is 5

$$K_2: x^2 + y^2 = 13$$
$$\text{Compare to: } x^2 + y^2 = r^2$$
$$\Rightarrow \qquad r^2 = 13$$
$$\Rightarrow \qquad r = \sqrt{13}$$
$\therefore$ radius of K_2 is $\sqrt{13}$

Example

A circle K has equation $25x^2 + 25y^2 = 49$.

Write down its radius length.

Find where K intersects the X and Y axes and draw the graph of K.

Solution:

$$25x^2 + 25y^2 = 49$$

$$x^2 + y^2 = \frac{49}{25} \quad \text{(divide across by 25)}$$

Compare to: $x^2 + y^2 = r^2$

$\Rightarrow \qquad\qquad r^2 = \frac{49}{25}$

$\Rightarrow \qquad\qquad r = \frac{7}{5}$

$\therefore$ radius of K is $\frac{7}{5}$

Diagram

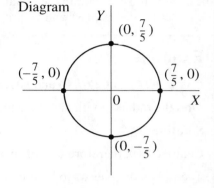

$25x^2 + 25y^2 = 49$

On the X axis, $y = 0$	On the Y axis, $x = 0$
$\Rightarrow \quad 25x^2 = 49$	$\Rightarrow \quad 25y^2 = 49$
$\Rightarrow \quad x^2 = \frac{49}{25}$	$\Rightarrow \quad y^2 = \frac{49}{25}$
$\Rightarrow \quad x = \pm\frac{7}{5}$	$\Rightarrow \quad y = \pm\frac{7}{5}$

Thus, the circle cuts the X axis at $(\frac{7}{5}, 0)$ and $(-\frac{7}{5}, 0)$

Thus, the circle cuts the Y axis at $(0, \frac{7}{5})$ and $(0, -\frac{7}{5})$

Example

(i) Find the equation of the circle, C, with centre $(3, -2)$ and radius $\sqrt{5}$.

(ii) Find the centre and radius length of the circle, C_2: $(x - 4)^2 + (y + 5)^2 = 9$.

Solution:

(i) Centre $(3, -2)$, radius $\sqrt{5}$

$\Rightarrow h = 3, \quad k = -2, \quad r = \sqrt{5}$

$\qquad (x - h)^2 + (y - k)^2 = r^2$

$\Rightarrow \qquad (x - 3)^2 + (y + 2)^2 = (\sqrt{5})^2$

$\Rightarrow \quad C_1: (x - 3)^2 + (y + 2)^2 = 5$

(ii) $\qquad\qquad (x - 4)^2 + (y + 5)^2 = 9$

Compare to: $(x - h)^2 + (y - k)^2 = 9$

$\Rightarrow -h = -4 \qquad -k = 5 \qquad r^2 = 9$

$\Rightarrow \quad h = 4 \qquad\quad k = -5 \qquad r = 3$

Thus, the centre of C_2 is $(4, -5)$

and the radius length $= 3$

Example

$a(3, 5)$ and $b(-1, -1)$ are the end points of a diameter of a circle K.

(i) Find the centre and radius length of K.

(ii) Find the equation of K.

(iii) K intersects the X axis at p and q, $p < q$. Find the coordinates of p and q.

Solution:

(i) Centre

The centre is the midpoint of $[ab]$

$(3, 5)$ $\qquad\qquad$ $(-1, -1)$

(x_1, y_1) $\qquad\qquad$ (x_2, y_2)

$\text{Centre} = \left(\dfrac{x_1 + x_2}{2}, \dfrac{y_1 + y_2}{2} \right) = \left(\dfrac{3-1}{2}, \dfrac{5-1}{2} \right) = \left(\dfrac{2}{2}, \dfrac{4}{2} \right) = (1, 2)$

Radius

The radius is the distance from the centre $(1, 2)$ to either $(3, 5)$ or $(-1, -1)$.

Distance from $(1, 2)$ to $(3, 5)$.

$\qquad\qquad (x_1, y_1)\ \ (x_2, y_2)$

Radius =

$\sqrt{(x_2 - x_1)^2 + (y_2 - y_1)^2} = \sqrt{(3-1)^2 + (5-2)^2} = \sqrt{2^2 + 3^2} = \sqrt{4+9} = \sqrt{13}$

(ii) Centre $(1, 2)$, radius $\sqrt{13}$

$\qquad h = 1, k = 2$ and $r = \sqrt{13}$

$\qquad (x - h)^2 + (y - k)^2 = r^2$

$\Rightarrow (x - 1)^2 + (y - 2)^2 = (\sqrt{13})^2$

$\Rightarrow K: (x - 1)^2 + (y - 2)^2 = 13$

(iii) On the X axis $y = 0$

$\therefore \quad (x - 1)^2 + (0 - 2)^2 = 13$ $\quad$ (put in $y = 0$)

$\Rightarrow \qquad x^2 - 2x + 1 + 4 = 13$

$\Rightarrow \qquad x^2 - 2x - 8 = 0$

$\Rightarrow \qquad (x + 2)(x - 4) = 0$

$\Rightarrow \qquad x + 2 = 0$ or $x - 4 = 0$

$\Rightarrow \qquad x = -2$ or $x = 4$

$\therefore$ K intersects the X axis at -2 and 4.

Diagram of the situation

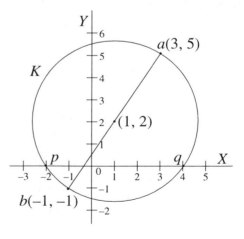

Thus, circle K has centre $(1, 2)$ and radius $\sqrt{13}$.

The equation of K is $(x - 1)^2 + (y - 2)^2 = 13$.

The coordinates where K intersects the X axis are $p\ (-2, 0)$ and $q\ (4, 0)$.

143

Example

$K_1: x^2 + y^2 - 6x + 8y - 11 = 0$ and $K_2: x^2 + y^2 - 10y + 9 = 0$ are the equations of two circles. Find the centre and radius of each circle. Do the circles intersect?

Solution:

The centres can be written down from inspection,

i.e. centre $= (-\frac{1}{2}$ number in front of x, $-\frac{1}{2}$ number in front of y)

$K_1: x^2 + y^2 - 6x + 8y - 11 = 0$	$K_2: \quad x^2 + y^2 - 10y + 9 = 0$
centre $= (3, -4) = (h, k)$	$\Rightarrow x^2 + y^2 + 0x - 10y + 9 = 0$
$h = 3, \qquad k = -4, \qquad c = -11$	centre $= (0, 5) = (h, k)$
Radius $= \sqrt{h^2 + k^2 - c}$	$h = 0, \qquad k = 5, \qquad c = 9$
$\quad = \sqrt{(3)^2 + (-4)^2 + 11}$	Radius $= \sqrt{h^2 + k^2 - c}$
$\quad = \sqrt{9 + 16 + 11}$	$\quad = \sqrt{(0)^2 + (5)^2 - 9}$
$\quad = \sqrt{36}$	$\quad = \sqrt{0 + 25 - 9}$
$\quad = 6$	$\quad = \sqrt{16}$
Thus, K_1 has centre $(3, -4)$ and radius 6	$\quad = 4$
	Thus, K_2 has centre $(0, 5)$ and radius 4

If two circles intersect the following fact holds:

$$\text{(distance between centres)} \leq \text{(sum of their radii)}$$

Their centres are $(3, -4)$ and $(0, 5)$.

$$(x_1, y_1) \qquad (x_2, y_2)$$

Distance between centres $= \sqrt{(x_2 - x_1)^2 + (y_2 - y_1)^2}$

$$= \sqrt{(0 - 3)^2 + (5 + 4)^2}$$

$$= \sqrt{(-3)^2 + (9)^2}$$

$$= \sqrt{9 + 81}$$

$$= \sqrt{90} \simeq 9.49$$

Sum of radii $= 6 + 4 = 10$

$$9.49 < 10$$

i.e. $\qquad$ (distance between centres) $<$ (sum of radii)

$\therefore$ the two circles intersect.

Example

Find the equation of the circle, C, with centre $(3, 2)$ which touches the X axis at one point only.

T is a tangent to C and T is parallel to the Y axis.

Find the two possible equations for T.

Solution:

Draw a diagram:

The centre $= (3, 2) = (h, k)$

C touches the X axis at $(3, 0)$

Radius $=$ distance from $(3, 2)$ to $(3, 0) = 2$

$h = 3, \quad k = 2, \quad r = 2$

$\quad (x - h)^2 + (y - k)^2 = r^2$

$\quad (x - 3)^2 + (y - 2)^2 = 2^2$

$C: (x - 3)^2 + (y - 2)^2 = 4$

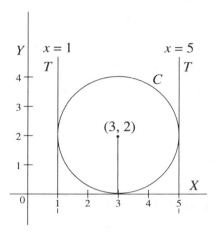

From the diagram the two tangents to C which are parallel to the Y axis are:

$$x = 1 \text{ and } x = 5$$

Example

The equation of the circle, C, is $(x - 3)^2 + (y + 2)^2 = 25$.

Determine if the points $(7, -3)$, $(-1, -5)$ and $(9, 2)$ are inside, on, or outside C.

Solution:

$C: (x - 3)^2 + (y + 2)^2 = 25$

$(7, -3)$	$(-1, -5)$	$(9, 2)$
put in $x = 7, y = -3$	put in $x = -1, y = -5$	put in $x = 9, y = 2$
$(7 - 3)^2 + (-3 + 2)^2$	$(-1 - 3)^2 + (-5 + 2)^2$	$(9 - 3)^2 + (2 + 2)^2$
$= (4)^2 + (-1)^2$	$= (-4)^2 + (-3)^2$	$= (6)^2 + (4)^2$
$= 16 + 1$	$= 16 + 9$	$= 36 + 16$
$= 17$	$= 25$	$= 52$
< 25	$= 25$	> 25
$\therefore \ (7, -3)$ is inside C	$\therefore \ (-1, -5)$ is on C	$\therefore \ (9, 2)$ is outside C

Example

The point $(5, k)$ is on the circle $(x - 2)^2 + (y - 3)^2 = 25$.

Find the two values of k.

Solution:

$$(x - 2)^2 + (y - 3)^2 = 25$$

$\therefore \quad (5 - 2)^2 + (k - 3)^2 = 25 \quad$ (put in $x = 5$ and $y = k$)

$\Rightarrow \quad (3)^2 + k^2 - 6k + 9 = 25$

$\Rightarrow 9 + k^2 - 6k + 9 - 25 = 0$

$\Rightarrow \qquad k^2 - 6k - 7 = 0$

$\Rightarrow \qquad (k - 7)(k + 1) = 0$

$\Rightarrow \qquad k - 7 = 0 \quad$ or $\quad k + 1 = 0$

$\Rightarrow \qquad k = 7 \quad$ or $\quad k = -1$

Thus, the two values of k are 7 or -1.

Example

The equation of the circle, C, is $(x + 1)^2 + (y - 1)^2 = 13$.

Find the centre and radius of C.

Show that the point $(2, -1)$ is on C and represent C on a diagram.

T is a tangent to C at $(2, -1)$. Find the equation of T.

K is a second tangent to C and $K \parallel T$. Find the equation of K and the distance between T and K.

Solution:

$$(x + 1)^2 + (y - 1)^2 = 13$$

Compare to: $(x - h)^2 + (y - k)^2 = r^2$

$\Rightarrow \quad -h = 1, \quad -k = -1, \quad r^2 = 13$

$\Rightarrow \quad\quad h = -1, \quad k = 1, \quad\quad r = \sqrt{13}$

Thus, the centre of C is $(-1, 1)$ and the radius is $\sqrt{13}$.

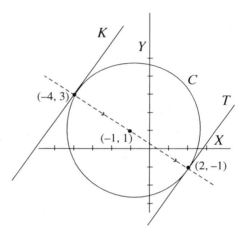

$C: (x + 1)^2 + (y - 1)^2 = 13$

Is $(2, -1)$ on the circle? Put in $x = 2$ and $y = -1$.

$(2 + 1)^2 + (-1 - 1)^2$

$= (3)^2 + (-2)^2$

$= 9 + 4$

$= 13$

$\therefore$ $(2, -1)$ is on the circle C.

Equation of T

Step 1: We find the slope of the radius from the centre $(-1, 1)$ to the point $(2, -1)$.

$$(-1, 1) \quad (2, -1)$$

$$(x_1, y_1) \quad (x_2, y_2)$$

Slope of radius $= m = \dfrac{y_2 - y_1}{x_2 - x_1} = \dfrac{-1 - 1}{2 + 1} = \dfrac{-2}{3} = -\dfrac{2}{3}$

Step 2: $\therefore$ Slope of $T = \dfrac{3}{2}$ $\quad\quad\quad\quad$ (turn upside down and change sign)

Step 3: Point $(2, -1)$ and slope $\frac{3}{2}$

$$x_1 = 2, \quad y_1 = -1, \quad m = \frac{3}{2}$$

$$(y - y_1) = m(x - x_1)$$

$\Rightarrow \qquad (y + 1) = \frac{3}{2}(x - 2)$

$\Rightarrow \qquad 2(y + 1) = 3(x - 2)$ \qquad (multiply both sides by 2)

$\Rightarrow \qquad 2y + 2 = 3x - 6$

$\Rightarrow -3x + 2y + 2 + 6 = 0$

$\Rightarrow \qquad -3x + 2y + 8 = 0$

$\Rightarrow \qquad 3x - 2y - 8 = 0$

Thus, the equation of T is $3x - 2y - 8 = 0$

$K \parallel T, \quad \therefore$ Slope of K is also $\frac{3}{2}$.

The image of $(2, -1)$ under a central symmetry in the centre $(-1, 1)$ will be a point on the tangent K.

$$(2, -1) \rightarrow (-1, 1) \rightarrow (-4, 3)$$

$\therefore$ the image of $(2, -1)$ under central symmetry in $(-1, 1)$ is $(-4, 3)$.

Thus, the point $(-4, 3)$ is on K and K has slope $\frac{3}{2}$.

Point $(-4, 3)$ and slope $= \frac{3}{2}$	Distance between T and K
$x_1 = -4, \qquad y_1 = 3, \qquad m = \frac{3}{2}$	distance between T and K
$(y - y_1) = m(x - x_1)$	= length of diameter
$(y - 3) = \frac{3}{2}(x + 4)$	= 2 (length of radius)
$2(y - 3) = 3(x + 4)$	$= 2(\sqrt{13})$
$2y - 6 = 3x + 12$	$= 2\sqrt{13}$
$-3x + 2y - 6 - 12 = 0$	Thus, the distance between T and K is $2\sqrt{13}$
$-3x + 2y - 18 = 0$	
$3x - 2y + 18 = 0$	[we could also find the distance between the points $(2, -1)$ and $(-4, 3)$]
$\therefore$ equation of K is $3x - 2y + 18 = 0$	

Example

$L: x - 3y + 10 = 0$ is a line and $C: x^2 + y^2 = 10$ is a circle.

Calculate the coordinates of any points in $L \cap C$ and state whether or not L is a tangent to C.

Solution:

$L: x - 3y + 10 = 0$ and $C: x^2 + y^2 = 10$

Step 1: $x - 3y + 10 = 0$

$x = (3y - 10)$ [x on its own from the line]

Step 2: $x^2 + y^2 = 10$

$\Rightarrow$ $(3y - 10)^2 + y^2 = 10$ [put in $(3y - 10)$ for x]

$\Rightarrow 9y^2 - 60y + 100 + y^2 = 10$

$\Rightarrow$ $10y^2 - 60y + 90 = 0$

$\Rightarrow$ $y^2 - 6y + 9 = 0$

$\Rightarrow$ $(y - 3)(y - 3) = 0$

$\Rightarrow$ $y - 3 = 0$ or $y - 3 = 0$

$\Rightarrow$ $y = 3$

Step 3:   Put in $y = 3$ into the equation of the line in Step 1 to find x.

$y = 3$

$x = 3y - 10$

$x = 3(3) - 10$

$x = 9 - 10$

$x = -1$

point $(-1, 3)$

$\therefore L \cap C = (-1, 3)$

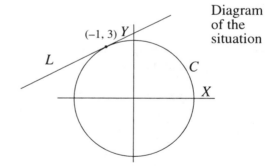

Diagram of the situation

Since there is only one point of contact, the line, L, is a tangent to the circle, C.

Example

The point $(2, \sqrt{21})$ is on a circle K, centre $(0, 0)$. Find the equation K.

The line $L: 2x - y + 5 = 0$ meets K at p and q. Calculate the coordinates of p and q.

Solution:

K is a circle with centre $(0, 0)$.

$\therefore$ K has equation $x^2 + y^2 = r^2$

$(2, \sqrt{21})$ is on K, so put in $x = 2$ and $y = \sqrt{21}$.

$$x^2 + y^2 = r^2$$
$$\Rightarrow (2)^2 + (\sqrt{21})^2 = r^2$$
$$\Rightarrow 4 + 21 = r^2$$
$$\Rightarrow 25 = r^2$$

$\therefore$ The equation of K is $x^2 + y^2 = 25$

Intersection of the line L: $2x - y + 5 = 0$ and the circle K: $x^2 + y^2 = 25$

Step 1: $\qquad 2x - y + 5 = 0$

$$-y = -2x - 5$$
$$y = (2x + 5) \qquad (y \text{ on its own from the line})$$

Step 2: $\qquad x^2 + y^2 = 25$

$$\Rightarrow x^2 + (2x + 5)^2 = 25 \qquad (\text{put in } (2x + 5) \text{ for } y)$$
$$\Rightarrow x^2 + 4x^2 + 20x + 25 = 25$$
$$\Rightarrow 5x^2 + 20x = 0$$
$$\Rightarrow x^2 + 4x = 0$$
$$\Rightarrow x(x + 4) = 0$$
$$\Rightarrow x = 0 \text{ or } x + 4 = 0$$
$$\Rightarrow x = 0 \text{ or } x = -4$$

Step 3: Put in separately $x = 0$ and $x = -4$ into the equation of the line in Step 1 to find the y coordinates.

$y = 2x + 5$	$y = 2x + 5$
$x = 0$	$x = -4$
$y = 2(0) + 5$	$y = 2(-4) + 5$
$y = 0 + 5$	$y = -8 + 5$
$y = 5$	$y = -3$
point p $(0, 5)$	point q $(-4, -3)$

Thus, $L \cap K$ at two points p $(0, 5)$ and q $(-4, -3)$.

It is straight forward to write down the equation of the image of a circle under S_X, axial symmetry in the X axis; S_Y, axial symmetry in the Y axis and S_o, central symmetry in the origin, $(0, 0)$. We concentrate on the coordinates of the centre of the circle and proceed as in coordinate geometry of the line.

Example

$(x - 2)^2 + (y + 5)^2 = 16$ is the equation of the circle C.

Write down the equation of the image of C under:

(i) S_X, axial symmetry in the X axis

(ii) S_Y, axial symmetry in the Y axis

(iii) S_o, central symmetry in the origin, $(0, 0)$.

Solution:

$$C: \quad (x - 2)^2 + (y + 5)^2 = 16$$

(i) $S_X(C)$: $(x - 2)^2 + (y - 5)^2 = 16$ (change sign of y coordinate of centre)

(ii) $S_Y(C)$: $(x + 2)^2 + (y + 5)^2 = 16$ (change sign of x coordinate of centre)

(iii) $S_o(C)$: $(x + 2)^2 + (y - 5)^2 = 16$ (change sign of both coordinates of centre)

Example

State the centre and radius length of the circle

$$K: (x + 1)^2 + (y - 3)^2 = 4$$

Find the equation of the image of K under the central symmetry in the point $(2, 1)$.

Solution:

Step 1: $(x + 1)^2 + (y - 3)^2 = 4$

Compare to: $(x - h)^2 + (y - k)^2 = r^2$

$\Rightarrow \quad -h = 1, \quad -k = -3, \quad r^2 = 4$

$\Rightarrow \quad h = -1, \quad k = 3, \quad r = 2$

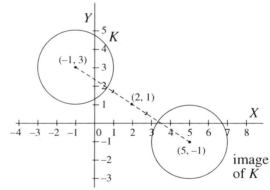

Thus, the centre of K is $(-1, 3)$

and its radius is 2.

Step 2: The new centre will be the

image of $(-1, 3)$ under a central symmetry in $(2, 1)$.

$(-1, 3) \rightarrow (2, 1) \rightarrow (5, -1)$

Thus, the new centre is $(5, -1)$.

Step 3: Centre $(5, -1)$, radius 2. (remember the radius does not change)

$$h = 5, \quad k = -1, \quad r = 2$$
$$(x - h)^2 + (y - k)^2 = r^2$$
$$(x - 5)^2 + (y + 1)^2 = 2^2$$
$$(x - 5)^2 + (y + 1)^2 = 4$$

Thus, the equation of the image of K is $(x - 5)^2 + (y + 1)^2 = 4$.

Example

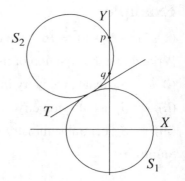

(i) Write down the length of the radius of the circle S_1: $x^2 + y^2 = 20$.

(ii) T: $x - 2y + 10 = 0$ is the equation of a tangent to S_1.

Show that the point of contact between T and S_1 is $(-2, 4)$.

(iii) S_2 is the image of S_1 under an axial symmetry in T. Write the equation of S_2.

(iv) Find the coordinates of p and q, points in which S_2 intersects the Y axis.

Solution:

(i) $$S_1: x^2 + y^2 = 20$$

Compare to: $x^2 + y^2 = r^2$

$\Rightarrow$ $$r^2 = 20$$

$\Rightarrow$ $$r = \sqrt{20}$$

Thus, the length of the radius of S_1 is $\sqrt{20}$.

(ii) $(-2, 4)$ should satisfy the equations of T and S_1.

T: $x - 2y + 10 = 0$	S_1: $x^2 + y^2 = 20$
$(-2) - 2(4) + 10$ (put in $x = -2, y = 4$)	$(-2)^2 + (4)^2$ (put in $x = -2, y = 4$)
$= -2 - 8 + 10$	$= 4 + 16$
$= 10 - 10$	$= 20$
$= 0$	$= 20$
$\therefore$ $(-2, 4)$ is on T	$\therefore$ $(-2, 4)$ is on S_1

As $(-2, 4)$ is on both T and S_1, it is the point of contact as we know that T is a tangent to S_1.

(iii) The radius of $S_2 = \sqrt{20}$ (same as the radius of S_1).

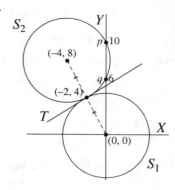

The centre of S_2 is the image of $(0, 0)$ under a central symmetry in $(-2, 4)$.

$(0, 0) \rightarrow (-2, 4) \rightarrow (-4, 8)$

$\therefore$ the centre of S_2 is $(-4, 8)$.

Equation of S_2: $(x + 4)^2 + (y - 8)^2 = (\sqrt{20})^2$

i.e. S_2: $(x + 4)^2 + (y - 8)^2 = 20$

(iv)   On the Y axis, $x = 0$

$$(x + 4)^2 + (y - 8)^2 = 20$$

$$(0 + 4)^2 + (y - 8)^2 = 20 \qquad \text{(put in } x = 0\text{)}$$

$\Rightarrow \qquad 16 + y^2 - 16y + 64 = 20$

$\Rightarrow \quad 16 + y^2 - 16y + 64 - 20 = 0$

$\Rightarrow \qquad y^2 - 16y + 60 = 0$

$\Rightarrow \qquad (y - 6)(y - 10) = 0$

$\Rightarrow \qquad y - 6 = 0 \text{ or } y - 10 = 0$

$\Rightarrow \qquad y = 6 \text{ or } \qquad y = 10$

$\therefore$ S_2 intersects the Y axis at 6 and 10.

Thus, the coordinates in which S_2 intersects the Y axis are q $(0, 6)$ and p $(0, 10)$.

9. GEOMETRY

Geometry Problems

Example

(i) Find the value of *x* and *y*.

(ii) Evaluate *X* + *Y* + *Z*.

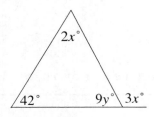

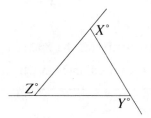

Solution:

(i)

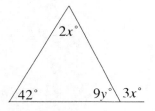

$3x = 2x + 42$ (exterior angle)

$\Rightarrow \quad 3x - 2x = 42$

$\Rightarrow \qquad\quad x = 42$

$9y + 3x = 180$

$\downarrow$

$\Rightarrow 9y + 3(42) = 180$

$\Rightarrow \quad 9y + 126 = 180$

$\Rightarrow \qquad 9y = 180 - 126$

$\Rightarrow \qquad 9y = 54$

$\Rightarrow \qquad\quad y = 6$

(ii)

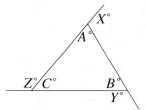

Mark angles *A*, *B* and *C*.

$X + A = 180, \ Y + B = 180 \ \text{and} \ Z + C = 180$

$\therefore \ X + A + Y + B + Z + C = 180 + 180 + 180$

$\therefore \ X + Y + Z + A + B + C = 540$

but $\qquad\qquad A + B + C = 180$

$\therefore \qquad\quad X + Y + Z + 180 = 540$

$\therefore \qquad\qquad\quad X + Y + Z = 540 - 180$

$\therefore \qquad\qquad\quad X + Y + Z = 360$

Example

(i) In a triangle, the perpendicular height is x cm, and the base is $(x + 5)$ cm. If the area of the triangle is 18 cm^2, calculate the value of x.

(ii) In a right-angled triangle the hypotenuse is x cm and the other two sides are $(x - 2)$ cm and $(x - 4)$ cm. Calculate the value of x.

Solution:

In both questions draw a diagram:

(i)

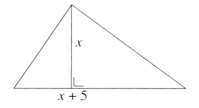

(ii)

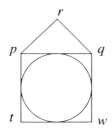

Equation given in disguise:

Area = 18 cm^2

$\Rightarrow \qquad \frac{1}{2}bh = 18$

$\Rightarrow \quad \frac{1}{2}(x + 5)(x) = 18$

$\Rightarrow \quad (x + 5)(x) = 36$

$\Rightarrow \quad x^2 + 5x - 36 = 0$

$\Rightarrow (x - 4)(x + 9) = 0$

$\Rightarrow \quad x - 4 = 0 \quad$ or $\quad x + 9 = 0$

$\Rightarrow \qquad x = 4 \quad$ or $\qquad x = -9$

(reject $x = -9$)

Thus, the value of x is 4

Given: Triangle is right-angled

$\therefore \qquad (x - 4)^2 + (x - 2)^2 = x^2$

$\Rightarrow x^2 - 8x + 16 + x^2 - 4x + 4 = x^2$

$\Rightarrow \qquad x^2 - 12x + 20 = 0$

$\Rightarrow \qquad (x - 10)(x - 2) = 0$

$\Rightarrow x - 10 = 0 \quad$ or $\quad x - 2 = 0$

$\Rightarrow \qquad x = 10 \quad$ or $\qquad x = 2$

(reject $x = 2$, because the triangle would not exist as side $x - 2 = 0$).

Thus, the value of x is 10.

Example

Find, in terms of π, the area of the circle inscribed in the square *ptwq* given that $|pr| = \sqrt{5}$ cm, $|qr| = 2$ cm and $|\angle qrp| = 90°$.

Solution:

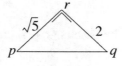

$$|pq|^2 = |pr|^2 + |rq|^2$$
$$|pq|^2 = (\sqrt{5})^2 + (2)^2$$
$$|pq|^2 = 5 + 4$$
$$|pq|^2 = 9$$
$$\Rightarrow \quad |pq| = 3$$

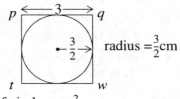

radius $= \frac{3}{2}$cm

Area of circle $= \pi r^2$
$$= \pi \times \frac{3}{2} \times \frac{3}{2}$$
$$= \frac{9}{4}\pi$$
$$= 2\frac{1}{4}\pi \ \text{cm}^2$$

Example

Find the values of x and y.

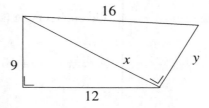

Solution:

Redraw both right-angled triangles separately and apply Pythagoras' theorem.

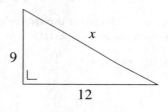

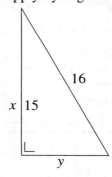

$$x^2 = 12^2 + 9^2$$
$$\Rightarrow \quad x^2 = 144 + 81$$
$$\Rightarrow \quad x^2 = 225$$
$$\Rightarrow \quad x = \sqrt{225}$$
$$\Rightarrow \quad x = 15$$

$$x^2 + y^2 = 16^2$$
$$\downarrow$$
$$\Rightarrow \quad 15^2 + y^2 = 16^2$$
$$\Rightarrow \quad 225 + y^2 = 256$$
$$\Rightarrow \quad y^2 = 256 - 225$$
$$\Rightarrow \quad y^2 = 31$$
$$\Rightarrow \quad y = \sqrt{31}$$

Example

k is the centre of the circle. If $|ab| = 2\sqrt{10}$ cm and the distance from k to ab is $\sqrt{8}$ cm, calculate the length of a diameter of the circle.

(Give your answer in the form $p\sqrt{q}$.)

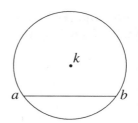

Solution:

Draw $kc \perp ab$.

$|ac| = \sqrt{10}$ and $|kc| = \sqrt{8}$ cm. $|ak| = $ radius

Using Pythagoras' theorem

$|ak|^2 = |ac|^2 + |ck|^2$

$\Rightarrow$ $|ak|^2 = (\sqrt{10})^2 + (\sqrt{8})^2$

$\Rightarrow$ $|ak|^2 = 10 + 8$

$\Rightarrow$ $|ak|^2 = 18$

$\Rightarrow$ $|ak| = \sqrt{18} = \sqrt{9 \times 2} = \sqrt{9}\sqrt{2} = 3\sqrt{2}$

Diameter $= 2|ak| = 2 \cdot 3\sqrt{2} = 6\sqrt{2}$

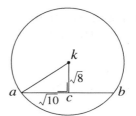

Congruent Triangles

Case 1

three sides of one triangle $=$ **three sides of the other triangle**

$\equiv$

S.S.S.

(three sides)

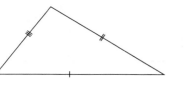
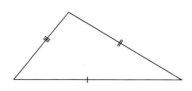

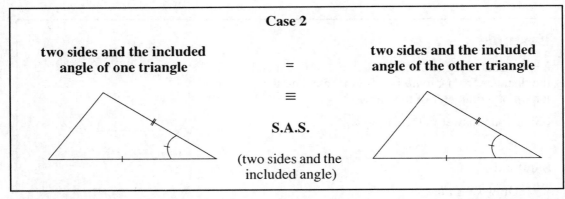

Case 2

two sides and the included angle of one triangle   =   **two sides and the included angle of the other triangle**

≡

S.A.S.

(two sides and the included angle)

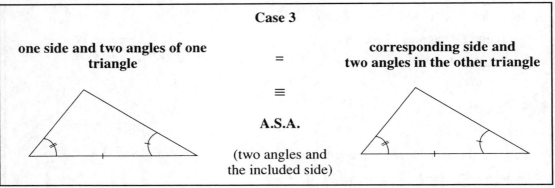

Case 3

one side and two angles of one triangle   =   **corresponding side and two angles in the other triangle**

≡

A.S.A.

(two angles and the included side)

Note: If any two pairs of angles are equal then the third pair of angles must also be equal. What is important is that the sides that are equal correspond to each other.

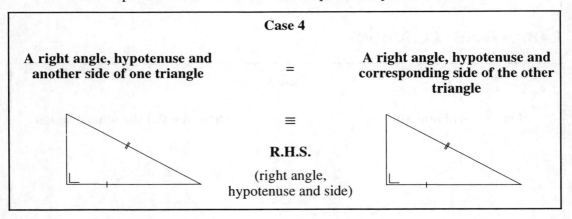

Case 4

A right angle, hypotenuse and another side of one triangle   =   **A right angle, hypotenuse and corresponding side of the other triangle**

≡

R.H.S.

(right angle, hypotenuse and side)

Geometry Theorems

There are 10 theorems to prove.

1.

> The sum of the degree-measures of the angles of a triangle is 180°.

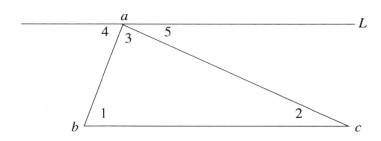

Proof:

Draw $L \parallel bc$

	$\angle 1 = \angle 4$	alternate angles
	$\angle 2 = \angle 5$	alternate angles
$\therefore$	$\angle 1 + \angle 2 + \angle 3 = \angle 4 + \angle 5 + \angle 3$	
but	$\angle 4 + \angle 5 + \angle 3 = 180°$	straight angle
$\therefore$	$\angle 1 + \angle 2 + \angle 3 = 180°$	

Corollary 1:

> The degree-measure of an exterior angle of a triangle is equal to the sum of the degree-measures of the two remote interior angles.

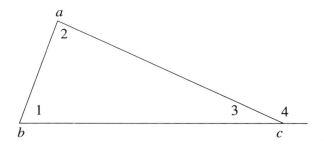

Proof:

	$\angle 1 + \angle 2 + \angle 3 = 180°$	3 angles of a triangle
	$\angle 3 + \angle 4 = 180°$	straight angle
$\therefore$	$\angle 1 + \angle 2 + \angle 3 = \angle 3 + \angle 4$	
$\therefore$	$\angle 1 + \angle 2 = \angle 4$	

Corollary 2: An exterior angle of a triangle is greater than either remote (opposite) interior angle.

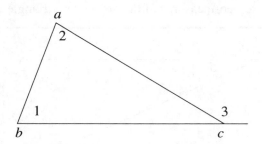

Proof:

$\angle 3 = \angle 1 + \angle 2$ exterior angle

but $\angle 1 > 0$ and $\angle 2 > 0$

$\therefore$ $\angle 3 > \angle 1$ and $\angle 3 > \angle 2$

---

2. Opposite sides of a parallelogram are equal in length.

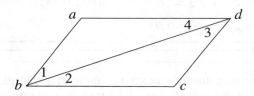

Proof:

In Δ's abd and cbd

     $\angle 1 = \angle 3$ alternate angles

     $\angle 2 = \angle 4$ alternate angles

     $|bd| = |bd|$ common side

$\therefore$ $\Delta abd \equiv \Delta cbd$ A.S.A.

$\therefore$ $|ab| = |dc|$ corresponding sides

and $|ad| = |bc|$ corresponding sides

3.

> If three parallel lines make intercepts of equal length on a transversal, then they will make intercepts of equal length on any other transversal.

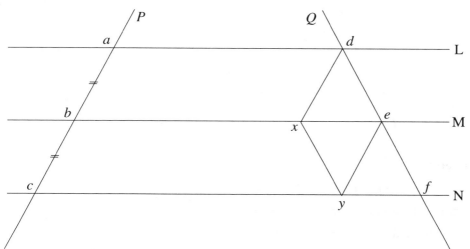

Construction:

Complete parallelograms *badx* and *edxy*.

Proof:

edxy is a parallelogram	construction
∴ |*xy*| = |*de*|	opposite sides
xy ∥ *ef*	construction
and *M* ∥ *N*	given
∴ *fexy* is a parallelogram	
∴ |*xy*| = |*ef*|	opposite sides
∴ |*de*| = |*ef*|	

161

4.

> A line which is parallel to one side-line of a triangle and cuts a second side will cut the third side in the same proportion as the second.

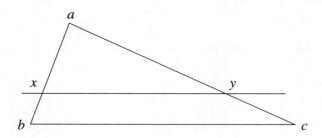

Proof:

Let x divide $[ab]$ in the ratio $m : n$, i.e. $\dfrac{|ax|}{|xb|} = \dfrac{m}{n}$.

Let $[ax]$ be divided into m equal parts.

Let $[xb]$ be divided into n equal parts.

Through each point thus obtained on $[ax]$ and $[xb]$ draw lines parallel to bc to meet ac.

$\therefore$ $[ay]$ is divided into m equal parts and $[yc]$ is divided into n equal parts.

$\therefore$ $\dfrac{|ay|}{|yc|} = \dfrac{m}{n}$

$\therefore$ $\dfrac{|ax|}{|xb|} = \dfrac{|ay|}{|yc|}$

5.

If the three angles of one triangle have degree-measures equal, respectively, to the degree-measures of the angles of a second triangle, then the lengths of the corresponding sides of the two triangles are proportional.

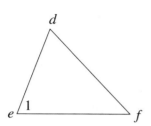

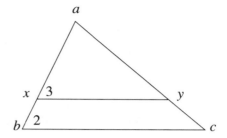

Construction:

Let Δaxy be the image of Δdef under a translation.

Proof:

$$\angle 1 = \angle 2 \qquad \text{given}$$

and $\quad \angle 1 = \angle 3 \qquad \text{same angle}$

$\therefore \quad \angle 2 = \angle 3$

$\therefore \quad xy \parallel bc$

$\therefore \quad \dfrac{|ab|}{|ax|} = \dfrac{|ac|}{|ay|}$

$\Rightarrow \quad \dfrac{|ab|}{|de|} = \dfrac{|ac|}{|df|}$

Similarly, $\dfrac{|ab|}{|de|} = \dfrac{|bc|}{|ef|}$

$\therefore \quad \dfrac{|ab|}{|de|} = \dfrac{|ac|}{|df|} = \dfrac{|bc|}{|ef|}$

6.

In a right-angled triangle, the square of the length of the side opposite to the right angle is equal to the sum of the squares of the lengths of the other two sides.

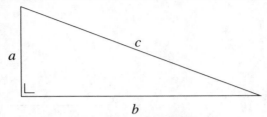

Construct a square using four congruent right-angled triangles.

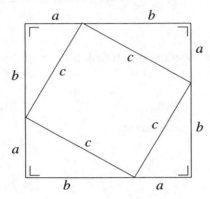

Area of larger square $= (a + b)^2 = 4(\text{area of one triangle}) + c^2$

$\Rightarrow \qquad\qquad (a + b)^2 = 4(\tfrac{1}{2}ab) + c^2$

$\Rightarrow \qquad\qquad a^2 + 2ab + b^2 = 2ab + c^2$

$\Rightarrow \qquad\qquad a^2 + b^2 = c^2$

7.

> If the square of the length of one side of a triangle is equal to the sum of the squares of the lengths of the other two sides, then the triangle has a right angle, and this is opposite the longest side.

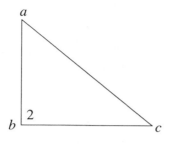 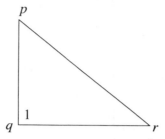

Construction:

Draw Δpqr such that $\angle 1 = 90°$

and $|pq| = |ab|$ and $|qr| = |bc|$.

Proof:

$|ab|^2 + |bc|^2 = |ac|^2$		given
but	$|pq|^2 + |qr|^2 = |pr|^2$	as $\angle 1 = 90°$
$\therefore$	$|pr| = |ac|$	
$\therefore$	$\Delta abc = \Delta pqr$	S.S.S.
$\therefore$	$\angle 2 = \angle 1 = 90°$	corresponding angles
$\therefore$	$\angle abc$ is a right angle and is opposite the longest side.	

8.

The products of the lengths of the sides of a triangle by the corresponding altitudes are equal.

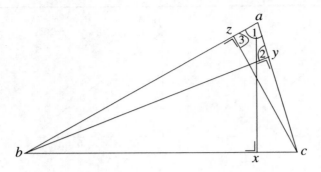

Proof:

In Δ's *aby* and *acz*,

$\angle 1 = \angle 1$ common angle

$\angle 2 = \angle 3 = 90°$ given

∴ Δ's *aby* and *acz* are equiangular

∴ $\dfrac{|ab|}{|ac|} = \dfrac{|by|}{|cz|}$ corresponding sides are in proportion

∴ $|ab| \cdot |cz| = |ac| \cdot |by|$ cross multiply

Similarly, $|ab| \cdot |cz| = |bc| \cdot |ax|$

∴ $|ab| \cdot |cz| = |ac| \cdot |by| = |bc| \cdot |ax|$

9.

> If the lengths of two sides of a triangle are unequal, then the degree-measures of the angles opposite to them are unequal, with the greater angle opposite the longer side.

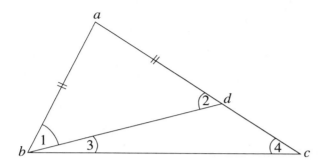

Construction:

Join b to d such that $|ab| = |ad|$.

Proof:

In $\triangle abd$,

$\quad |ab| = |ad|$ construction

$\therefore \quad \angle 1 = \angle 2$

In $\triangle bcd$,

$\quad \angle 2 > \angle 4$ exterior angle

$\therefore \quad \angle 1 > \angle 4$

$\therefore \quad \angle 1 + \angle 3 > \angle 4$

$\therefore \quad \angle abc > \angle acb$

10.

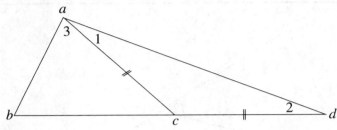

Construction:

Join c to d such that $|ac| = |cd|$.

Proof:

In $\triangle acd$,

$|ac| = |cd|$ construction

$\therefore$ $|\angle 1| = |\angle 2|$

$\therefore$ $|\angle 1| + |\angle 3| > |\angle 2|$

$\therefore$ $|bd| > |ab|$ side opposite greater angle

but $|bd| = |bc| + |cd|$

       $= |bc| + |ac|$

$\therefore$ $|bc| + |ac| > |ab|$

168

Enlargements

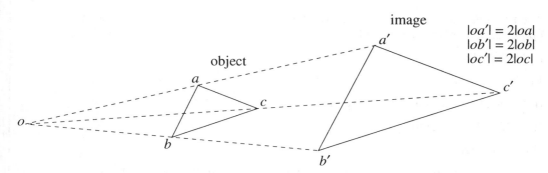

In the diagram above:

The Δabc is the **object** (the starting shape) and $\Delta a'b'c'$ is the **image** (the enlarged shape).

$\Delta a'b'c'$ is the image of Δabc under the enlargement, centre o, scale factor 2.

Note: The centre of enlargement can be a vertex on the object figure or inside it.

Properties of Enlargements

1. The shape of the image is the same as the shape of the object (only size has changed).

2. The amount by which a figure is enlarged is called the 'scale factor' and denoted by k.

3. image length $= k$(object length)   or $k = \dfrac{\text{image length}}{\text{object length}}$

4. area of image $= k^2$(area object)   or $k^2 = \dfrac{\text{area of image}}{\text{area of object}}$

Notes:

1. The scale factor can be less than one (i.e. $0 < k < 1$). In these cases, the image will be smaller than the object. Though smaller, the image is still called an enlargement.

2. If a figure B is an enlargement of figure A under a scale factor k, then the figure A is an enlargement of B under a scale factor $\frac{1}{k}$ (turn upside down), with the same centre of enlargement.

Example

The triangle *ors* is the image of the triangle *opq* under an enlargement, centre *o*.

|*op*| = 4, |*pr*| = 6.

Find

(i) the scale factor of the enlargement

(ii) If |*oq*| = 3·2, find |*qs*|

(iii) |*pq*| : |*rs*|

(iv) the area of the triangle *ors* given the area of Δ*opq* to be 6 square units

Solution:

Divide the figure into two separate similar triangles. Mark in known lengths.

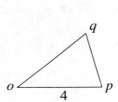
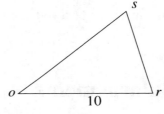

(i) Scale factor = k = $\dfrac{\text{image length}}{\text{object length}}$ = $\dfrac{|or|}{|op|}$ = $\dfrac{10}{4}$ = 2·5

(ii) |*qs*|

$|os| = k|oq| = (2{\cdot}5)(3{\cdot}2) = 8$

$|qs| = |os| - |oq| = 8 - 3{\cdot}2 = 4{\cdot}8$

(iii) |*pq*| : |*rs*| = |*op*| : |*or*| = 4 : 10 = 2 : 5

(iv)   area of image = k^2(area of object)

⇒   area of Δ*ors* = k^2(area of Δ*opq*)

$= (2{\cdot}5)^2(6)$

$= (6{\cdot}25)(6)$

$= 37{\cdot}5$

Thus, the area of Δ*ors* = 37·5 square units

Example

The rectangle *aefg* is an enlargement of the rectangle *abcd* with |*ac*| = 5, |*cf*| = 3.

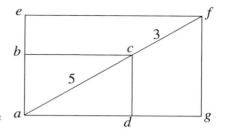

(i) Write down the centre of enlargement.

(ii) Find *k*, the scale factor of the enlargement.

(iii) If the area of the rectangle *aefg* is 62·72 square units, find the area of the rectangle *abcd*.

(iv) A further enlargement will map rectangle *aefg* back onto rectangle *abcd*.

Find the scale factor, if the centre of enlargement remains the same.

Solution:

(i) The centre of enlargement is *a* (as *a* is common to both rectangles)

(ii) Divide the figure into two separate similar rectangles. Mark in known lengths.

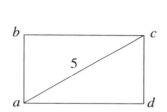 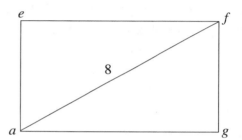

$$\text{Scale factor} = k = \frac{\text{image length}}{\text{object length}} = \frac{|af|}{|ac|} = \frac{8}{5} = 1\cdot6$$

(iii) (area of image) = k^2(area of object)

$\Rightarrow$ area of rectangle *aefg* = k^2(area of rectangle *abcd*)

$$62\cdot72 = (1\cdot6)^2(\text{area of rectangle } abcd)$$

$$62\cdot72 = 2\cdot56(\text{area of rectangle } abcd)$$

$$\frac{62\cdot72}{2\cdot56} = \text{area of rectangle } abcd$$

$$24\cdot5 = \text{area of rectangle } abcd$$

Thus, the area of rectangle *abcd* is 24·5 square units.

(iv) rectangle *aefg* is mapped onto rectangle *abcd* under an enlargement of scale factor $\frac{1}{k}$.

$$k = \frac{8}{5}, \therefore \frac{1}{k} = \frac{5}{8} \text{ (turn upside down)}$$

Thus, rectangle *aefg* is mapped onto rectangle *abcd* under an enlargement of scale factor $\frac{5}{8}$.

Example

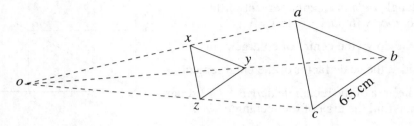

Δxyz is the image of Δabc, under an enlargement, centre o.

If area of $\Delta abc = 40$ cm^2 and the area of $\Delta xyz = 25 \cdot 6$ cm^2, find:

(i)   the scale factor of enlargement, k

(ii) $|yz|$ if $|bc| = 6 \cdot 5$ cm.

Solution:

(i)   area of image $= k^2$(area of object)

$\Rightarrow$ area of $\Delta xyz = k^2$(area of Δabc)

$\Rightarrow$ $25 \cdot 6 = k^2(40)$

$\Rightarrow$ $\dfrac{25 \cdot 6}{40} = k^2$

$\Rightarrow$ $0 \cdot 64 = k^2$

$\Rightarrow$ $0 \cdot 8 = k$

Thus, the scale factor of enlargement is $0 \cdot 8$

(ii)   image length $= k$(object length)

$\Rightarrow$ $|yz| = k|bc|$

                    $= (0 \cdot 8)(6 \cdot 5)$

                    $= 5 \cdot 2$

Thus, $|yz| = 5 \cdot 2$ cm

Enlargements and Coordinate Geometry

If the centre of enlargement is (0, 0) do the following:

> Multiply each part of the coordinates by the scale factor, i.e.
> $$(x, y) \rightarrow (kx, ky)$$

If the given centre of enlargement is **not** the origin do the following:

1. Find the translation which maps the centre of enlargement to the origin and apply this translation to the coordinates of the vertices of the original figure.

2. Multiply each part of these coordinates by the scale factor k.

3. Apply the inverse of the translation in Step 1 to find their images under the enlargement from the original centre of enlargement.

Remember: | translation | $\rightarrow$ | multiply by k | $\rightarrow$ | inverse translation |

Always keep this order if the centre of enlargement is not (0, 0).

If the figure is given in terms of its coordinates and the centre of enlargement is (0, 0) then the scale factor is given by:

$$k = \left| \frac{\text{any } x \text{ coordinate on image}}{\text{corresponding } x \text{ coordinate on object}} \right| \quad \text{or } k = \left| \frac{\text{any } y \text{ coordinate on image}}{\text{corresponding } y \text{ coordinate on object}} \right|$$

If the centre of enlargement is not (0, 0) then find the translation which maps the centre of enlargement to (0, 0), apply this translation to the given vertices and then find k using the fact above.

Example

$p(2, 7)$, $q(6, 3)$ and $r(-4, -9)$ are the coordinates of the vertices of $\triangle pqr$. Find the coordinates of the vertices of its image, $\triangle p'q'r'$, under an enlargement of scale factor $1\frac{1}{2}$, with (-2, 3) as the centre of enlargement.

Solution:

1. Centre of enlargement is (-2, 3). Map it to (0, 0).

   $(-2, 3) \rightarrow (0, 0)$ [Rule add 2 to x, take 3 from y]

   $p(2, 7)$ $q(6, 3)$ $r(-4, -9)$
       $\downarrow$ $\downarrow$ $\downarrow$

      (4, 4)   (8, 0)   (-2, -12)   (add 2 to x, take 3 from y)
       $\downarrow$ $\downarrow$ $\downarrow$

2.   (6, 6)   (12, 0)   (-3, -18)   (multiply coordinates by $1\frac{1}{2}$)
       $\downarrow$ $\downarrow$ $\downarrow$

3.   (4, 9)   (10, 3)   (-5, -15)   (inverse translation, take 2 from x, add 3 to y)

Thus, the images are $p'(4, 9)$, $q'(10, 3)$ and $r'(-5, -15)$.

Example

$a(12,15)$, $b(6, 3)$ and $c(3, 9)$ are the coordinates of the vertices of $\triangle abc$. Under an enlargement, of centre $(0, 0)$, the vertices are mapped onto $a'(8, 10)$, $b'(4, 2)$ and $c'(2, 6)$, respectively.

(i) Find the scale factor of enlargement, k.

(ii) Verify that $\dfrac{\text{Area of } \triangle a'b'c'}{\text{Area of } \triangle abc} = k^2$

Solution:

The centre of enlargement is $(0, 0)$:

$$\therefore k = \left| \frac{\text{any } x \text{ coordinate on image}}{\text{corresponding } x \text{ coordinate on object}} \right| \text{ or}$$

$$k = \left| \frac{\text{any } y \text{ coordinate on image}}{\text{corresponding } y \text{ coordinate on object}} \right|$$

$$a(12,15) \to a'(8,10)$$

$\therefore k = \dfrac{8}{12} = \dfrac{2}{3}$ or $k = \dfrac{10}{15} = \dfrac{2}{3}$

Thus, the scale factor is $\dfrac{2}{3}$

Area of $\triangle abc$	Area of $\triangle a'b'c'$
$(12,15)$ $(6, 3)$ $(3, 9)$	$(8, 10)$ $(4, 2)$ $(2, 6)$
$\downarrow$ $\downarrow$ $\downarrow$	$\downarrow$ $\downarrow$ $\downarrow$
$(9, 6)$ $(3, -6)$ $(0, 0)$	$(6, 4)$ $(2, -4)$ $(0, 0)$
(x_1, y_1) (x_2, y_2)	(x_1, y_1) (x_2, y_2)
$A = \frac{1}{2}\lvert x_1 y_2 - x_2 y_1 \rvert$	$A = \frac{1}{2}\lvert x_1 y_2 - x_2 y_1 \rvert$
$= \frac{1}{2}\lvert (9)(-6) - (3)(6) \rvert$	$= \frac{1}{2}\lvert (6)(-4) - (2)(4) \rvert$
$= \frac{1}{2}\lvert -54 - 18 \rvert$	$= \frac{1}{2}\lvert -24 - 8 \rvert$
$= \frac{1}{2}\lvert -72 \rvert$	$= \frac{1}{2}\lvert -32 \rvert$
$= \frac{1}{2}\lvert 72 \rvert$	$= \frac{1}{2}\lvert 32 \rvert$
$= 36$	$= 16$

$$\therefore \quad \frac{\text{Area of } \triangle a'b'c'}{\text{Area of } \triangle abc} = \frac{16}{36} = \frac{4}{9}$$

$$k^2 = \left(\frac{2}{3} \right)^2 = \frac{4}{9}$$

Thus, $\dfrac{\text{Area of } \triangle a'b'c'}{\text{Area of } \triangle abc} = k^2$

10. TRIGONOMETRY

1. Trigonometric ratios

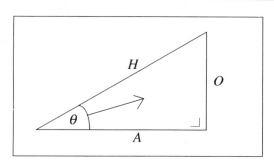

$$\sin\theta = \frac{\text{Opposite}}{\text{Hypotenuse}} = \frac{O}{H}$$

$$\cos\theta = \frac{\text{Adjacent}}{\text{Hypotenuse}} = \frac{A}{H}$$

$$\tan\theta = \frac{\text{Opposite}}{\text{Adjacent}} = \frac{O}{A}$$

Memory Aid: Oh Hell, Another Hour, Of Algebra, sin, cos and tan.

2. Special right-angled triangles

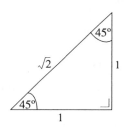
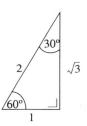

The above trigonometrical ratios are given on page 9 of the mathematical tables where $\pi = 180°$

A	0	π	$\dfrac{\pi}{2}$	$\dfrac{\pi}{3}$	$\dfrac{\pi}{4}$	$\dfrac{\pi}{6}$
$\cos A$	1	-1	0	$\dfrac{1}{2}$	$\dfrac{1}{\sqrt{2}}$	$\dfrac{\sqrt{3}}{2}$
$\sin A$	0	0	1	$\dfrac{\sqrt{3}}{2}$	$\dfrac{1}{\sqrt{2}}$	$\dfrac{1}{2}$
$\tan A$	0	0	gan sain-mhíniú not defined	$\sqrt{3}$	1	$\dfrac{1}{\sqrt{3}}$

3. Unit circle

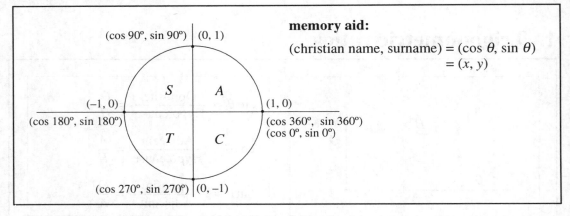

memory aid:

(christian name, surname) = (cos θ, sin θ)
                          = (x, y)

4. Angles between 0° and 360°

The trigonometric ratio of an angle between 0° and 360° can be found with the following steps:

1. Make a rough diagram of the angle on a unit circle.

2. Use $\begin{array}{c|c} S & A \\ \hline T & C \end{array}$ to find whether this ratio is positive or negative.

3. Find its **reference** angle, the acute angle to the X axis.

4. Use the calculator or special triangles, to find the value of this reference angle and use the sign in Step 2.

5. Given the values of sin, cos and tan

Between 0° and 360° there may be two angles with the same trigonometric ratio.

e.g. $\cos 120° = -\frac{1}{2}$ and $\cos 240° = -\frac{1}{2}$.

To find the two values we do the following:

1. Ignore the sign and evaluate the reference angle using special triangles or calculator.

2. From the sign of the given ratio decide in which quadrants the angles can lie.

3. Using a diagram, state the angles between 0° and 360°.

6. Angle of elevation and depression

The **angle of elevation** of an object as seen by an observer is the angle between the horizontal and the line from the object to the observer's eye (the line of vision).

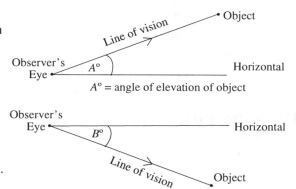

$A°$ = angle of elevation of object

If the object is below the level of the observer, then the angle between the horizontal and the observer's line of vision is called the **angle of depression**.

$B°$ = angle of depression of object

7. Compass directions

The **direction** to a point is stated as a number of degrees East or West of North or South.

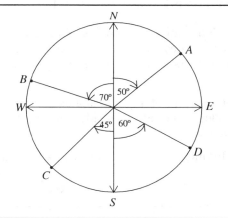

A is $N\ 50°\ E$

B is $N\ 70°\ W$

C is $S\ 45°\ W$

D is $S\ 60°\ E$

Note: $N\ 50°\ E$ means $50°$ East of North.

8. Notation

The diagram shows the **usual notation** for a triangle in trigonometry:

Vertices: a, b, c

Angles: A, B, C

Length of Sides: a, b, c

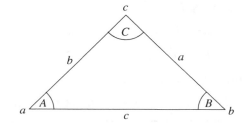

The lengths of the sides are denoted by a lower case letter, and named after the angle they are opposite, *i.e.* a is opposite angle A, b is opposite angle B, and c is opposite angle C.

9. Area of a triangle

Area of $\triangle abc = \frac{1}{2}ab \sin C = \frac{1}{2}ac \sin B = \frac{1}{2}bc \sin A$

or: Area of triangle = half the product of the lengths of two of its sides by the sine of the included angle.

(The first form is given on page 6 of the tables.)

10. Sine rule

In any $\triangle abc$

$$\frac{a}{\sin A} = \frac{b}{\sin B} = \frac{c}{\sin C}$$

or: $\dfrac{\sin A}{a} = \dfrac{\sin B}{b} = \dfrac{\sin C}{c}$

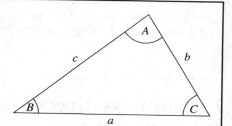

(The first form is given on page 9 of the tables.)

In words: **The sine of the angles of a triangle are in the same ratio to the lengths of the opposite sides.** This is known as the **sine rule**, and it applies to any triangle, including a right-angled triangle. It is used to find unknown sides and angles when given:

1. The measure of any two angles and the length of any side.
2. The lengths of any two sides and the measure of one angle opposite one of these given sides.

Note: In practice we only use two parts of the sine rule, *e.g.*

$$\frac{p}{\sin P} = \frac{q}{\sin Q}$$

11. Cosine Rule

In any $\triangle abc$:

$a^2 = b^2 + c^2 - 2bc \cos A$

or: $b^2 = a^2 + c^2 - 2ac \cos B$

or: $c^2 = a^2 + b^2 - 2ab \cos C$

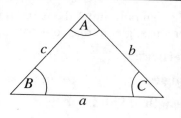

(The first form is given on page 9 of the tables.)

The cosine rule, in this form, is used to find the length of the third side of a triangle when given the lengths of the two other sides and the included angle. (In this case we would not be able to use the sine rule.)

178

Alternative Form of the cosine rule.

$$a^2 = b^2 + c^2 - 2bc \cos A$$

$$\Rightarrow 2bc \cos A = b^2 + c^2 - a^2$$

$$\Rightarrow \cos A = \frac{b^2 + c^2 - a^2}{2bc}$$

Similarly: $\cos B = \dfrac{c^2 + a^2 - b^2}{2ac}$ and $\cos C = \dfrac{a^2 + b^2 - c^2}{2ab}$

(This form is **not** given on page 9 of the tables.)

The cosine rule, in this form, is used to find angles when given the lengths of the three sides.

(In this case we would not be able to use the sine rule.)

Note: If the angle is greater than 90° its cosine is negative.

12. Compound Angles

1.	$\cos (A + B)$	$=$	$\cos A \cos B - \sin A \sin B$
2.	$\cos (A - B)$	$=$	$\cos A \cos B + \sin A \sin B$
3.	$\sin (A + B)$	$=$	$\sin A \cos B + \cos A \sin B$
4.	$\sin (A - B)$	$=$	$\sin A \cos B - \cos A \sin B$

1 and 3 are on page 9 of the tables.

2 and 4 can be gotten by changing the signs in the middle on both sides of 1 and 3.

Note: 1. Always make sure your calculator is in 'degree mode'.

2. Check the manual on how to correctly use your calculator as many calculators use a different sequence for entering data.

Example

An upright pole of 18 m above the ground casts a shadow 50 m long.

Find the angle of elevation of the sun, correct to the nearest degree.

Solution:

Represent the situation with a right-angled triangle.

Let $A°$ = angle of elevation of the sun.

We have the opposite and adjacent, $\therefore$ use tan.

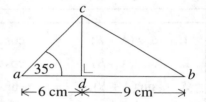

$$\tan A = \frac{18}{50}$$

$$\tan A = 0.36$$

$\Rightarrow \qquad A = 19.798876°$ [Press: $\boxed{0.36}$ $\boxed{\text{INV}}$ $\boxed{\text{TAN}}$]

Thus, the angle of elevation of the sun is 20°.

Example

$|ad| = 6$ cm, $|db| = 9$ cm,

$|\angle cad| = 35°$ and $cd \perp ab$.

Find,

(i) $|cd|$, correct to one decimal place.

(ii) $|\angle cbd|$, correct to the nearest degree.

Solution:

Redraw both right-angled triangles separately.

(i)

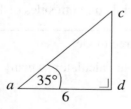

$$\tan 35° = \frac{|cd|}{6}$$

$\Rightarrow \qquad 6\tan 35° = |cd|$

$\Rightarrow \qquad 6(0.7002075) = |cd|$

$\Rightarrow \qquad 4.2012452 = |cd|$

Thus, $|cd| = 4.2$ cm

(ii)

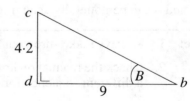

$$\tan B = \frac{4.2}{9}$$

$\Rightarrow \qquad B = 25.016893°$

[Press: $\boxed{4.2}$ $\boxed{\div}$ $\boxed{9}$ $\boxed{=}$ $\boxed{\text{INV}}$ $\boxed{\text{TAN}}$]

Thus, $|\angle cbd| = 25°$

Example

In $\triangle abc$, $|ac| = 7$ cm, $|\angle abc| = 30°$ and $|\angle acb| = 80°$.

Find $|ab|$, correct to the nearest cm.

Solution:

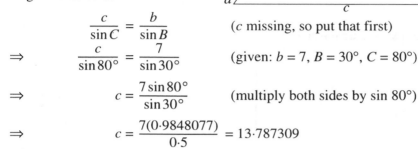

Using the sine rule:

$$\frac{c}{\sin C} = \frac{b}{\sin B} \qquad \text{(c missing, so put that first)}$$

$$\Rightarrow \qquad \frac{c}{\sin 80°} = \frac{7}{\sin 30°} \qquad \text{(given: $b = 7$, $B = 30°$, $C = 80°$)}$$

$$\Rightarrow \qquad c = \frac{7 \sin 80°}{\sin 30°} \qquad \text{(multiply both sides by sin 80°)}$$

$$\Rightarrow \qquad c = \frac{7(0 \cdot 9848077)}{0 \cdot 5} = 13 \cdot 787309$$

Thus, $c = 14$ cm

Example

A plot of land has a triangular shape pqr, as shown.

Find:

(i)   the area of triangle pqr, correct to the nearest m²

(ii) $|qr|$, correct to the nearest metre.

Solution:

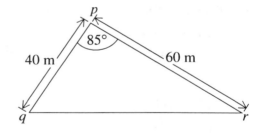

(i) $q = 60$, $r = 40$, $p = 85°$

Area of $\triangle pqr = \frac{1}{2} qr \sin P$

$$= \frac{1}{2}(60)(40)(\sin 85°)$$

$$= \frac{1}{2}(60)(40)(0 \cdot 9961947)$$

$$= 1195 \cdot 4336$$

Thus, area of $\triangle pqr = 1195$ m²

(ii)   We know two sides and included angle

$\therefore$ use the cosine rule

$$p^2 = q^2 + r^2 - 2qr \cos P$$

$$p^2 = (60)^2 + (40)^2 - 2(60)(40)(\cos 85°)$$

$$p^2 = 3600 + 1600 - 2(60)(40)(0 \cdot 0871557)$$

$$p^2 = 5200 - 418 \cdot 34757$$

$$p^2 = 4781 \cdot 6524$$

$$p = \sqrt{4781 \cdot 6524} = 69 \cdot 149493$$

Thus, $|qr| = 69$ m

181

Example

A garden *pqrs* is in the shape of a quadrilateral.

|*pq*| = 15 m, |*ps*| = 8 m, |*rs*| = 9 m, the angle at *p* is 90° and |∠*qrs*| = 80°.

Find the value of

(i) |*qs*|

(ii) |∠*rqs*| to the nearest degree.

Solution:

Divide figure into two separate triangles.

(i)

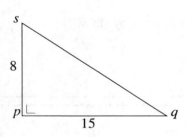

Use Pythagoras' Theorem to find |*qs*|

$$|qs|^2 = |qp|^2 + |ps|^2$$
$$= (15)^2 + (8)^2$$
$$= 225 + 64$$
$$= 289$$
$$\Rightarrow \quad |qs| = \sqrt{289} = 17$$

Thus, |*qs*| = 17 m

(ii)

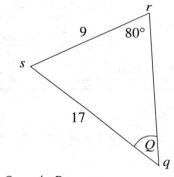

$$\frac{\sin Q}{q} = \frac{\sin R}{r} \qquad \text{(sine rule)}$$

$$\frac{\sin Q}{9} = \frac{\sin 80°}{17}$$

$$\frac{\sin Q}{9} = \frac{0 \cdot 9848077}{17}$$

$$\sin Q = \frac{9(0 \cdot 9848077)}{17}$$

$$\sin Q = 0 \cdot 5213688$$

$$\Rightarrow \quad Q = 31 \cdot 424113°$$

[Press: $\boxed{0 \cdot 5213688}$ $\boxed{\text{INV}}$ $\boxed{\text{SIN}}$]

Thus, |∠*rqs*| = 31°

Example

Find the size of the greatest angle of the triangle which has sides of length 3, 5 and 7.

(rough diagram)

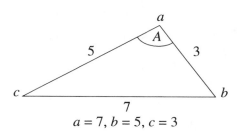

$a = 7, b = 5, c = 3$

Solution:

The largest angle is opposite the largest side.

We know the lengths of the three sides but we do not know any angles.

$\therefore$ use the cosine rule

$$a^2 = b^2 + c^2 - 2bc \cos A \quad \text{(page 9)}$$

$\Rightarrow \qquad 7^2 = 5^2 + 3^2 - 2(5)(3) \cos A$

$\Rightarrow \qquad 49 = 25 + 9 - 30 \cos A$

$\Rightarrow \qquad 49 = 34 - 30 \cos A$

$\Rightarrow \quad 30 \cos A = 34 - 49$

$\Rightarrow \quad 30 \cos A = -15$

$\Rightarrow \qquad \cos A = -\dfrac{15}{30}$

$\Rightarrow \qquad \cos A = -0 \cdot 5$

$\Rightarrow \qquad A = 120° \qquad$ [Press: $\boxed{0 \cdot 5}$ $\boxed{+/-}$ $\boxed{\text{INV}}$ $\boxed{\text{COS}}$]

Thus, the largest angle is 120°.

Example

In Δpqr, |pq| = 20 cm, |pr| = 7 cm. If the area of Δpqr = 28 cm^2, find |$\angle qpr$|, correct to the nearest degree.

(rough diagram)

Solution:

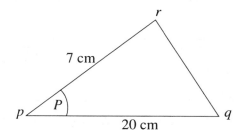

Equation given in disguise:

Area of $\Delta pqr = 28$

$\Rightarrow \qquad \dfrac{1}{2} qr \sin P = 28$

$\Rightarrow \dfrac{1}{2}(7)(20) \sin P = 28$

$\Rightarrow \qquad 70 \sin P = 28$

$\Rightarrow \qquad \sin P = \dfrac{28}{70}$

$\Rightarrow \qquad \sin P = 0 \cdot 4$

$\Rightarrow \qquad P = 23 \cdot 578178° \quad$ [Press: $\boxed{0 \cdot 4}$ $\boxed{\text{INV}}$ $\boxed{\text{SIN}}$]

$\therefore \qquad |\angle qpr| = 24°$

183

Example

opq is a sector of a circle with a radius of length 10.

Calculate the area of the shaded portion, correct to two places of decimals.

Take $\pi = 3\cdot14$.

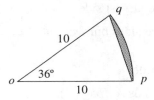

Solution:

Area of sector *opq*

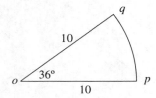

Area of sector $= \dfrac{36}{360} \pi r^2$

$\qquad = \dfrac{1}{10}(3\cdot14)(10)(10)$

$\qquad = 31\cdot4$

Area of Δopq

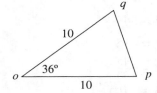

Area of $\Delta = \dfrac{1}{2}$ |*op*| . |*oq*| sin 36°

$\qquad = \dfrac{1}{2}(10)(10)(0\cdot5877852)$

$\qquad = 29\cdot389263$

Area of shaded region = Area of sector *opq* – Area of Δopq

$\qquad\qquad = 31\cdot4 - 29\cdot389263$

$\qquad\qquad = 2\cdot0107374$

$\qquad\qquad = 2\cdot01$

Example

A ship, *q*, is 7 km from a port, *p*. The direction of *q* from *p* is *N* 45° *E*.

A second ship, *r*, is 4·2 km from *q*. The direction of *r* from *q* is *S* 75° *E*.

Calculate the distance from the port *p* to the ship *r*.

Solution:

From the information in the question we construct a triangle.

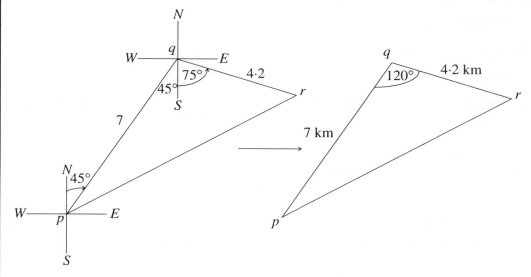

Two sides and included angle, ∴ use cosine rule.

$$|pr|^2 = |pq|^2 + |qr|^2 - 2|pq| \cdot |qr| \cdot \cos 120°$$

$$= (7)^2 + (4\cdot2)^2 - 2(7)(4\cdot2)(-0\cdot5)$$

$$= 49 + 17\cdot64 + 29\cdot4$$

$$= 96\cdot04$$

$$\Rightarrow \quad |pr| = \sqrt{96\cdot04} = 9\cdot8$$

Thus, the distance between the port p and ship r is 9·8 km

Example

Find cos 210°, leaving your answer in surd form.

Solution:

Surd form, ∴ cannot use calculator.

1. The diagram shows the angle 210°.

2. 210° is in the 3rd quadrant.

   cos is negative in the 3rd quadrant.

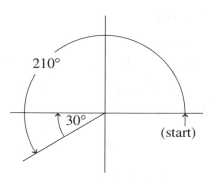

3. Reference angle is 30°.

4. ∴ $\cos 210° = -\cos 30° = -\dfrac{\sqrt{3}}{2}$ (page 9 of tables)

Example

If cos $A = -0.7914$, find the two values of A in $0 \leq A \leq 360°$.

Solution:

1. Find reference angle (ignore sign).

If cos $A = 0.7914$

$\Rightarrow \qquad A = 37°41'$

[Press: $\boxed{0.7914}$ $\boxed{\text{INV}}$ $\boxed{\text{COS}}$ $\boxed{\text{INV}}$ $\boxed{\text{DMS}}$]

2. cos is negative in the 2nd and 3rd quadrant.

3. Rough diagram

A in the 2nd quadrant

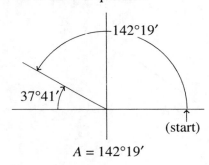

$A = 142°19'$

A in the 3rd quadrant

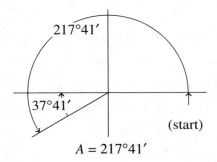

$A = 217°41'$

Thus, if cos $A = -0.7914$, $\quad A = 142°19'$ or $A = 217°41'$.

Example

$\sin \theta = \dfrac{\sqrt{3}}{2}$

Write two values for θ in $0 \leq \theta \leq 180°$.

Hence write the two corresponding values for cos θ.

Solution:

1. Find reference angle.

If $\sin \theta = \dfrac{\sqrt{3}}{2}$

$\Rightarrow \qquad \theta = 60° \qquad\qquad$ (page 9)

2. sin is positive in the 1st and 2nd quadrant.

3. Rough diagram

θ in the 1st quadrant

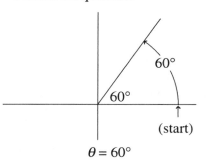

(start)

$\theta = 60°$

θ in the 2nd quadrant

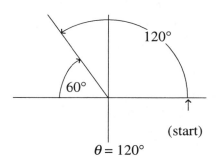

120°

60°

(start)

$\theta = 120°$

Thus, if $\sin \theta = \dfrac{\sqrt{3}}{2}$, $\quad\quad \theta = 60°$ or $\theta = 120°$

$\theta = 60° \Rightarrow \cos \theta = \cos 60° = \dfrac{1}{2}$

$\theta = 120° \Rightarrow \cos \theta = \cos 120° = -\dfrac{1}{2}$

Example

(i) Find the value of A for which $\cos A = -1$, $0° \le A \le 360°$.

(ii) If $0° \le A \le 360°$, find the value of A for which $\sin A = 1$.

(iii) If $0° \le A \le 360°$, find the values of A for which $\cos A = 0$.

(iv) Evaluate $\sin^2 270$.

Solution:

Draw the unit circle.

Remember: (christian name, surname) = $(\cos \theta, \sin \theta) = (x, y)$.

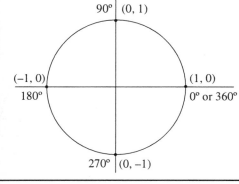

(i) $\cos A = -1$

$\Rightarrow A = 180°$

(iii) $\cos A = 0$

$\Rightarrow A = 90°$ or $270°$

(ii) $\sin A = 1$

$\Rightarrow A = 90°$

(iv) $\sin^2 270$

$= (\sin 270)^2$

$= (-1)^2 = 1$

Example

If $\sin A = \frac{4}{5}$ and $\cos B = \frac{5}{13}$, $A < 90°$, $B < 90°$. Find:

(i) $\cos A$ **(ii)** $\sin B$ **(iii)** $\sin (A + B)$.

Show that $\sin^2 A + \cos^2 A = 1$.

Solution:

Draw two right-angled triangles from the given information and use Pythagoras' theorem to find the missing sides.

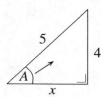 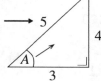 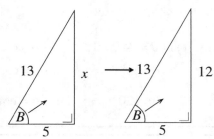

Given: $\sin A = \frac{4}{5}$

$$x^2 + 4^2 = 5^2$$
$$\Rightarrow \quad x^2 + 16 = 25$$
$$\Rightarrow \quad x^2 = 25 - 16$$
$$\Rightarrow \quad x^2 = 9$$
$$\Rightarrow \quad x = 3$$

Given: $\cos B = \frac{5}{13}$

$$x^2 + 5^2 = 13^2$$
$$\Rightarrow \quad x^2 + 25 = 169$$
$$\Rightarrow \quad x^2 = 169 - 25$$
$$\Rightarrow \quad x^2 = 144$$
$$\Rightarrow \quad x = 12$$

(i) $\cos A = \frac{3}{5}$

(ii) $\sin B = \frac{12}{13}$

(iii) $\sin (A + B) = \sin A \cos B + \cos A \sin B$

$$= \frac{4}{5} \times \frac{5}{13} + \frac{3}{5} \times \frac{12}{13}$$
$$= \frac{20}{65} + \frac{36}{65}$$
$$= \frac{56}{65}$$

$\sin^2 A + \cos^2 A$

$$= \left(\frac{4}{5}\right)^2 + \left(\frac{3}{5}\right)^2$$
$$= \frac{16}{25} + \frac{9}{25}$$
$$= \frac{25}{25} = 1$$

Example

Write cos 75° in surd form.

Solution:

We first express 75° as a combination of 30°, 45° or 60° and use page 9 of the tables.

$\cos 75° = \cos (45°+30°)$

$\qquad = \cos 45° \cos 30° - \sin 45° \sin 30°$

$\qquad = \dfrac{1}{\sqrt{2}} \cdot \dfrac{\sqrt{3}}{2} - \dfrac{1}{\sqrt{2}} \cdot \dfrac{1}{2}$

$\qquad = \dfrac{\sqrt{3}}{2\sqrt{2}} - \dfrac{1}{2\sqrt{2}}$

$\qquad = \dfrac{\sqrt{3}-1}{2\sqrt{2}}$

$75° = 45° + 30°$

$\cos (A + B) = \cos A \cos B - \sin A \sin B$

let $A = 45°$ and $B = 30°$

$\dfrac{\pi}{4} = \dfrac{180°}{4} = 45° = A$

$\dfrac{\pi}{6} = \dfrac{180°}{6} = 30° = B$

11. PERMUTATIONS, COMBINATIONS AND PROBABILITY

Permutations

A permutation is a selection of a number of items in a certain order.

A permutation is also called an **arrangement**.

An aid to solving problems is to represent each choice with an empty box at the beginning of the problem. Always start with the choice, or operation, in the arrangement whose choice from the given set is **most** restricted.

Example

(i) How many different arrangements can be made of the letters of the word *C O M P A N Y*?

(ii) How many of these begin with the letter *C*?

(iii) How many begin with *C* and end with *Y*?

Solution:

Represent each choice with a box.

(i) We have 7 letters to fill into 7 spaces.

$$\boxed{7}.\boxed{6}.\boxed{5}.\boxed{4}.\boxed{3}.\boxed{2}.\boxed{1} = 7 . 6 . 5 . 4 . 3 . 2 . 1 = 5\,040$$

(ii) Begin with *C*.

Thus, the first place can only be filled in one way, with *C*.

C
$$\boxed{1}.\boxed{6}.\boxed{5}.\boxed{4}.\boxed{3}.\boxed{2}.\boxed{1} = 1 . 6 . 5 . 4 . 3 . 2 . 1 = 720$$

(iii) Begin with *C* and end with *Y*.

Thus, the first place can only be filled in one way, with *C*, and the last place can only be filled in one way, with *Y*.

C   *Y*
$$\boxed{1}.\boxed{5}.\boxed{4}.\boxed{3}.\boxed{2}.\boxed{1}.\boxed{1} = 1 . 5 . 4 . 3 . 2 . 1 . 1 = 120$$

Example

How many different arrangements can be made from the letters *V*, *W*, *X*, *Y*, *Z*, taking all the letters at a time, if *V* must be second and *Z* can never be last?

Solution:

Represent each choice with a box.

The second place can only be filled in one way, with *V*. The last place can only be filled in 3 ways (cannot use *V* or *Z*). These choices must be filled in first, then fill in the other places.

$$\underset{}{\boxed{3}} . \underset{V}{\boxed{1}} . \underset{}{\boxed{2}} . \underset{}{\boxed{1}} . \underset{no\ Z}{\boxed{3}} = 3 . 1 . 2 . 1 . 3 = 18$$

Example

A number-plate is to consist of three letters of the English alphabet and two digits. If no letter or digit can be repeated and 0 can never be used as the first digit, how many different plates can be manufactured?

B	A	T	4	5

(an example)

Solution:

Represent each choice with a box.

$$\underset{}{\boxed{26}} . \underset{}{\boxed{25}} . \underset{}{\boxed{24}} . \underset{no\ 0}{\boxed{9}} . \underset{}{\boxed{9}} = 26 . 25 . 24 . 9 . 9 = 1\,263\,600$$

Example

How many different arrangements, taking 3 letters at a time, can be formed from the word *P H O E N I X*

Solution:

Represent each choice with a box. We only use 3 boxes because our choice is restricted to 3 letters at a time.

$$\boxed{7} . \boxed{6} . \boxed{5} = 7 . 6 . 5 = 210$$

Example

How many different five digit numbers can be formed from the digits, 1, 2, 3, 4 and 5, if no digit can be repeated and:

(i)   there are no restrictions on digits

(ii) the number is odd

(iii) the number is even

(iv) the number is greater than 30 000

Solution:

Represent each choice with a box.

(i) no restrictions

$$\boxed{5}.\boxed{4}.\boxed{3}.\boxed{2}.\boxed{1}$$

$$= 5.4.3.2.1 = 120$$

(ii) must be odd.

Thus, the last place can be filled in only 3 ways (1, 3 or 5). Fill this in first, then fill in the other places.

$$\boxed{4}.\boxed{3}.\boxed{2}.\boxed{1}.\boxed{3}$$

$$= 4.3.2.1.3 = 72$$

1, 2, 3, 4 / 5

(iii) must be even.

Thus, the last place can be filled in only 2 ways (2 or 4). Fill this in first, then fill in the other places.

$$\boxed{4}.\boxed{3}.\boxed{2}.\boxed{1}.\boxed{2}$$

$$= 4.3.2.1.2 = 48$$

(iv) must be greater than 30 000. Thus, the first place can be filled in only 3 ways (3, 4 or 5). Fill this in first, then fill in the other places.

$$\boxed{3}.\boxed{4}.\boxed{3}.\boxed{2}.\boxed{1}$$

$$= 3.4.3.2.1 = 72$$

Factorial Notation

The product of all whole numbers from 1 to n is called factorial n, and is denoted by $n!$

Thus: $n! = n(n-1)(n-2)(n-3) .... 3.2.1$

The shorthand used is to write an exclamation mark after the number.

For example:

$1! = 1$

$2! = 2.1 = 2$

$3! = 3.2.1 = 6$

$4! = 4.3.2.1 = 24$

$5! = 5.4.3.2.1 = 120$, etc.

You can also use the $\boxed{n!}$ button on your calculator.

Example

(i) Evaluate $\dfrac{9!}{6!4!}$

(ii) If $k6! = 6! + 7!$, find the value of k.

Solution:

(i) $\dfrac{9!}{6!4!} = \dfrac{362\ 880}{(720)\ (24)} = \dfrac{362\ 880}{17\ 280} = 21$

(ii) $k6! = 6! + 7!$

   $\Rightarrow \quad k(720) = 720 + 5040$

   $\Rightarrow \quad 720k = 5760$

   $\Rightarrow \quad\quad k = 8$

Combinations

A combination is a selection where the order is not important.

$\binom{n}{r}$ gives the number of ways of choosing r items from n different items.

Thus, n = the number of items we have to choose from.

         r = the number of items we choose.

In short: $\binom{n}{r} = \binom{\text{Have}}{\text{Choose}}$

Before attempting a problem on combinations it is good practice to write down the values of n (number we have to choose from) and r (the number we choose).

Example

Seven people take part in a chess competition. How many games will be played if each person must play each of the others?

Solution:

We **have** 7 people to choose from, of whom we want to **choose** 2 (as 2 people play in each game).

Thus, $n = 7$, $r = 2$

$$\binom{7}{2} = \frac{7 \cdot 6}{2 \cdot 1} \begin{array}{l} \rightarrow \text{ Start at 7, go down two terms} \\ \rightarrow \text{ Start at 2, go down two terms} \end{array}$$

$$= \frac{42}{2} = 21$$

Example

Ten points are taken on the circumference of a circle (as shown). A chord is a line segment joining any two of these points. Calculate the number of such chords that can be drawn. With these points as vertices, how many triangles can be drawn?

Solution:

Number of chords.	Number of triangles.
We have 10 points.	We have 10 points.
Each chord uses 2 points.	Each triangle uses 3 points.
Thus, $n = 10$, $r = 2$	Thus, $n = 10$, $r = 3$

$$\binom{10}{2} = \frac{10 \cdot 9}{2 \cdot 1} = \frac{90}{2} = 45$$

$$\binom{10}{3} = \frac{10 \cdot 9 \cdot 8}{3 \cdot 2 \cdot 1} = \frac{720}{6} = 120$$

$\therefore$ number of chords is 45

$\therefore$ number of triangles is 120

Example

In how many ways can a selection of 5 books be made from 12?

(a) If a certain book must always be chosen, in how many ways can the selection be made?

(b) If a certain book must never be chosen, in how many ways can the selection be made?

Solution:

We **have** 12 books, of which we want to **choose** 5.

Thus, $n = 12$, $r = 5$.

$$\binom{12}{5} = \frac{12 \cdot 11 \cdot 10 \cdot 9 \cdot 8}{5 \cdot 4 \cdot 3 \cdot 2 \cdot 1} = \frac{95\,040}{120} = 792$$

(a) A certain book must always be one of the five.

$\therefore$ we **have** 11 books, of which we want to **choose** 4 (already chosen one).

Thus, $n = 11$, $r = 4$

$$\binom{11}{4} = \frac{11 \cdot 10 \cdot 9 \cdot 8}{4 \cdot 3 \cdot 2 \cdot 1} = \frac{7\,920}{24} = 330$$

(b) A certain book must never be one of the five.

$\therefore$ We **have** 11 books, of which we want to **choose** 5.

Thus $n = 11$, $r = 5$

$$\binom{11}{5} = \frac{11 \cdot 10 \cdot 9 \cdot 8 \cdot 7}{5 \cdot 4 \cdot 3 \cdot 2 \cdot 1} = \frac{55\,440}{120} = 462$$

Probability

Laws of Probability

1.	$p(E) = \dfrac{\text{no. of desirable outcomes}}{\text{no. of possible outcomes}}$
2.	$0 \le p(E) \le 1$ i.e. answer must be between 0 and 1.
3.	$p(A \text{ and } B) = p(A) \cdot p(B)$ (Key word: And $\Rightarrow$ Multiply)
4.	$p(A \text{ or } B) = p(A) + p(B) - p(A \text{ and } B)$ (Key word: Or $\Rightarrow$ Add)
5.	$p(E) + p(\text{not } E) = 1$ Very useful in the 'at least one' type of problem $p(\text{at least once}) = 1 - p(\text{does not happen at all})$

Example

A letter is selected at random from the letters of the word $MISSISSIPPI$.

Find the probability that the letter is:

(i) M **(ii)** S or P **(iii)** a vowel

Solution:

There are 11 letters in the word $MISSISSIPPI$.

(i) There is just one M

$\therefore p(M) = \frac{1}{11}$

(ii) There are 4 S's and 2 P's (6 altogether)

$\therefore p(S \text{ or } P) = \frac{6}{11}$

(iii) There is just one vowel, I. However, I occurs 4 times.

$\therefore p(\text{vowel}) = p(I) = \frac{4}{11}$

Example

There are 40 people in a club, 24 male, 16 female.

Four of the males and two of the females wear glasses.

When a person is selected at random what is the probability that the person is a:

(i) male?

(ii) female not wearing glasses?

(iii) female wearing glasses or a male not wearing glasses?

(iv) male, given that the person wears glasses?

Solution:

Represent the information with a table:

	Male	Female
Glasses	4	2
No Glasses	20	14

40 persons altogether.

(i) There are 24 males

$\therefore p(\text{male}) = \frac{24}{40} = \frac{3}{5}$

(ii) There are 14 females not wearing glasses.

$\therefore p(\text{female not wearing glasses}) = \frac{14}{40} = \frac{7}{20}$

(iii) There are 2 females wearing glasses and 20 males not wearing glasses.

$\therefore p(\text{female wearing glasses or a male not wearing glasses}) = \frac{22}{40} = \frac{11}{20}$

(iv) We are told that the person chosen wears glasses.

6 persons wear glasses, 4 males wear glasses.

$\therefore p(\text{male, given that the person wear glasses})$

$= \dfrac{\text{number of males wearing glasses}}{\text{number of persons wearing glasses}} = \frac{4}{6} = \frac{2}{3}$

Example

A coin and a die are thrown.

Write down the probability of obtaining:

(i) a tail and an odd number

(ii) a head or a number ≥ 5.

Solution:

Method 1: Using two-way tables.

There are 12 possible outcomes (6 for the die, 2 for the coin, $6 \times 2 = 12$)

(i)

T	•		•		•	
H						
	1	2	3	4	5	6

p(a tail and an odd number) $= \frac{3}{12} = \frac{1}{4}$

Method 2: Using the laws of probability

(i) p(a tail and an odd number)   [Key word 'and' $\therefore$ use multiplication law]

$= p$(a tail) $.\ p$ (odd number)

$= \frac{1}{2} \cdot \frac{1}{2}$

$= \frac{1}{4}$

(ii)

T					•	•
H	•	•	•	•	•	•
	1	2	3	4	5	6

p(a head or a number ≥ 5) $= \frac{8}{12} = \frac{2}{3}$

(ii) p(a head or a number ≥ 5)   [Key word 'or' $\therefore$ use addition law]

$= p$(head) $+ p$(number ≥ 5) $- p$(head and a number ≥ 5).

$= \frac{1}{2} + \frac{2}{6} - \frac{2}{12}$ ———————→ a head and a number ≥ 5 occurs twice

$= \frac{6}{12} + \frac{4}{12} - \frac{2}{12}$ i.e. $(H, 5)$ and $(H, 6)$

These were counted twice,

$= \frac{8}{12} = \frac{2}{3}$ thus we subtract $\frac{2}{12}$

Example

A bag contains 5 red and 3 yellow discs only. When a disc is drawn from the bag, it is returned before the next draw. What is the probability that two draws will yield

(i) both discs yellow?

(ii) both discs the same colour?

Solution:

Method 1:

Using the laws of probability. There are 8 discs altogether.

p(red) $= \frac{5}{8}$ p(yellow) $= \frac{3}{8}$

(i) p(both discs yellow) $= p$(yellow and then a yellow)

$= p$(yellow) $.\ p$(yellow)

$= \frac{3}{8} \cdot \frac{3}{8} = \frac{9}{64}$

(ii) If the two discs are the same colour we could get, a yellow and then a yellow **or** a red and then a red

p(both discs the same colour)

$= p$(both discs yellow) $+ p$(both discs red)

$= p$(yellow) $\cdot p$(yellow) $+ p$(red) $\cdot p$(red)

$= \dfrac{3}{8} \cdot \dfrac{3}{8} + \dfrac{5}{8} \cdot \dfrac{5}{8}$

$= \dfrac{9}{64} + \dfrac{25}{64} = \dfrac{34}{64} = \dfrac{17}{32}$

Method 2: Using two-way tables:

There are 64 possible outcomes ($8 \times 8 = 64$).

(i)

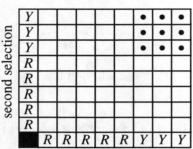

first selection

p(both yellow discs) $= \dfrac{9}{64}$

(ii)

second selection

					•	•	•
Y					•	•	•
Y					•	•	•
Y					•	•	•
R	•	•	•	•	•			
R	•	•	•	•	•			
R	•	•	•	•	•			
R	•	•	•	•	•			
R	•	•	•	•	•			

R R R R R Y Y Y

first selection

p(both discs the same colour)

$= \dfrac{34}{64} = \dfrac{17}{32}$

Example

Two unbiased dice are thrown, one red and the other black, and the scores are added.

The faces of the red die are numbered 1, 2, 3, 4, 5 and 6.

The faces of the black die are numbered 1, 1, 2, 3, 3 and 4.

Find the probability of obtaining:

(i) a score of 5 **(ii)** a score of 6 or more **(iii)** a score less than 4.

Solution:

Make out a two-way table:

	①	②	③	④	⑤	⑥
④	5	6	7	8	9	10
③	4	5	6	7	8	9
③	4	5	6	7	8	9
②	3	4	5	6	7	8
①	2	3	4	5	6	7
①	2	3	4	5	6	7

black die

red die

There are 36 possible outcomes
$(6 \times 6 = 36)$

(i) $p(\text{a score of 5}) = \frac{6}{36} = \frac{1}{6}$

(ii) $p(\text{a score of 6 or more}) = \frac{20}{36} = \frac{5}{9}$

(iii) $p(\text{a score less than 4}) = \frac{5}{36}$

Example

A game consists of spinning an unbiased arrow on a square board and throwing an unbiased die.

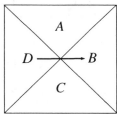

The board contains the letters A, B, C and D. The board is so designed that when the arrow stops spinning it can only point at one letter and it is equally likely to point at A or B or C or D.

List all possible outcomes of the game, that is, of spinning the arrow and throwing the die. Find the probability that in any one game the outcome will be:

(i) an A and a 6

(ii) a B and an even number

(iii) an A and an even number or a B and an odd number

(iv) a C and a number ≥ 4 or a D and a number ≤ 2

Solution:

Method 1: Make out a two-way table for each question.

There are 24 possible outcomes (6 numbers, 4 letters, $6 \times 4 = 24$)

(i)

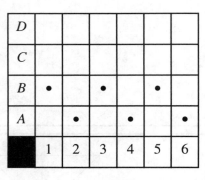

$$p(\text{an } A \text{ and a } 6) = \frac{1}{24}$$

(ii)

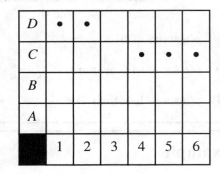

$$p(\text{a } B \text{ and an even number}) = \frac{3}{24} = \frac{1}{8}$$

(iii)

$$p\left(\begin{array}{c}\text{an } A \text{ and an even number or}\\ \text{a } B \text{ and an odd number}\end{array}\right) = \frac{6}{24} = \frac{1}{4}$$

(iv)

$$p\left(\begin{array}{c}\text{a } C \text{ and a number} \ge 4 \text{ or}\\ \text{a } D \text{ and a number} \le 2\end{array}\right) = \frac{5}{24}$$

Method 2:   Write out al the possible couples (number, letter).

(1, A)	(1, B)	(1, C)	(1, D)
(2, A)	(2, B)	(2, C)	(2, D)
(3, A)	(3, B)	(3, C)	(3, D)
(4, A)	(4, B)	(4, C)	(4, D)
(5, A)	(5, B)	(5, C)	(5, D)
(6, A)	(6, B)	(6, C)	(6, D)

There are 24 couples.

(i) $p(\text{an } A \text{ and a } 6) = \frac{1}{24}$

(ii) $p(\text{a } B \text{ and an even number}) = \frac{3}{24} = \frac{1}{8}$

(iii) $p\left(\begin{array}{c}\text{an } A \text{ and an even number or}\\ \text{a } B \text{ and an odd number}\end{array}\right) = \frac{6}{24} = \frac{1}{4}$

(iv) $p\left(\begin{array}{c}\text{a } C \text{ and a number} \ge 4 \text{ or}\\ \text{a } D \text{ and a number} \le 2\end{array}\right) = \frac{5}{24}$

Be careful if after the first selection there is no replacement, as in the next example.

Example

A girl selects two different numbers at random, one after another without replacement, from the whole numbers 1, 2, 3, 4 and 5 and uses these to form a two digit number in the order in which she selects them.

(i) How many outcomes are possible?

(ii) Calculate the probability that the sum of the numbers is less than 7.

Solution:

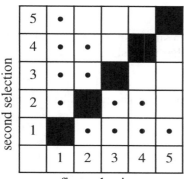

first selection

The shaded regions indicate you can't pick the same number again if it was chosen on the first choice. There are 20 blank spaces, hence there are 20 possible outcomes.

The dots indicate where the two numbers added together are less than 7.

There are 12 dots.

(i) There are 20 possible outcomes.

(ii) p(total is less than 7) $= \frac{12}{20} = \frac{3}{5}$

Example

A bag contains 20 identical marbles, except for colour, 8 of which are white and the remainder black.

Three marbles are removed at random, one at a time, without replacement.

Find the probability that:

(i) all are black   **(ii)** at least one is white

Solution:

(i) There are 20 identical marbles, 8 white, 12 black.

p(1st black) $= \frac{12}{20}$

p(2nd black $= \frac{11}{19}$ (as one black marble has been removed)

p(3rd black) $= \frac{10}{18}$ (as two black marbles have been removed)

p(all black) $= p$(1st black) . p(2nd black) . p(3rd black)

$$= \frac{12}{20} \times \frac{11}{19} \times \frac{10}{18}$$

$$= \frac{11}{57}$$

(ii) $p(\text{at least one white}) = 1 - p(\text{none are white})$

$$\downarrow$$

$$= 1 - p(\text{all black})$$

$$= 1 - \frac{11}{57}$$

$$= \frac{46}{57}$$

Example

The probability that a woman will hit the target with a single shot at a rifle range is $\frac{2}{5}$. Find the probability that she first hits the target with her third shot.

Solution:

$p(\text{hit}) + p(\text{miss}) = 1$ (either she hits the target or she misses it)

$$p(\text{hit}) = \frac{2}{5}$$

$$p(\text{miss}) = 1 - p(\text{hit}) = 1 - \frac{2}{5} = \frac{3}{5}$$

$p(\text{she first hits the target on the third shot})$

$= p(\text{misses on 1st shot}) \cdot p(\text{misses on 2nd shot}) \cdot p(\text{hits target on 3rd shot})$

$$= \frac{3}{5} \times \frac{3}{5} \times \frac{2}{5} = \frac{18}{125}$$

12. STATISTICS

Mean and Standard Deviation of an Array of Numbers

$$\text{Mean} = \bar{x} = \frac{\Sigma x}{n}$$

$$\text{Standard Deviation} = \sigma = \sqrt{\frac{\Sigma d^2}{n}}$$
where $d = |x - \bar{x}|$

n is the number of values of x.

Example

Calculate **(i)** the mean and **(ii)** the standard deviation, correct to two decimal places, of the following array of numbers 2, 5, 6, 8, 10, 11.

Solution:

(i) $\text{Mean} = \bar{x} = \frac{\Sigma x}{n} = \frac{2 + 5 + 6 + 8 + 10 + 11}{6} = \frac{42}{6} = 7$

(ii) Make out a table:

x	d	d^2
2	5	25
5	2	4
6	1	1
8	1	1
10	3	9
11	4	16
		56

$d = |x - \bar{x}|$

$$\sigma = \sqrt{\frac{\Sigma d^2}{n}} = \sqrt{\frac{56}{6}} = \sqrt{9 \cdot 3333333} = 3 \cdot 06$$

Example

The mean of eight numbers is 9. When one of the numbers is taken away the mean is increased by 1. Find the number that was taken away.

Solution:

Old Situation	**New Situation**
The mean of the 8 numbers is 9.	The mean of the remaining 7 numbers is 10.
∴ the numbers must add up to 72.	∴ the numbers must add up to 70.
i.e. $\dfrac{72}{8} = 9$	i.e. $\dfrac{70}{7} = 10$

$$72 - 70 = 2$$

∴ the number taken away was 2.

Mean and Standard Deviation of a Frequency Distribution

$$\text{Mean} = \bar{x} = \frac{\Sigma f x}{\Sigma f}$$

$$\sigma = \sqrt{\frac{\Sigma f d^2}{\Sigma f}}$$

where $d = |x - \bar{x}|$

f is the frequency attached to each value of x.

Example

20 pupils were given a problem to solve. The following grouped frequency distribution table gives the number of pupils who solved the problem in the given time interval.

Time (minutes)	0 – 4	4 – 12	12 – 24	24 – 40
Frequency	3	8	7	2

Assuming the data can be taken at the mid-interval values, calculate:

(i) the mean   **(ii)** the standard deviation, correct to 2 places of decimals.

Solution:

The table can be re-written using the mid-interval values.

Time (minutes)	2	8	18	32
Frequency	3	8	7	2

(i) Mean $= \bar{x} = \dfrac{\Sigma fx}{\Sigma f} = \dfrac{3(2) + 8(8) + 7(18) + 2(32)}{3 + 8 + 7 + 2}$

$$= \dfrac{6 + 64 + 126 + 64}{20} = \dfrac{260}{20} = 13$$

(ii) Make out a table:

f	x	d	d^2	fd^2
3	2	11	121	363
8	8	5	25	200
7	18	5	25	175
2	32	19	361	722
20				1 460

$d = |x - \bar{x}|$

$$\sigma = \sqrt{\dfrac{\Sigma f d^2}{\Sigma f}} = \sqrt{\dfrac{1\,460}{20}} = \sqrt{73} = 8{\cdot}54$$

Weighted Mean

$$\text{Weighted mean} = \bar{x}_w = \frac{\Sigma wx}{\Sigma w}$$

w is the weight attached to each value of x.

Example

Subject	Physics	Chemistry	Mathematics	Irish
Mark	74	65	82	58
Weight	3	4	5	2

The table shows a student's marks and the weights given to these marks.

Calculate the weighted mean mark for the student.

Solution:

$$\text{Weighted mean} = \bar{x}_w = \frac{\Sigma wx}{\Sigma w} = \frac{3(74) + 4(65) + 5(82) + 2(58)}{3 + 4 + 5 + 2}$$

$$= \frac{222 + 260 + 410 + 116}{14}$$

$$= \frac{1\,008}{14}$$

$$= 72$$

Thus, the student had a weighted mean mark of 72.

Given the Mean

Often we are given the mean and we need to find one of the values or frequencies. Basically, we are given an equation in disguise. We use this equation to find the missing value or frequency.

Example

The table below shows the frequency of 0, 1, 2 or 3 goals scored in a number of football matches:

Number of goals scored	0	1	2	3
Number of matches	1	x	1	5

If the mean number of goals scored per match is 2, find the value of x.

The area (frequencies) are circled in each rectangle.

Completed table:

Distances (km)	0 – 2	2 – 4	4 – 8	8 – 14	14 – 16	16 – 24
No. of Students	16	10	8	24	12	56

Total number of students = 16 + 10 + 8 + 24 + 12 + 56 = 126

Cumulative Frequency Distribution

In a cumulative frequency distribution the frequencies are accumulated. Each accumulated frequency is the combined total of all the previous frequencies up to that particular value. If we fill in the accumulated frequencies in tabular form we have what is called a cumulative **frequency distribution table**.

The graph of a cumulative frequency distribution is called a **cumulative frequency curve** or **ogive**. We can use the curve to estimate the median and the interquartile range.

The following cumulative frequency curve shows how to estimate the median and the interquartile range.

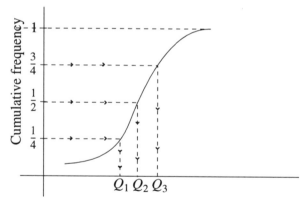

(i)　Median = Q_2

(ii)　Interquartile range = $Q_3 - Q_1$

Note:　If the data is given as a grouped frequency distribution always make sure the **upper class limits** are plotted against the cumulative frequencies.

Example

The table show the number of people who saved money in a School Credit Union.

€(20 – 40) means 20 is included but 40 is not, etc.

Amount Saved in €	0 – 20	20 – 40	40 – 60	60 – 80	80 – 100	100 – 120
Number of People	10	24	44	32	22	8

Construct a cumulative frequency table. Draw a cumulative frequency curve.

Use the curve to estimate

(i) the median amount of money saved per person, correct to the nearest €.

(ii) the interquartile range.

Solution:

Cumulative frequency table:

Amount Saved in €	< 20	< 40	< 60	< 80	< 100	< 120
Number of People	10	34	78	110	132	140

Cumulative frequency curve:

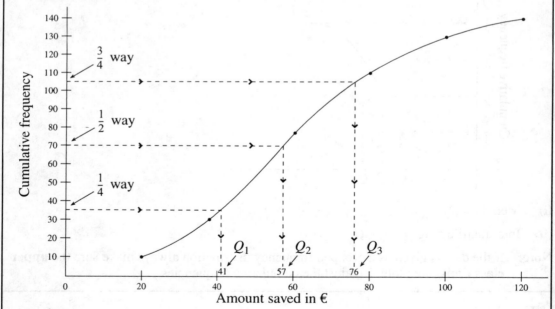

(i) Median = Q_2 = €57

(ii) Interquartile range = $Q_3 - Q_1$ = €76 – €41 = €35

A cumulative frequency curve can be used to estimate the number of values that lie **below**, or **above**, a particular value or to estimate the number of values that lie **between** two values. Consider the next example.

Example

The cumulative frequency table below shows the marks obtained by 100 students in a school test.

Marks	≤ 20	≤ 40	≤ 60	≤ 80	≤ 100
Cumulative Frequency	9	19	57	92	100

Draw a cumulative frequency curve.

(i) Use the curve to estimate the number of students who got less than 50 marks.

(ii) The school decides that the 15 highest marked students will each receive a prize.

Use the curve to estimate the least mark a student must obtain in order to qualify for a prize.

(iii) Complete the corresponding frequency table:

Marks	0 – 20	20 – 40	40 – 60	60 – 80	80 – 100
No. of students					

Solution:

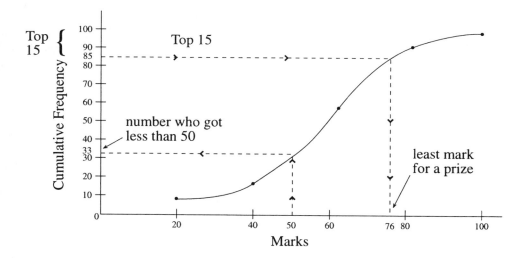

213

(i) Number of students who got less than 50 marks = 33

(ii) Least mark for a prize = 76

(iii) Grouped frequency table:

When the cumulative frequency table was constructed the frequencies were added.

Therefore, to return to the frequency table we simply do the reverse, **subtract the frequencies**.

$80 - 100 : 100 - 92 = 8$ $60 - 80 : 92 - 57 = 35$

$40 - 60 : 57 - 19 = 38$ $20 - 40 : 19 - 9 = 10$

$0 - 20 : = 9$ (remains the same)

Marks	0 – 20	20 – 40	40 – 60	60 – 80	80 – 100
No. of students	9	10	38	35	8

13. LINEAR INEQUALITIES AND LINEAR PROGRAMMING

Linear Inequalities

To graph the region (half-plane) represented by a linear inequality of the form $ax + by \geq k$ or $ax + by \leq k$ do the following:

> **Step 1:** Graph the line $ax + by = k$ by finding two points on the line, and drawing a line through these points.
>
> The usual points are where the line cuts the X and Y axes.
>
> (**Remember:** on the X axis $y = 0$, on the Y axis $x = 0$)
>
> **Step 2:** Test a point not on the line, usually $(0, 0)$, in the inequality.
>
>   **(a)**   If the inequality is **true** the arrows point towards the point being tested.
>
>   **(b)**   If the inequality is **false** the arrows point away from the point being tested.

Example

Graph the inequality $3x + 2y \geq 12$, indicating the correct half-plane.

Solution:

Step 1: Graph the line $3x + 2y = 12$

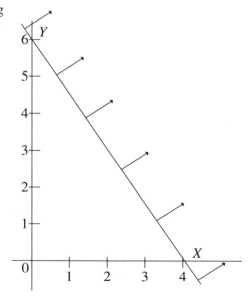

$$3x + 2y = 12$$

$y = 0$	$x = 0$
$3x = 12$	$2y = 12$
$x = 4$	$y = 6$
$(4, 0)$	$(0, 6)$

Plot the points $(4, 0)$ and $(0, 6)$ and draw a line through them.

Step 2: Test $(0, 0)$ in $3x + 2y \geq 12$

$$3(0) + 2(0) \geq 12$$

$$0 \geq 12 \text{ false}$$

$(0, 0)$ does not satisfy the inequality, hence, the set of all the points on the opposite side of the line to $(0, 0)$, indicated by arrows in the diagram, is the required region.

Note: If a line passes through the origin, $(0, 0)$, the intercept method of drawing the line will not work. If this happens, choose a suitable value for x (e.g. the coefficient of y) and find the corresponding value of y, or vice versa.

Consider the next example.

Example

Graph the solution set of $x - 3y \geq 0$, indicating the correct half-plane.

Solution:

Step 1: Graph the line $x - 3y = 0$.

One point on this line is $(0, 0)$ as there is no constant term.

Let $x = 3$ (coefficient of y)

$x - 3y = 0$
↓
$3 - 3y = 0$ (put in 3 for x)

$-3y = -3$

$3y = 3$

$y = 1$

point $(3, 1)$

Plot the points $(0, 0)$ and $(3, 1)$ and draw a line through them.

Step 2: Test $(2, 0)$, which is not on the line, in $x - 3y \geq 0$

$$2 - 3(0) \geq 0$$

$$2 \geq 0 \text{ True}$$

$(2, 0)$ satisfies the inequality, hence, the set of all the points on the same side of the line as $(2, 0)$, indicated by the arrows in the diagram, is the required region.

Sometimes we are given the graph of a linear inequality and asked to write down, algebraically, the region that the inequality represents.

When this happens do the following:

Step 1: Find the equation of the line in the form $ax + by + c = 0$ (if not given).

Step 2: Pick a point not on the line, $(0, 0)$ if possible, and decide if the point is in the region represented by the inequality.

Step 3: Put the coordinates of the point into the equation of the line.

Step 4: (a) If the point is in the region represented by the inequality keep the direction of the inequality sign found in Step 3.

   (b) If the point is not in the region represented by the inequality reverse the direction of the inequality sign found in Step 3.

Example

Write down the inequity which defines the region indicated by the arrows.

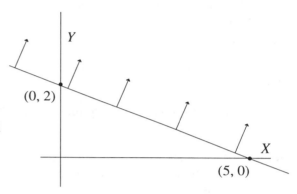

Solution:

Step 1: Find the equation of the line.

Since the slope is missing, we first find the slope and use **either** point with this slope to find the equation.

$(5, 0)$ $(0, 2)$

(x_1, y_1) (x_2, y_2)

$$m = \frac{y_2 - y_1}{x_2 - x_1}$$

$$= \frac{2 - 0}{0 - 5}$$

$$= \frac{2}{-5}$$

$$= -\frac{2}{5}$$

$\therefore$ slope of line is $-\frac{2}{5}$

containing $(5, 0)$ with slope $-\frac{2}{5}$

$x_1 = 5$ $y_1 = 0$ $m = -\frac{2}{5}$

$$(y - y_1) = m(x - x_1)$$

$$(y - 0) = -\frac{2}{5}(x - 5)$$

$$5(y - 0) = -2(x - 5)$$

(multiply both sides by 5)

$$5y = -2x + 10$$

$$2x + 5y - 10 = 0$$

Step 2: $(0, 0)$ is not on the line and is **not** in the region represented by the arrows.

Step 3: Test $(0, 0)$ in $2x + 5y - 10 = 0$

$$2(0) + 5(0) - 10$$

$$= 0 + 0 + -10$$

$$= -10 < 0$$

217

Step 4: As (0, 0) is not in the required region we reverse the direction of the inequality sign found in Step 3.

Thus, the required inequality is: $2x + 5y - 10 \geq 0$

Example

The equation of the line M is $x - y + 1 = 0$ and the equation of the line N is $x + y - 6 = 0$.

Write down the three inequalities which define the triangular region indicated in the diagram.

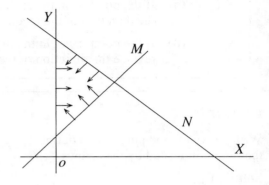

Solution:

The first inequality is $x \geq 0$, i.e. on the Y axis and to the right.

Step 1: Given the equation of the line.

    M: $x - y + 1 = 0$

Step 2: (0, 0) is not on the line and is **not** in the region represented by the arrows.

Step 3: Test (0, 0) in $x - y + 1 = 0$

    $0 - 0 + 1$

    $= 1 > 0$

Step 4: As (0, 0) is not in the required region we reverse the direction of the inequality sign in Step 3.

Thus, the required inequality is:

    $x - y + 1 \leq 0$

Step 1: Given the equation of the line.

    N: $x + y - 6 = 0$

Step 2: (0, 0) is not on the line and is in the region represented by the arrows.

Step 3: Test (0, 0) in $x + y - 6 = 0$

    $0 + 0 - 6$

    $= -6 < 0$

Step 4: As (0, 0) is in the required region we keep the direction of the inequality sign found in Step 3.

Thus, the required inequality is:

    $x + y - 6 \leq 0$

Thus, the three required inequalities are:

$x \geq 0$, $x - y + 1 \leq 0$ and $x + y - 6 \leq 0$

Maximising and Minimising

Often it is required to find a region which is common to more than one inequality. This common region is often called the 'feasible region'. Having found the common region of three or more inequalities we may be asked to find the coordinates of the point that will give the maximum or minimum value in the region according to a given rule.

The following is very important:

> The maximum and minimum values of a region bounded by straight lines will **always** occur at one of the vertices of the region.

The maximum or minimum value of the common region is found with the following steps:

> **Step 1:** Do all the calculations to draw the lines and determine the direction of the arrows.
>
> **Step 2:** Draw a diagram and shade in the common region and label each vertex.
>
> **Step 3:** Find the coordinates of the vertices of the common region using simultaneous equations (do not read from your graph). However, any vertex which lies on the X or Y axis can be written down from the graph. Put in the coordinates of each vertex on your diagram.
>
> **Step 4:** Substitute the coordinates of the vertices of the common region into the given rule, using a table, to find the maximum or minimum values.

Example

Using the same axes and scales and taking $x, y \in R$ graph each of the following half-planes:

$A = \{(x, y)|y \geq 0\}$

$B = \{(x, y)|x + 2y \leq 140\}$

$C = \{(x, y)|5x + 4y \geq 400\}$

Indicate the set of points $D = A \cap B \cap C$.

Calculate the coordinates of the vertices of D (it is not sufficient to read these coordinates from your graph).

Find the couple $(x, y) \in D$ for which $30x + 10y$ is a maximum and write down this maximum.

Solution:

Step 1: A: $y \geq 0$, this is the set of points on and above the X axis.

$\therefore$ arrows on the X axis and pointing upwards.

B: $x + 2y \leq 140$	C: $5x + 4y \geq 400$

Line : $x + 2y = 140$

$$x + 2y = 140$$

$y = 0$	$x = 0$
$x = 140$	$2y = 140$
	$y = 70$
(140, 0)	(0, 70)

Test (0, 0) in $x + 2y \leq 140$

$$(0) + 2(0) \leq 140$$

$$0 \leq 140 \text{ True}$$

∴ arrows point towards (0, 0)

Line : $5x + 4y = 400$

$$5x + 4y = 400$$

$y = 0$	$x = 0$
$5x = 400$	$4y = 400$
$x = 80$	$y = 100$
(80, 0)	(0, 100)

Test (0, 0) in $5x + 4y \geq 400$

$$5(0) + 4(0) \geq 400$$

$$0 \geq 400 \text{ False}$$

∴ arrows point away from (0, 0)

Step 2:

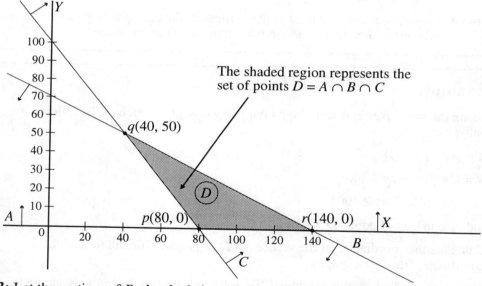

The shaded region represents the set of points $D = A \cap B \cap C$

Step 3: Let the vertices of D, the shaded region, be p, q and r (as shown).

We have already shown that $p = (80, 0)$ and $r = (140, 0)$.

We now solve the simultaneous equations $x + 2y = 140$ and $5x + 4y = 400$ to find the coordinates of q.

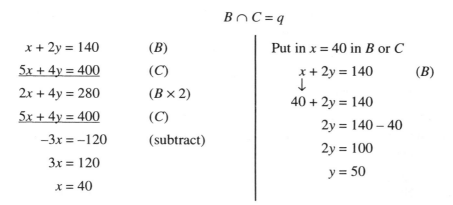

$$B \cap C = q$$

$x + 2y = 140$ (B)	Put in $x = 40$ in B or C
$5x + 4y = 400$ (C)	$x + 2y = 140$ (B)
$2x + 4y = 280$ (B × 2)	↓
$5x + 4y = 400$ (C)	$40 + 2y = 140$
$-3x = -120$ (subtract)	$2y = 140 - 40$
$3x = 120$	$2y = 100$
$x = 40$	$y = 50$

Thus, the coordinates of q are (40, 50).

Thus, the coordinates of D are p(80, 0), q(40, 50) and r(140, 0).

Step 4: Using a table, the coordinates of p, q and r are substituted, separately, into $30x + 10y$, to find the maximum value.

Vertex	$30x$	$10y$	$30x + 10y$	
p(80, 0)	2 400	0	2 400	
q(40, 50)	1 200	500	1 700	
r(140, 0)	4 200	0	4 200	← Maximum value

4 200 is the maximum value of $30x + 10y$ and it occurs at (140, 0).

Linear Programming

Linear inequalities can be used to solve practical problems. When used in this way we call it **Linear Programming**. Linear programming deals with trying to find the best solution, usually the maximum or minimum, to a wide range of problems within certain limitations called **constraints**. When solving a problem in linear programming, read the question carefully a few times and do the following:

1. Let x equal one unknown number and let y equal the other unknown number that is required (unless given in the question).

2. Using the information in the question convert the constraints into linear inequalities in terms of x and y (using a table can be useful).

3. Graph each of the inequalities and shade in the feasible region.

4. Find the coordinates of the vertices of this common region.

5. Write the objective function, the expression to be maximised or minimised, in terms of x and y.

6. Substitute, separately, the coordinates of the vertices of the feasible region (obtained in **Step 4**) into the objective function, using a table, to find the maximum or minimum values.

Note: In certain questions the inequalities $x \geq 0$ and $y \geq 0$ will be given in disguise. This is because in many cases it is physically impossible for x and y to be negative.

Example

A farmer has not more than $2\,000$ m^2 of ground for planting apple trees and blackcurrant bushes. The ground space required for an apple tree is 50 m^2 and for a blackcurrant bush is 5 m^2.

The planting of an apple tree costs €20 and the planting of a blackcurrant bush costs €4. The farmer has at most €1000 to spend on planting.

If the farmer plants x apple trees and y blackcurrant bushes, write two inequalities in x and y and illustrate these on graph paper.

When fully grown, each apple tree will produce a crop worth €90 and each blackcurrant bush a crop worth €15.

How many of each should be planted so that the farmer's gross income is a maximum?

Calculate the farmer's maximum profit.

Solution:

There are two constraints, space and costs.

Step 1: Given: x = number of apple trees and y = number of blackcurrant bushes.

Step 2: The inequalities given in disguise are $x \geq 0$ and $y \geq 0$.

(It is impossible to plant a negative number of trees or bushes.)

We use a table to help us to write down the other two inequalities.

	x	y	
Space	50	5	≤ 2000
Costs	20	4	≤ 1000

Space constraint: $50x + 5y \leq 2000$	Costs constraint: $20x + 4y \leq 1000$
$\Rightarrow \qquad 10x + y \leq 400$	$\Rightarrow \qquad 5x + y \leq 250$
(divide across by 5)	(divide across by 4)

The four inequalities are:

$x \geq 0, \qquad\qquad y \geq 0, \qquad\qquad 10x + y \leq 400, \qquad 5x + y \leq 250$ **True**

Step 3: $x \geq 0$, this is the set of points on and to the right of the Y axis.

$\therefore$ arrows on the Y axis and pointing right.

$y \geq 0$, this is the set of points on and above the X axis.

$\therefore$ arrow on the X axis and pointing upwards.

$10x + y \leq 400$	$5x + y \leq 250$
Line: $10x + y = 400$	Line: $5x + y = 250$

$10x + y = 400$

$y = 0$	$x = 0$
$10x = 400$	$y = 400$
$x = 40$	
$(40, 0)$	$(0, 400)$

$5x + y = 250$

$y = 0$	$x = 0$
$5x = 250$	$y = 250$
$x = 50$	
$(50, 0)$	$(0, 250)$

Test $(0, 0)$ in $10x + y \leq 400$

$\qquad 10(0) + (0) \leq 400$

$\qquad\qquad\qquad 0 \leq 400$ **True**

$\therefore$ arrows point towards $(0, 0)$

Test $(0, 0)$ in $5x + y \leq 250$

$\qquad 5(0) + (0) \leq 250$

$\qquad\qquad\qquad 0 \leq 250$

$\therefore$ arrows point towards $(0, 0)$

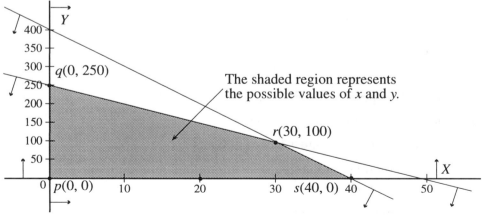

The shaded region represents the possible values of x and y.

Step 4: Let the vertices of the shaded region be p, q, r and s (as shown).

$p = (0, 0)$ and we have already shown that $q = (0, 250)$ and $s = (40, 0)$.

We now solve the simultaneous equations $10x + y = 400$ and $5x + y = 250$ to find the coordinates of r (cannot be read from the graph).

$10x + y = 400$

$\underline{5x + y = 250}$

$\Rightarrow \quad\quad 5x = 150 \quad\quad$ (subtract)

$\Rightarrow \quad\quad x = 30$

Put in $x = 30$ into one of the equations

$10x + y = 400$

$\downarrow$

$10(30) + y = 400 \quad$ (put in $x = 30$)

$\Rightarrow \quad 300 + y = 400$

$\Rightarrow \quad y = 400 - 300$

$\Rightarrow \quad y = 100$

Thus, the coordinates of r are $(30, 100)$.

Step 5: Gross income on each apple tree is €90 and on each blackberry bush is €15.

$\therefore$ the gross income will be €$(90x + 15y)$

$\therefore$ the objective function is $90x + 15y$

Step 6: Using a table, the coordinates of p, q, r and s are substituted, separately, into $90x + 15y$, to find the maximum gross income.

Vertex	$90x$	$15y$	$90x + 15y$	
$p(0, 0)$	0	0	0	
$q(0, 250)$	0	3 750	3 750	
$r(30, 100)$	2 700	1 500	4 200 ← maximum value	
$s(40, 0)$	3 600	0	3 600	

Thus, the farmer should plant 30 apple trees and 100 blackberry bushes in order to get a maximum gross income of €4 200.

Maximum Profit:

The cost of planting 30 apple trees = €20 × 30 = €600

The cost of planting 100 blackberry bushes = €4 × 100 = €400

Thus, the total cost = €600 + €400 = €1 000

Maximum profit = Maximum gross income – Costs

$\quad\quad\quad\quad$ = €4 200 – €1 000

$\quad\quad\quad\quad$ = €3 200

Thus, the maximum profit is €3 200.

Example

A ship has space for at most 200 containers, which are of two types – refrigerated and unrefrigerated. Each refrigerated container carries a load of 3 tonnes and each unrefrigerated container carries a load of 8 tonnes. The maximum load the ship can carry is 1 200 tonnes.

Freight charges on each refrigerated container are €100 and on each unrefrigerated container €80.

Graph the set showing the possible numbers of each type of container that the ship can carry. If operating costs on each journey amount to €14 000 indicate by the letter K that region of your graph where the ship is not operating at a loss. Calculate the maximum profit if a ready supply of each container is available and state the number of each type of container the ship should carry to achieve this maximum profit.

Solution:

There are two constraints, the number of containers and the total weight.

Step 1: Let x = number of refrigerated containers and
y = number of unrefrigerated containers.

Step 2: The inequalities given in disguise are $x \geq 0$ and $y \geq 0$

(It is impossible to have a negative number of containers.)

We use a table to write down the other two inequalities.

	x	y	
Number	1	1	≤ 200
Weight	3	8	$\leq 1\,200$

Number constraint: $x + y \leq 200$ Weight constraint: $3x + 8y \leq 1\,200$

Step 3: $x \geq 0$, this is the set of points on and to the right of the Y axis.

∴ arrows on the Y axis and pointing right.

$y \geq 0$, this is the set of points on and above the X axis.

∴ arrows on the X axis and pointing upwards.

$$x + y \leq 200$$
Line: $x + y = 200$

$$x + y = 200$$

$y = 0$	$x = 0$
$x = 200$	$y = 200$
$(200, 0)$	$(0, 200)$

Test $(0, 0)$ in $x + y \leq 200$

$$0 + 0 \leq 200$$

$$0 \leq 200 \text{ True}$$

∴ arrows point towards $(0, 0)$

$$3x + 8y \leq 1\,200$$
Line: $3x + 8y = 1\,200$

$$3x + 8y = 1\,200$$

$y = 0$	$x = 0$
$3x = 1200$	$8y = 1200$
$x = 400$	$y = 150$
$(400, 0)$	$(0, 150)$

Test $(0, 0)$ in $3x + 8y \leq 1\,200$

$$3(0) + 8(0) \leq 1\,200$$

$$0 \leq 1\,200 \text{ True}$$

∴ arrows point towards $(0, 0)$

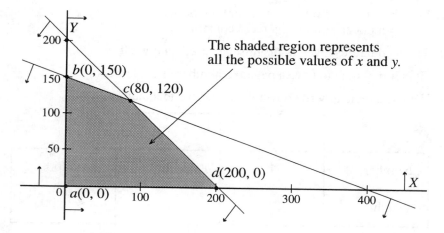

The shaded region represents all the possible values of x and y.

Step 4: Let the vertices of the shaded region be a, b, c and d (as shown).
$a = (0, 0)$ and we have already shown that $b = (0, 150)$ and $d = (200, 0)$.

We now solve the simultaneous equations $x + y = 200$ and $3x + 8y = 1\,200$ to find the coordinates of c (cannot be read from the graph).

$x + y = 200$ ①
$3x + 8y = 1\,200$ ②
$3x + 3y = 600$ ① × 3
$3x + 8y = 1\,200$ ②
$-5y = -600$ (subtract)
$5y = 600$
$y = 120$

Put in $y = 120$ into ① or ②
$x + y = 200$ ①
↓
$x + 120 = 200$
$x = 200 - 120$
$x = 80$

Thus, the coordinates of c are $(80, 120)$.

226

Step 5: Freight charges (income)

Freight charges on each refrigerated container are €100.

Freight charges on each unrefrigerated container are €80.

∴ Freight charges will be € $(100x + 80y)$

We require that the freight charges be at least €14 000,
i.e. Freight charges ≥ 14 000

∴ $\qquad 100x + 80y \geq 14\,000$

⇒ $\qquad 10x + 8y \geq 1\,400$

⇒ $\qquad 5x + 4y \geq 700$

We now graph the inequality $5x + 4y \geq 700$

Line: $5x + 4y = 700$		Test $(0, 0)$ in $5x + 4y \geq 700$

$5x + 4y = 700$		$5(0) + 4(0) \geq 700$
$y = 0$	$x = 0$	$0 \geq 700$ **False**
$5x = 700$	$4y = 700$	∴ arrows point away from $(0, 0)$
$x = 140$	$y = 175$	
$(140, 0)$	$(0, 175)$	

The region K, where the freight charges are at least €14 000, is indicated on the graph.

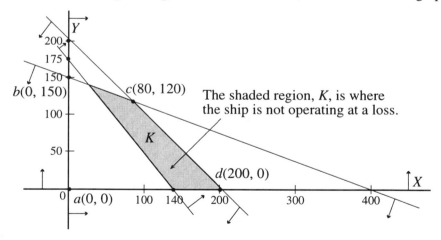

The shaded region, K, is where the ship is not operating at a loss.

227

Step 6: Using a table, the coordinates of a, b, c and d are substituted, separately, into $100x + 8y$, to find maximum income.

Vertex	$100x$	$80y$	$100x + 80y$
$a(0, 0)$	0	0	0
$b(0, 150)$	0	12 000	12 000
$c(80, 120)$	8 000	9 600	17 600
$d(200, 0)$	20 000	0	20 000 ← maximum income

Maximum profit = Maximum income − Costs
= €20 000 − €14 000 = €6 000

Thus, the maximum profit is €6 000 and this occurs when the ship carries 200 refrigerated containers and no unrefrigerated containers.

EXAM PAPERS

AN ROINN OIDEACHAIS AGUS EOLAÍOCHTA

LEAVING CERTIFICATE EXAMINATION, 2002

MATHEMATICS – ORDINARY LEVEL – PAPER 1 (300 marks)

THURSDAY, 6 JUNE – MORNING, 9.30 to 12.00

Attempt **SIX QUESTIONS** (50 marks each)

WARNING: Marks will be lost if all necessary work is not clearly shown.

---

1. **(a)** Copper and zinc are mixed in the ratio 19:6.
   The amount of copper used is 133 kg.
   How many kilogrammes of zinc are used?

   (b) Four telephone calls cost €3.85, €7.45, €8.40 and €11.55.

   (i) John estimates the total cost of the four calls by ignoring the cent part in the cost of each call. Calculate the percentage error in his estimate.

   (ii) Anne estimates the total cost of the four calls by rounding the cost of each call to the nearest euro. Calculate the percentage error in her estimate.

   (c) A raffle to raise money for a charity is being held.

   The first prize is €100, the second is €85, the third is €65 and the fourth is €50.

   The cost of printing tickets is €42 for the first 500 tickets and €6 for each additional 100 tickets. The smallest number of tickets that can be printed is 500.

   Tickets are being sold at €1.50 each.

   (i) What is the minimum possible cost of holding the raffle?

   (ii) If 500 tickets are printed, how many tickets must be sold in order to avoid a loss?

   (iii) If 1 000 tickets are printed and 65% of the tickets are sold, how much money will be raised for the charity?

2. **(a)** Solve for x

$$\frac{x-7}{2} = \frac{x+3}{6}.$$

   (b) **(i)** Show that $x + 2$ is a factor of $2x^3 + 7x^2 + x - 10$.

   (ii) Hence, or otherwise, find the three roots of $2x^3 + 7x^2 + x - 10 = 0$.

   (c) **(i)** Express b in terms of a and c where $\dfrac{8a - 5b}{b} = c$.

   (ii) Hence, or otherwise, evaluate b when $a = 2^{\frac{5}{2}}$ and $c = 3^3$.

3. **(a)** Solve the inequality $5x + 1 \geqslant 4x - 3$ for $x \in \mathbf{R}$ and illustrate the solution set on a number line.

(b) **(i)** Solve for x and y

$$y = 10 - 2x$$
$$x^2 + y^2 = 25.$$

(ii) Hence, find the two possible values of $x^3 + y^3$.

(c) Let $f(x) = x^2 + ax + t$ where $a, t = \mathbf{R}$.

(i) Find the value of a, given that $f(-5) = f(-1)$.

(ii) Given that there is only one value of x for which $f(x) = 0$, find the value of t.

4. **(a)** Given that $i^2 = -1$, simplify

$$2(3 - i) + i(4 + 5i)$$

and write your answer in the form $x + yi$ where $x, y \in \mathbf{R}$.

(b) Let $z = 5 + 4i$.

(i) Plot z and $\bar{z}$ on an Argand diagram, where $\bar{z}$ is the complex conjugate of z.

(ii) Calculate $z\bar{z}$.

(iii) Express $\dfrac{z}{\bar{z}}$ in the form $u + vi$ where $u, v \in \mathbf{R}$.

(c) p and k are real numbers such that $p(2 + i) + 8 - ki = 5k - 3 - i$.

(i) Find the value of p and the value of k.

(ii) Investigate if $p + ki$ is a root of the equation $z^2 - 4z + 13 = 0$.

5. **(a)** Write down the next three terms in each of the following arithmetic sequences

(i) $-10, -8, -6, \ldots\ldots$

(ii) $4.1, 4.7, 5.3, \ldots\ldots$

(b) The sum of the first n terms of an arithmetic series is given by

$$S_n = \frac{3n}{2}(n + 3).$$

(i) Calculate the first term of the series.

(iii) By calculating S_9 and S_{10}, find T_{10} (the tenth term of the series).

(c) The first three terms of a geometric sequence are

$$k - 3, 2k - 4, 4k - 3, \ldots\ldots$$

where k is a real number.

(i) Find the value of k.

(ii) Hence, write down the value of each of the first four terms of the sequence.

6. **(a)** Let $f(x) = \dfrac{1}{3}(x - 8)$ for $x \in \mathbf{R}$.

Evaluate $f(5)$.

(b) **(i)** Find $\dfrac{dy}{dx}$ where $y = (x - 1)^7$ and evaluate your answer at $x = 2$.

(ii) Find $\dfrac{dy}{dx}$ where $y = (x^3 - 3)(x^2 - 4)$ and simplify your answer.

(c) Let $f(x) = x^3 - ax + 7$ for all $x \in \mathbf{R}$ and for $a \in \mathbf{R}$

(i) The slope of the tangent to the curve $y = f(x)$ at $x = 1$ is -9. Find the value of a.

(ii) Hence, find the co-ordinates of the local maximum point and the local minimum point on the curve $y = f(x)$.

7. **(a)** Differentiate $7x^3 - 3x^2 + 9x$ with respect to x.

(b) **(i)** Differentiate $x^5 - 17 + \dfrac{1}{x^5}$ with respect to x.

(ii) Differentiate $\dfrac{2x}{x - 1}$ with respect to x and simplify your answer.

(c) A marble rolls along the top of a table. It starts to move at $t = 0$ seconds.

The distance that it has travelled at t seconds is given by

$$s = 14t - t^2$$

where s is in centimetres.

(i) What distance has the marble travelled when $t = 2$ seconds?

(ii) What is the speed of the marble when $t = 5$ seconds?

(iii) When is the speed of the marble equal to zero?

(iv) What is the acceleration of the marble?

8. Let $f(x) = \dfrac{1}{x + 2}$.

(i) Find $f(-6), f(-3), f(-1), f(0)$ and $f(2)$.

(ii) For what real value of x is $f(x)$ not defined?

(iii) Draw the graph of $f(x) = \dfrac{1}{x + 2}$ for $-6 \leqslant x \leqslant 2$.

(iv) Find $f'(x)$, the derivative of $f(x)$.

(v) Find the two values of x at which the slope of the tangent to the graph is $-\dfrac{1}{9}$.

(vi) Show that there is no tangent to the graph of f that is parallel to the x-axis.

EXAM PAPERS

AN ROINN OIDEACHAIS AGUS EOLAÍOCHTA

LEAVING CERTIFICATE EXAMINATION, 2002

MATHEMATICS – ORDINARY LEVEL – PAPER 2 (300 marks)

MONDAY, 10 JUNE – MORNING, 9.30 to 12.00

Attempt FIVE questions from **Section A** and **ONE** question from **Section B**.

Each question carries 50 marks.

WARNING: Marks will be lost if all necessary work is not clearly shown.

SECTION A

Attempt FIVE questions from this section.

1. **(a)** Each side of an equilateral triangle measures 4 units. Calculate the area of the triangle, giving your answer in surd form.

   Note: Area of a triangle $= \dfrac{1}{2}\,ab\sin C$.

   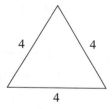

   (b) The diagram shows the curve $y = x^2 + 1$ in the domain $0 \leqslant x \leqslant 4$.

   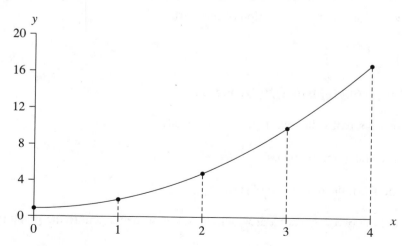

(i) Copy the following table. Then, complete it using the equation of the curve:

x	0	1	2	3	4
y					

(ii) Hence, use Simpson's Rule to estimate the area between the curve and the x-axis.

(c) A solid is in the shape of a hemisphere surmounted by a cone, as in the diagram.

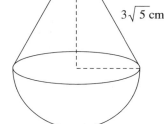

(i) The volume of the hemisphere is 18π cm^3.
Find the radius of the hemisphere.

(ii) The slant height of the cone is $3\sqrt{5}$ cm.
Show that the vertical height of the cone is 6 cm.

(iii) Show that the volume of the cone equals the volume of the hemisphere.

(iv) This solid is melted down and recast in the shape of a solid cylinder. The height of the cylinder is 9 cm. Calculate its radius.

2. **(a)** Find the co-ordinates of the point of intersection of the line $4x + y = 5$ and the line $3x - 2y = 12$.

(b) The line L has equation $4x - 5y = -40$.
$a(0, 8)$ and $b(-10, 0)$ are two points.

(i) Verify that a and b lie on L.

(ii) What is the slope of L?

(iii) The line K is perpendicular to L and it contains b. Find the equation of K.

(iv) K intersects the y-axis at the point c. Find the co-ordinates of c.

(v) d is another point such that $abcd$ is a rectangle. Calculate the area of $abcd$.

(vi) Find the co-ordinates of d.

3. **(a)** Write down the co-ordinates of any three points that lie on the circle with equation $x^2 + y^2 = 100$.

(b) The circle C has equation $(x - 2)^2 + (y + 1)^2 = 8$.

(i) Find the co-ordinates of the two points at which C cuts the y-axis.

(ii) Find the equation of the tangent to C at the point $(4, 1)$.

(c) $a(-5, 1)$, $b(3, 7)$ and $c(9, -1)$ are three points.

(i) Show that the triangle abc is right-angled.

(ii) Hence, find the centre of the circle that passes through a, b and c and write down the equation of the circle.

4. (a) The area of the triangle *rpt* is 30 cm². *rd* is perpendicular to *pt*.

Given that $|pt| = 12$ cm, calculate $|rd|$.

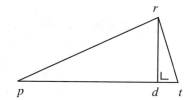

(b) Prove that if three parallel lines make intercepts of equal length on a transversal, then they will also make intercepts of equal length on any other transversal.

(c) The triangle *a'b'c'* is the image of the triangle *abc* under an enlargement.

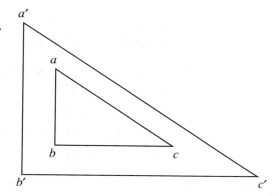

(i) Find, by measurement, the scale factor of the enlargement.

(ii) Copy the diagram and show how to find the centre of the enlargement.

(iii) Units are chosen so that $|bc| = 8$ units.

How many of these units is $|b'c'|$?

(iv) Find the area of triangle *abc*, given that the area of *a'b'c'* is 84 square units.

5. (a) Use the information given in the diagram to show that

$$\sin\theta + \cos\theta > \tan\theta.$$

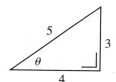

(b) A circle has radius 24 cm and centre *o*.

(i) Calculate the area of a sector which has 70° at *o*.

Take $\pi = \dfrac{22}{7}$.

(ii) An arc of length 48 cm subtends an angle *A* at *o*. Calculate *A*, correct to the nearest degree.

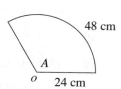

(c) In the quadrilateral $abcd$, $|ac| =$
5 units, $|bc| = 4$ units, $|\angle bca| = 110°$,
$|\angle acd| = 33°$ and $|\angle cda| = 23°$.

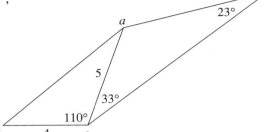

(i) Calculate $|ab|$, correct to
two decimal places.

(ii) Calculate $|cd|$, correct to
two decimal places.

6. **(a)** There are eight questions on an examination paper.

(i) In how many different ways can a candidate select six questions?

(ii) In how many different ways can a candidate select six questions if one
particular question must always be selected?

(b) A meeting is attended by 23 men and 21 women.
Of the men, 14 are married and the others are single.
Of the women, 8 are married and the others are single.

(i) A person is picked at random. What is the probability that the person is a
woman?

(ii) A person is picked at random. What is the probability that the person is
married?

(iii) A man is picked at random. What is the probability that he is married?

(iv) A woman is picked at random. What is the probability that she is single?

(c) The digits 0, 1, 2, 3, 4, 5 are used to form four-digit codes. A code cannot begin with
0 and no digit is repeated in any code.

(i) Write down the largest possible four-digit code.

(ii) Write down the smallest possible four-digit code.

(iii) How many four-digit codes can be formed?

(iv) How many of the four-digit codes are greater than 4000?

7. (a) Calculate the mean of the following numbers:

$$1, 0, 1, 5, 2, 3, 9.$$

(b) The following cumulative frequency table refers to the ages of 70 guests at a wedding:

Age (in years)	<20	<40	<60	<90
Number of guests	6	23	44	70

(i) Copy and complete the following frequency table:

Age (in years)	0–20	20–40	40–60	60–90
Number of guests				

[Note: 20–40 means 20 years old or more but less than 40 etc.]

(ii) Using mid-interval values, calculate the mean age of the guests.

(iii) What is the greatest number of guests who could have been over 65 years of age?

(c) The grouped frequency table below refers to the marks obtained by 85 students in a test:

Marks	0–40	40–55	55–70	70–100
Number of students	16	18	27	24

[Note: 40–55 means 40 marks or more but less than 55 etc.]

(i) What percentage of students obtained 55 marks or higher?

(ii) Name the interval in which the median lies.

(iii) Draw an accurate histogram to represent the data.

SECTION B

Attempt ONE question from this section

8. (a) x and y are two points on a circle with centre o.
px and py are tangents to the circle, as shown.

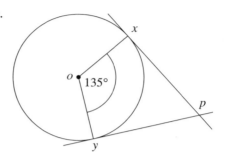

    (i) Write down $|\angle pxo|$.

    (ii) Given that $|\angle xoy| = 135°$, find $|\angle ypx|$.

(b) Prove that an angle between a tangent ak and a chord $[ab]$ of a circle has degree-measure equal to that of any angle in the alternate segment.

(c) The lines kd and kr are tangents to a circle at d and r respectively.

s is a point on the circle as shown.

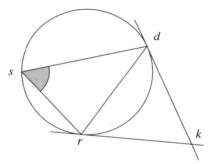

    (i) Name two angles in the diagram equal in measure to $\angle dsr$.

    (ii) Find $|\angle rkd|$, given that $|\angle dsr| = 65°$.

    (iii) Is $|dk| = |rk|$? Give a reason for your answer.

9. (a) Let $\vec{p} = -\vec{i} + 2\vec{j}$ and $\vec{w} = 3\vec{i} - 4\vec{j}$.

Express, in terms of $\vec{i}$ and $\vec{j}$,

    (i) $2\vec{w}$

    (ii) $2\vec{w} - \vec{p}$.

(b) $abcd$ is a parallelogram. The diagonals intersect at the point m.

Express each of the following as a single vector

    (i) $\vec{ab} + \vec{bm}$

    (ii) $\vec{ab} + \vec{ad}$

    (iii) $\vec{ac} + \vec{ab}$

    (iv) $\frac{1}{2}\vec{ac} + \frac{1}{2}\vec{db}$.

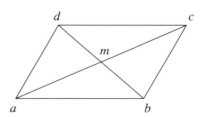

(c) Let $\vec{x} = 3\vec{i} + 4\vec{j}$ and $\vec{y} = 5\vec{i} + 12\vec{j}$.

    (i) Show that $|\vec{x}| + |\vec{y}| > |\vec{x} + \vec{y}|$.

    (ii) Write down $\vec{x}^{\perp}$ in terms of $\vec{i}$ and $\vec{j}$ and hence, show that $|\vec{x}|^2 + |\vec{x}^{\perp}|^2 = |\vec{x} - \vec{x}^{\perp}|^2$.

10. (a) (i) Calculate each of the following to three decimal places

$$\left(\frac{1}{2}\right)^6, \left(\frac{1}{2}\right)^7, \left(\frac{1}{2}\right)^8, \left(\frac{1}{2}\right)^9.$$

    (ii) Hence, write down $\displaystyle\lim_{n \to \infty}\left(\frac{1}{2}\right)^n$.

(b) The first term of a geometric series is 3. The second term of the series is 12.

    (i) Write down the common ratio.

    (ii) What is the fifth term of the series?

    (iii) Calculate the sum of the first nine terms of the series.

(c) (i) €100 is invested at 10% compound interest per annum.

    Show that the value of the investment is less than €1 000 after 24 years and more than €1 000 after 25 years.

    (ii) The sum to infinity of a geometric series is 2. The common ratio and the first term of the series are equal. Find the common ratio.

11. (a) The equation of the line M is $2x + y = 10$.
The equation of the line N is $4x - y = 8$.

Write down the three inequalities that define the shaded region in the diagram.

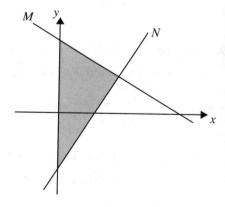

(b)   A new ship is being designed. It can have two types of cabin accommodation for passengers – type A cabins and type B cabins.

Each type A cabin accommodates 6 passengers and each type B cabin accommodates 3 passengers. The maximum number of passengers that the ship can accommodate is 330.

Each type A cabin occupies 50 m^2 of floor space. Each type B cabin occupies 10 m^2 of floor space. The total amount of floor space occupied by cabins cannot exceed 2300 m^2.

(i)   Taking x to represent the number of type A cabins and y to represent the number of type B cabins, write down two inequalities in x and y and illustrate these on graph paper.

(ii)   The income on each voyage from renting the cabins to passengers is €600 for each type A cabin and €180 for each type B cabin. How many of each type of cabin should the ship have so as to maximise income, assuming that all cabins are rented?

(iii)   What is the maximum possible income on each voyage from renting the cabins?

ANSWERS

Leaving Certificate Examination, 2002

Ordinary Level

Paper 1

1. (a) 42 (b) (i) 7.2% (ii) 0.8% (c) (i) €342 (ii) 228 (iii) €603 (profit)

2. (a) 12 (b) (ii) $-2, 1, \frac{5}{2}$ (c) (i) $\dfrac{8a}{c+5}$ (ii) $\sqrt{2}$ or $2\frac{1}{2}$

3. (a) $x \geqslant -4$ (b) (i) $x = 5, y = 0$ or $x = 3, y = 4$ (ii) 125 or 91 (c) (i) 6 (ii) 9

4. (a) $1 + 2i$ (b) (ii) 41 (iii) $\frac{9}{41} + \frac{40}{41}i$ (c) (i) $p = 2; k = 3$ (ii) yes

5. (a) (i) $-4, -2, 0$ (ii) 5.9, 6.5, 7.1 (b) (i) 6 (ii) $T_{10} = S_{10} - S_9 = 195 - 161 = 33$
   (c) (i) 7 (ii) 4, 10, 25, 62.5

6. (a) -1 (b) (i) $7(x-1)^6; 7$ (ii) $5x^4 - 12x^2 - 6x$
   (c) (i) 12 (ii) max $(-2, 23)$; min $(2, -9)$

7. (a) $21x^2 - 6x + 9$ (b) (i) $5x^4 - 5x^{-6}$ or $5x^4 - \dfrac{5}{x^6}$ (ii) $\dfrac{-2}{(x-1)^2}$
   (c) (i) 24 m (ii) 4 m/s (iii) $t = 7$ (iv) -2 m/s^2

8. (a) (i) $-\frac{1}{4}, -1, 1, \frac{1}{2}, \frac{1}{4}$ (ii) -2 (iv) $\dfrac{-1}{(x+2)^2}$ (v) -5 or 1

Paper 2

1. (a) $4\sqrt{3}$ (b) (i)

x	0	1	2	3	4
y	1	2	5	10	17

   (ii) $\frac{76}{3}$ (c) (i) 3 cm (iv) 2 cm

2. (a) $(2, -3)$ (b) (ii) $\frac{4}{5}$ (iii) $5x + 4y + 50 = 0$ (iv) $(0, -\frac{25}{2})$ (v) 205 (vi) $(10, -\frac{9}{2})$

3. (a) $(10, 0), (0, -10), (0, 10), (0, -10), (8, 6), (-8, -6), (6, -8), (-6, 8)$ etc.
   (b) (i) $(0, 1), (0, -3)$ (ii) $x + y - 5 = 0$ (c) (ii) $(x-2)^2 + y^2 = 50$ or $x^2 + y^2 - 4x - 46 = 0$

4. (a) 5 cm (c) (i) 2 (iii) 16 (iv) 21 sq. units

5. (a) $\frac{3}{5} + \frac{4}{5} > \frac{3}{4}$ (b) (i) $352\ \text{cm}^2$ (ii) $115°$ (c) (i) 7.39 (ii) 10.61

6. (a) (i) 28 (ii) 21 (b) (i) $\frac{21}{44}$ (ii) $\frac{1}{2}$ (iii) $\frac{14}{23}$ (iv) $\frac{13}{21}$
(c) (i) $5\,432$ (ii) $1\,023$ (iii) 300 (iv) 120

7. (a) 3 (b) (i)

Age (in years)	0–20	20–40	40–60	60–90
Number of guests	6	17	21	26

(ii) 51 (iii) 26 (c) (i) 60% (ii) 55–70

8. (a) (i) $90°$ (ii) $45°$ (c) (i) $\angle krd$ or $\angle kdr$ (ii) $50°$ (iii) yes, because $\triangle krd$ is isosceles or kd and kr are tangents

9. (a) (i) $6\vec{i} - 8\vec{j}$ (ii) $7\vec{i} - 10\vec{j}$ (b) (i) $\overrightarrow{am}$ or $\overrightarrow{mc}$ (ii) $\overrightarrow{ac}$ (iii) $\overrightarrow{ad}$ or $\overrightarrow{bc}$ (iv) $\overrightarrow{ab}$ or $\overrightarrow{dc}$
(c) (i) $5 + 13 > \sqrt{320}$ (ii) $-4\vec{i} + 3\vec{j}$; $25 + 25 = 50$

10. (a) (i) 0.016; 0.008; 0.004; 0.002 (ii) 0 (b) (i) 4 (ii) 768 (iii) $262\,143$
(c) (i) 24 years amounts to €984.97; 25 years amounts to €1\,083.47 (ii) $\frac{2}{3}$

11. (a) $2x + y \leqslant 10$; $4x - y \leqslant 8$; $x \geqslant 0$ (b) (i) $6x + 3y \leqslant 330$ or $2x + y \leqslant 110$;
$50x + 10y \leqslant 2\,300$ or $5x + y \leqslant 230$ (ii) 40 type A and 30 type B (iii) €29\,400

AN ROINN OIDEACHAIS AGUS EOLAÍOCHTA

LEAVING CERTIFICATE EXAMINATION, 2001

MATHEMATICS – ORDINARY LEVEL – PAPER 1 (300 marks)

THURSDAY, 7 JUNE – MORNING, 9.30 to 12.00

Attempt SIX QUESTIONS (50 marks each)

WARNING: Marks may be lost if all necessary work is not clearly shown.

---

1. **(a)** A cookery book gives the following instruction for calculating the amount of time for which a turkey should be cooked:

'Allow 15 minutes per 450 grammes plus an extra 15 minutes.'

For how many hours and minutes should a turkey weighing 9 kilogrammes be cooked?

(b) **(i)** The answer to $3.58 + 2.47$ was given as 6.50.

What was the percentage error correct to one decimal place?

(ii) Calculate the value of
$$\frac{3.1 \times 10^5 - 1.5 \times 10^4}{5.9 \times 10^6}$$

and write your answer as a decimal number.

(c) €5000 was invested for 3 years at compound interest.
The rate for the first year was 4%. The rate for the second year was $4\frac{1}{2}\%$.

(i) Find the amount of the investment at the end of the second year.

At the beginning of the third year a further €4000 was invested.
The rate for the third year was $r\%$.
The total investment at the end of the third year was €9811.36.

(ii) Calculate the value of r.

2. **(a)** Find the solution set of
$$11 - 2n > 3, \qquad n \in \mathbf{N}.$$

(b) Solve for x and y
$$x + 2y = 3$$
$$x^2 - y^2 = 24.$$

(c) Solve each of the following equations for p

   (i) $9^p = \dfrac{1}{\sqrt{3}}$

   (ii) $2^{3p-7} = 2^6 - 2^5$.

3.   **(a)**   Given that $u^2 + 2as = v^2$, calculate the value of a when $u = 10$, $s = 30$ and $v = 20$.

   (b)   **(i)**   Simplify $(x + \sqrt{x})(x - \sqrt{x})$ when $x > 0$.

          (ii)   Hence, or otherwise, find the value of x for which
$$(x + \sqrt{x})(x - \sqrt{x}) = 6.$$

   (c)   Let $f(x) = x^3 + ax^2 + bx - 6$ where a and b are real numbers.

       Given that $x - 1$ and $x - 2$ are factors of $f(x)$

       (i)   find the value of a and the value of b

       (ii)   hence, find the values of x for which $f(x) = 0$.

4.   **(a)**   Let $w = 3 - 2i$ where $i^2 = -1$.

       Plot

       (i) w

       (ii) iw

       on an Argand diagram.

   (b)   Solve
$$(x + 2yi)(1 - i) = 7 + 5i$$

       for real x and for real y.

   (c)   Let $z_1 = 3 + 4i$ and $z_2 = 12 - 5i$.

       $\bar{z}_1$ and $\bar{z}_2$ are the complex conjugates of z_1 and z_2, respectively.

       (i)   Show that $z_1\bar{z}_2 + \bar{z}_1 z_2$ is a real number.

       (ii)   Investigate if $|z_1| + |z_2| = |z_1 + z_2|$.

5.   **(a)**   5, 13, 21, 29, ... is an arithmetic sequence.

       Which term of the sequence is 813?

   (b)   The nth term of a geometric series is given by
$$\text{T}_n = 3^n.$$

       (i)   What is the value of a, the first term?

       (ii)   What is the value of r, the common ratio?

(iii) Show that S_{10}, the sum of the first 10 terms, is $\frac{3}{2}(3^{10} - 1)$.

(c) The sum of the first n terms of an arithmetic series is given by

$$S_n = 4n^2 - 8n.$$

(i) Use S_1 and S_2 to find the first term and the common difference.

(ii) Starting with the first term, how many terms of the series must be added to give a sum of 252?

6. **(a)** Let $g(x) = \dfrac{1}{x^2 + 1}$ for $x \in \mathbf{R}$.

Evaluate

(i) $g(2)$

(ii) $g(3)$ and write your answers as decimals.

(b) Let $f(x) = 2 - 9x + 6x^2 - x^3$ for $x \in \mathbf{R}$.

(i) Find $f(-1), f(2)$ and $f(5)$.

(ii) Find $f'(x)$, the derivative of $f(x)$.

(iii) Find the co-ordinates of the local maximum and the local minimum of $f(x)$.

(iv) Draw the graph of $f(x)$ in the domain $-1 \leqslant x \leqslant 5$.

(v) Use your graph to find the range of real values of k for which $f(x) = k$ has more than one solution.

7. **(a)** Differentiate with respect to x

(i) $6x^5 + x^2$

(ii) $(x - 3)(x + 3)$.

(b) **(i)** Find $\dfrac{dy}{dx}$ when $y = \dfrac{x^2}{x - 4}$, $x \neq 4$.

(ii) Find the value of $\dfrac{dy}{dx}$ at $x = 0$ when $y = (x^2 - 7x + 1)^5$.

(c) Two fireworks were fired straight up in the air at $t = 0$ seconds.
The height, h metres, which each firework reached above the ground t seconds after it was fired is given by

$$h = 80t - 5t^2.$$

The first firework exploded 5 seconds after it was fired.

(i) At what height was the first firework when it exploded?

(ii) At what speed was the first firework travelling when it exploded?

The second firework failed to explode and it fell back to the ground.

(iii) After how many seconds did the second firework reach its maximum height?

8. (a) Let $g(x) = x^4 - 32x$ for $x \in \mathbf{R}$.

     (i) Write down $g'(x)$, the derivative of $g(x)$.

     (ii) For what value of x is $g'(x) = 0$?

  (b) Differentiate $3x^2 - x$ from first principles with respect to x.

  (c) Let $f(x) = \dfrac{1}{x+1}$ for $x \in \mathbf{R}$ and $x > -1$.

     (i) Find $f'(x)$.

     (ii) Find the co-ordinates of the point on the curve of $f(x)$ at which the tangent has slope of $-\dfrac{1}{4}$.

     (iii) Find the equation of the tangent to the curve which has slope of $-\dfrac{1}{4}$.

LEAVING CERTIFICATE EXAMINATION, 2001

MATHEMATICS — ORDINARY LEVEL — PAPER 2 (300 marks)

MONDAY, 11 JUNE — MORNING, 9.30 to 12.00

Attempt **FIVE Questions** from Section **A** and **ONE Question** from Section **B**

Each question carries 50 marks.

Marks may be lost if all necessary work is not clearly shown.

SECTION A

Attempt FIVE questions from this section.

1. **(a)** A running track is made up of two straight parts and two semicircular parts as shown in the diagram.

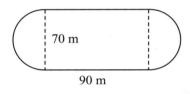

The length of each of the straight parts is 90 metres.

The diameter of each of the semicircular parts is 70 metres.

Calculate the length of the track correct to the nearest metre.

(b) The sketch shows a flood caused by a leaking underground pipe that runs from a to b.

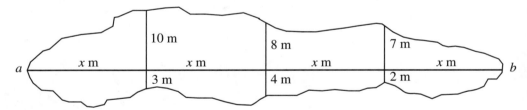

At equal intervals of x m along $[ab]$ perpendicular measurements are made to the edges of the flood. The measurements to the top edge are 10 m, 8 m and 7 m. The measurements to the bottom edge are 3 m, 4 m and 2 m. At a and b the measurements are 0 m.

Using Simpson's Rule the area of the flood is estimated to be 672 m^2.

Find x and hence, write down the length of the pipe.

(c) Sweets, made from a chocolate mixture, are in the shape of solid spherical balls. The diameter of each sweet is 3 cm.

36 sweets fit exactly in a rectangular box which has internal height 3 cm.

(i) The base of the box is a square. How many sweets are there in each row?

(ii) What is the internal volume of the box?

(iii) The 36 sweets weigh 675 grammes.
What is the weight of 1 cm^3 of the chocolate mixture? Give your answer correct to one decimal place.

2. **(a)** The point $(t, 2t)$ lies on the line $3x + 2y + 7 = 0$.
Find the value of t.

(b) $a(4, 2)$, $b(-2, 0)$ and $c(0, 4)$ are three points.

(i) Prove that $ac \perp bc$.

(ii) Prove that $|ac| = |bc|$.

(iii) Calculate the area of the triangle bac.

(iv) The diagonals of the square $bahg$ intersect at c.
Find the co-ordinates of h and the co-ordinates of g.

(v) Find the equation of the line bc and show that h lies on this line.

3. **(a)** The circle S has equation $(x - 3)^2 + (y - 4)^2 = 25$.

(i) Write down the centre and the radius of S.

(ii) The point $(k, 0)$ lies on S. Find the two real values of k.

(b) Prove that the line $x - 3y = 10$ is a tangent to the circle with equation $x^2 + y^2 = 10$ and find the co-ordinates of the point of contact.

(c) C is a circle with centre $(0, 0)$. It passes through the point $(1, -5)$.

(i) Write down the equation of C.

(ii) The point (p, p) lies inside C where $p \in \mathbf{Z}$.
Find all the possible values of p.

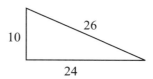

4. **(a)** Prove that the triangle with sides of lengths 10 units, 24 units and 26 units is right-angled.

(b) Prove that a line which is parallel to one side-line of a triangle, and cuts a second side, will cut the third side in the same proportion as the second.

(c) **(i)** Draw a square with sides 7 cm and mark o, the point of intersection of the diagonals.

(ii) Draw the image of the square under the enlargement with centre o and scale factor $\frac{1}{2}$.

(iii) Calculate the area of the image square.

(iv) Under another enlargement the area of the image of the square with sides 7 cm is 196 cm^2.
What is the scale factor of this enlargement?

5. **(a)** $\sin\theta = \dfrac{3}{5}$ where $0° < 0 < 90°$.

Find, without using the Tables or a calculator, the value of

    (i) $\cos\theta$

    (ii) $\cos2\theta$. [Note: $\cos 2\theta = \cos^2\theta - \sin^2\theta$.]

(b) In the triangle abc, $|ab| = 3$ units, $|bc| = 7$ units and $|\angle abc| = 67°$.

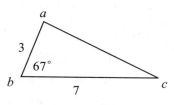

    (i) Calculate the area of the triangle abc, correct to one decimal place.

    (ii) Calculate $|ac|$, correct to the nearest whole number.

(c) s and t are two points 300 m apart on a straight path due north.

From s the bearing of a pillar is N 40° E.
From t the bearing of the pillar is N 70° E.

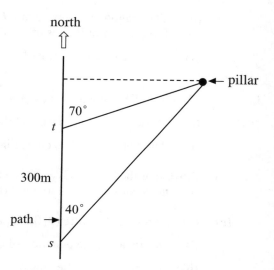

    (i) Show that the distance from t to the pillar is 386 m, correct to the nearest metre.

    (ii) Find the shortest distance from the path to the pillar, correct to the nearest metre.

6. **(a)** Sarah and Jim celebrate their birthdays in a particular week (Monday to Sunday inclusive).

Assuming that the birthdays are equally likely to fall on any day of the week, what is the probability that

    (i) Sarah's birthday is on Friday
    (ii) Sarah's birthday and Jim's birthday are both on Friday?

(b) **(i)** How many different arrangements can be made using all the letters of the word IRELAND?

    (ii) How many arrangements begin with the letter I?

    (iii) How many arrangements end with the word LAND?

    (iv) How many begin with I and end with LAND?

(c) **(i)** Eight points lie on a circle, as in the diagram.

How many different lines can be drawn by joining any two of the eight points?

(ii) Find the value of the natural number n such that

$$\binom{n}{2} = 105. \qquad \text{[Note: } \binom{n}{2} \text{ may also be written as } {}''C_2.\text{]}$$

7. **(a)** **(i)** Calculate the mean of the following numbers

$$2, 3, 5, 7, 8.$$

(ii) Hence, calculate the standard deviation of the numbers correct to one decimal place.

(b) The following table shows the distribution of the amounts spent by 40 customers in a shop:

Amount Spent	€0–€8	€8–€12	€12–€16	€16–€20	€20–32
Number of Customers	2	9	13	10	6

[Note: €8–€12 means €8 or over but less than €12 etc.]

(i) Taking mid-interval values, estimate the mean amount spent by the customers.

(ii) Copy and complete the following cumulative frequency table:

Amount Spent	€8	€12	€16	€20	€32
Number of Customers					

(iii) Draw a cumulative frequency curve (ogive).

(iv) Use your curve to estimate the number of customers who spent €25 or more.

SECTION B

Attempt ONE question from this section.

8. **(a)** The points f, g, h and m lie on a circle with centre o.

Given that $|\angle foh| = 80°$, find

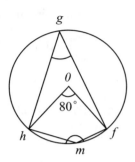

  (i) $|\angle fgh|$
  (ii) $|\angle fmh|$.

(b) Prove that if $[ab]$ and $[cd]$ are chords of a circle and the lines ab and cd meet at the point k which is inside the circle, then $|ak|.|kb| = |ck|.|kd|$.

(c) $[xy]$ and $[rs]$ are chords of a circle which intersect at a point p outside the circle. pt is a tangent to the circle at the point t.

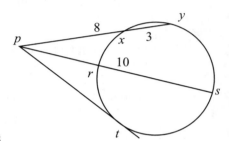

Given that $|py| = 8$, $|xy| = 3$ and $|ps| = 10$,

  (i) write down $|px|$

  (ii) calculate $|rs|$

  (iii) calculate $|pt|$, giving your answer in its simplest surd form.

9. **(a)** Given that $\vec{p} = 5\vec{i} - 12\vec{j}$,

  (i) calculate $|\vec{p}|$

  (ii) write down $\vec{p}^{\perp}$ in terms of $\vec{i}$ and $\vec{j}$.

(b) **(i)** Find the scalars k and t such that $2(3\vec{i} - t\vec{j}) + k(-\vec{i} + 2\vec{j}) = t\vec{i} - 8\vec{j}$.

  (ii) $oacb$ is a parallelogram where o is the origin. p is the point of intersection of the diagonals. m is the midpoint of $[ac]$.

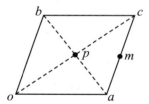

  Express $\vec{p}$ and $\vec{m}$ in terms of $\vec{a}$ and $\vec{b}$.

(c) Let $\vec{x} = \vec{i} + 2\vec{j}$ and $\vec{y} = 6\vec{i} + 2\vec{j}$.

  (i) Calculate $\vec{x}.\vec{y}$.

  (ii) Hence, find the measure of the angle between $\vec{x}$ and $\vec{y}$.

10. **(a)** Expand $(1 + x)^3$ fully.
Expand $(1 - x)^3$ fully.

Hence, find the real numbers a and k such that

$$(1 + x)^3 + (1 - x)^3 = a + kx^2.$$

(b) The nth term of a geometric series is given by $T_n = 27(\frac{2}{3})^n$.

    (i) Write out the first three terms of the series.

    (ii) Find an expression for the sum of the first five terms.

    (iii) Find the sum to infinity of the series.

(c) €100 was invested at the beginning of each year for twenty consecutive years at 4% per annum compound interest.

Calculate the total value of the investment at the end of the twenty years, correct to the nearest €.

11. (a) Using graph paper, illustrate the set of points (x, y) that simultaneously satisfy the three inequalities:

$$y \geqslant 2$$
$$x + 2y \leqslant 8$$
$$5x + y \geqslant -5.$$

(b) Houses are to be built on 9 hectares of land.
Two types of houses, bungalows and semi-detached houses, are possible.

Each bungalow occupies one-fifth of a hectare.
Each semi-detached house occupies one-tenth of a hectare.

The cost of building a bungalow is €80 000.
The cost of building a semi-detached house is €50 000.
The total cost of building the houses cannot be greater than €4 million.

    (i) Taking x to represent the number of bungalows and y to represent the number of semi-detached houses, write down two inequalities in x and y and illustrate these on graph paper.

    (ii) The profit on each bungalow is €10 000. The profit on each semi-detached house is €7000. How many of each type of house should be built so as to maximise profit?

ANSWERS

Leaving Certificate Examination, 2001
Ordinary Level

Paper 1

1. **(a)** 5 hours and 15 minutes **(b) (i)** 7.4% **(ii)** 0.05 **(c) (i)** €5434 **(ii)** $r = 4$

2. **(a)** 0, 1, 2, 3 **(b)** $x = -7, y = 5$ or $x = 5, y = -1$ **(c) (i)** $p = -\frac{1}{4}$ **(ii)** $p = 4$

3. **(a)** 5 **(b) (i)** $x^2 - x$ **(ii)** $x = 3$ or $x = -2$ **(c) (i)** $a = -6; b = 11$ **(ii)** 1, 2, 3

4. **(b)** $x = 1, y = 3$ **(c) (i)** 32, a real number **(ii)** no, $18 \neq \sqrt{226}$

5. **(a)** 102 or u_{102} **(b) (i)** 3 **(ii)** 3 **(c) (i)** $a = -4, d = 8$ **(ii)** 9

6. **(a) (i)** 0.2 **(ii)** 0.1 **(b) (ii)** 18, 0, −18 **(ii)** $-9 + 12x - 3x^2$
   (iii) $(1, -2)$ min. point; $(3, 2)$ max. point **(v)** $-2 \leqslant k \leqslant 2$

7. **(a) (i)** $30x^4 + 2x$ **(ii)** $2x$ **(b) (i)** $\dfrac{x^2 - 8x}{(x-4)^2}$ **(ii)** −35
   (c) (i) 275 m **(ii)** 30 m/s **(iii)** 8 seconds

8. **(a) (i)** $4x^3 - 32$ **(ii)** $x = 2$ **(c) (i)** $-\dfrac{1}{(x+1)^2}$ **(ii)** $(1, \frac{1}{2})$ **(iii)** $x + 4y - 3 = 0$

Paper 2

1. **(a)** 400 m **(b)** $x = 18; 72$ m **(c) (i)** 6 **(ii)** 972 cm^3 **(iii)** 1.3 g

2. **(a)** $t = -1$ **(b) (i)** $-\frac{1}{2} \times 2 = -1, \therefore ac \perp bc$ **(ii)** $\sqrt{20} = \sqrt{20}, \therefore |ac| = |bc|$
   (iii) 10 **(iv)** $h(2, 8), g(-4, 6)$ **(v)** $2x - y + 4 = 0$

3. **(a) (i)** centre $= (3, 4)$; Radius $= 5$ **(ii)** $k = 0$ or $k = 6$ **(b)** $(1, -3)$
   (c) (i) $x^2 + y^2 = 26$ **(ii)** $-5 \leqslant p \leqslant 5, p \in z$ or $p = 0, \pm 1, \pm 2, \pm 3$

4. **(c) (iii)** 12.25 cm^2 **(iv)** 2

5. **(i)** $\frac{4}{5}$ or 0.8 **(ii)** $\frac{7}{25}$ or 0.28 **(b) (i)** 9.7 **(ii)** 6 **(c) (ii)** 362 m

6. **(a) (i)** $\frac{1}{7}$ **(ii)** $\frac{1}{49}$ **(b) (i)** 7! or 5040 **(ii)** 6! or 720 **(iii)** 6 **(iv)** 2
   (c) (i) 28 **(ii)** 15

7. **(a)** **(i)** 5 **(ii)** 2.3 **(b)** **(i)** €15.40

(ii)

Amount Spent	< €8	< €12	< €16	< €20	< €32
Number of Customers	2	11	24	34	40

(iv) 1

8. **(a)** **(i)** $40°$ **(ii)** $140°$ **(c)** **(i)** 5 **(ii)** 6 **(iii)** $2\sqrt{10}$

9. **(a)** **(i)** 13 **(ii)** $12\vec{i} + 5\vec{j}$ **(b)** **(i)** $k = 1; t = 5$ **(ii)** $\vec{p} = \frac{1}{2}\vec{a} + \frac{1}{2}\vec{b}; \vec{m} = \vec{a} + \frac{1}{2}\vec{b}$

(c) **(i)** 10 **(ii)** $45°$ or $\dfrac{\pi}{4}$

10. **(a)** $1 + 3x + 3x^2 + x^3; 1 - 3x + 3x^2 - x^3; a = 2, k = 6$

(b) **(i)** 18, 12, 8 **(ii)** $\dfrac{18[1 - (\frac{2}{3})^5]}{1 - \frac{2}{3}}$ or $54[1 - (\frac{2}{3})^5]$ **(iii)** 54 **(c)** €3097

11. **(b)** **(i)** $\frac{1}{5}x + \frac{1}{10}y \leqslant 9$ or $2x + y \leqslant 90$, $80\ 000x + 50\ 000y \leqslant 4\ 000{,}000$ or $8x + 5y \leqslant 400$
(ii) No bungalows and 80 semi-detached houses.

http://217.169.30.165/data/order.aspf

PIW = 13328412 & SRC = PMBIR